Android Game Programming by Example

Harness the power of the Android SDK by building three immersive and captivating games

John Horton

BIRMINGHAM - MUMBAI

Android Game Programming by Example

First published: June 2015

Production reference: 1250615

Published by Packt Publishing Ltd.
Livery Place
35 Livery Street
Birmingham B3 2PB, UK.

ISBN 978-1-78528-012-2

www.packtpub.com

Credits

Author
John Horton

Reviewers
Håvard Kindem
José Rodriguez-Rivas

Commissioning Editor
Nadeem N. Bagban

Acquisition Editor
Tushar Gupta

Content Development Editor
Siddhesh Salvi

Technical Editor
Prajakta Mhatre

Copy Editor
Charlotte Carneiro

Project Coordinator
Nidhi Joshi

Proofreader
Safis Editing

Indexer
Tejal Soni

Production Coordinator
Melwyn D'sa

Cover Work
Melwyn D'sa

About the Author

John Horton is a technology enthusiast based in the UK. When he is not creating apps and writing books or blog articles for `http://www.gamecodeschool.com`, he can be found playing or making video games with his two sons.

About the Reviewers

Håvard Kindem is a game developer from Norway who has a long-lived passion for games and game development. He started programming at an early age, which later resulted in an MSc in game technology. During his studies, Håvard became the founding member and CEO of Fallen Leaves Interactive, a group focusing on PC, Xbox, and Android development. The company made games for clients such as KLM Royal Dutch Airlines and contributed to Games4Health.

Currently, Håvard is employed at the National Lottery Association in Norway, where he works as a concept developer. In order to find new exciting products for its about 2.8 million customers, he has, among other things, worked on and published multiple mobile games. Håvard remains an avid gamer, and when he is not busy releasing a new project, he loves to return to the old classics or spend the evenings playing his bass guitar.

I would like to thank my mentor, Simon McCallum, for always challenging me and pushing me toward new technologies. I would also like to thank my nephew and niece for being my motivation and allowing me to stay a kid forever; I love you guys! Last but not least, I would like to thank my partner in crime, Sara, for her support and striving for perfection.

José Rodriguez-Rivas is a young game developer. He loves to dream big about his future, often picturing himself as a head developer for a huge game company that he started. He first started developing games using RPG Maker VX Ace when he was in the eighth grade. As soon as he got into high school, he wanted to learn how to actually program a video game. He first learned Java with the libGDX framework, which allows him to port his games to both PC and Android. He is really into web design as well, and has designed two websites, one for his own company, Tiny Country Games (`https://tinycountrygames.com/`), and another for the Young Entrepreneurs Association of California, YEACAL (`http://yeacal.org/`). He enjoys learning new things, even if they don't directly relate to game development. For example, he likes to practice instruments such as the guitar, ukulele, and electric bass.

First of all, I would thank my computer science teacher, Mark Sheinberg, for always pushing me to improve my coding skills and learn new things. I would like to thank my best friend, Charli-Anne Hanna-Baker, for always supporting my work and keeping my morale high with her amazing attitude. Annika Pašeta, thank you for giving me the opportunity of being the webmaster of YEACAL, which inspired me to learn ASP.NET and C#. Last but not least, I would like to thank my family for their constant support and love.

---

www.PacktPub.com

Support files, eBooks, discount offers, and more

For support files and downloads related to your book, please visit www.PacktPub.com.

Did you know that Packt offers eBook versions of every book published, with PDF and ePub files available? You can upgrade to the eBook version at www.PacktPub.com and as a print book customer, you are entitled to a discount on the eBook copy. Get in touch with us at service@packtpub.com for more details.

At www.PacktPub.com, you can also read a collection of free technical articles, sign up for a range of free newsletters and receive exclusive discounts and offers on Packt books and eBooks.

https://www2.packtpub.com/books/subscription/packtlib

Do you need instant solutions to your IT questions? PacktLib is Packt's online digital book library. Here, you can search, access, and read Packt's entire library of books.

Why subscribe?

- Fully searchable across every book published by Packt
- Copy and paste, print, and bookmark content
- On demand and accessible via a web browser

Free access for Packt account holders

If you have an account with Packt at www.PacktPub.com, you can use this to access PacktLib today and view 9 entirely free books. Simply use your login credentials for immediate access.

Table of Contents

Preface   **vii**

Chapter 1: Player 1 UP   **1**

A closer look at the games   **2**
  Tappy Defender   2
  Tough retro platformer   3
  Asteroids simulator   5
Setting up your development environment   **6**
  Installing the JDK   7
  Installing Android Studio   10
Summary   **12**

Chapter 2: Tappy Defender – First Step   **13**

Planning the first game   **13**
  Backstory   13
  The game mechanics   14
  Rules for the game   15
  The design   15
    Control   15
    Model   16
    View   16
    Design pattern reality check   16
  The game code structure   16
    The Android Activity lifecycle   16
  The Android Studio file structure   18
Building the home screen   **19**
  Creating the project   19
    What we did   20
  Building the home screen UI   21
    What we did   24
  Coding the functionality   24

Creating GameActivity	27
What we did	27
Configuring the AndroidManifest.xml file	27
What we did	28
Coding the game loop	**28**
Building the view	28
Creating a new class for the view	29
What we did	30
Structuring the class code	30
The game activity	32
The PlayerShip object	**34**
Drawing the scene	**37**
Plotting and drawing	37
Drawing PlayerShip	38
The Canvas and Paint objects	39
Controlling the frame rate	41
Deploying the game	**41**
Debugging on an Android device	41
Summary	**43**
Chapter 3: Tappy Defender – Taking Flight	**45**
Controlling the spaceship	**45**
Detecting touches	46
Adding boosters to the spaceship	47
Detecting the screen resolution	50
Building the enemies	**52**
Designing the enemy	53
Spawning the enemy	53
Making the enemy think	55
The thrill of flight – scrolling the background	**58**
Things that go bump – collision detection	**62**
Collision detection options	62
Rectangle intersection	62
Radius overlapping	63
The crossing number algorithm	65
Optimizations	65
Multiple hitboxes	65
Neighbor checking	65
Best options for Tappy Defender	66
Summary	**70**

Chapter 4: Tappy Defender – Going Home   **71**

Displaying a HUD   **71**

Implementing the rules   **74**

Ending the game   **78**

     Restarting the game   81

Adding sound FX   **82**

     Generating the FX   82

     The SoundPool class   85

     Coding the sound FX   85

Adding persistence   **87**

Iteration   **89**

     Multiple different enemy graphics   89

     An exercise in balance   91

     Format time   96

     Handle the back button   97

The finished game   **98**

Summary   **98**

Chapter 5: Platformer – Upgrading the Game Engine   **99**

The game   **100**

     The backstory   100

     The game mechanics   101

     Rules for the game   101

Upgrading the game engine   **101**

     The platform activity   101

     Locking the layout to landscape   104

     The PlatformView class   105

         The basic structure of PlatformView   106

         The GameObject class   109

         The view through a viewport   116

         Creating the levels   122

         The enhanced update method   131

         The enhanced draw method   132

Summary   **135**

Chapter 6: Platformer – Bob, Beeps, and Bumps   **137**

The SoundManager class   **137**

Introducing Bob   **141**

Multiphase collision detection   **150**

Player input   **157**

Animating Bob   **165**

Summary   **171**

Chapter 7: Platformer – Guns, Life, Money, and the Enemy	**173**
Ready aim fire	**173**
Pickups	180
The drone	190
The guard	195
Summary	**203**
Chapter 8: Platformer – Putting It All Together	**205**
Bullet collision detection	**205**
Adding some fire tiles	**207**
Eye candy	**211**
The new platform tiles	212
The new scenery objects	218
Scrolling parallax backgrounds	226
Pause menu with moveable viewport	234
Levels and game rules	236
Traveling between levels	236
The level designs	242
The cave	243
The city	244
The forest	245
The mountains	246
The HUD	247
Summary	**248**
Chapter 9: Asteroids at 60 FPS with OpenGL ES 2	**251**
Asteroids simulator	**252**
The game controls	252
Rules for the game	252
Introducing OpenGL ES 2	**252**
Why use it and how does it work?	252
What is neat about Version 2?	253
How we will use OpenGL ES 2?	254
Preparing OpenGL ES 2	**255**
Locking the layout to landscape	255
Activity	255
The view	257
A class to manage our game	258
Managing simple shaders	259
The game's main loop – the renderer	264
Building an OpenGL-friendly, GameObject super class	**271**
The spaceship	**281**
Drawing at 60 + FPS	**283**
Summary	**285**

Chapter 10: Move and Draw with OpenGL ES 2   287

Drawing a static game border   **287**

Twinkling stars   **290**

Bringing the spaceship to life   **293**

Rapid fire bullets   **298**

Reusing existing classes   **301**

   Adding the SoundManager class   302

   Adding the InputController class   304

Drawing and moving the asteroids   **309**

Scores and the HUD   **314**

   Adding control buttons   315

   Tally icons   319

   Life icons   323

     Declaring, initializing, and drawing the HUD objects   326

Summary   **328**

Chapter 11: Things That Go Bump – Part II   329

Planning for collision detection   **329**

   Colliding with the border   330

     The first phase of border collision detection   330

   Colliding with an asteroid   331

     The crossing number   331

     The first phase and overview of asteroid collision detection   332

   The CollisionPackage class   333

     Adding collision packages to the objects and making them accessible   336

   The CD class outline   341

     Implementing radius overlapping for asteroids and ships   342

     Implementing rectangle intersection for the border   343

Performing the checks   **344**

   Helper methods   344

     Destroying a ship   344

     Destroying an asteroid   345

   Testing for collisions in update()   346

Precise collision detection with the border   **350**

Precise collision detection with an asteroid   **352**

Finishing touches   **357**

Summary   **358**

Index   359

Preface

Making games is addictive and very rewarding, it can be hard to stop once you get started. The problem comes when we reach a stumbling block because we don't know how to implement a feature, or perhaps integrate it into our game. This book is a whirlwind tour of as many Android 2D gaming features that can possibly be squeezed into 11 chapters.

Every line of the code used to build three games of increasing difficulty is shown in the text of the book and explained in a straightforward manner.

Steadily build up to implement a flexible and advanced game engine that uses OpenGL ES 2 for fast smooth frame rates. This is achieved by starting with a simple game and gradually increasing the complexity of the three complete games built step by step.

Implement cool features like sprite sheet character animation and scrolling parallax backgrounds. Design and implement genuinely challenging and playable platform game levels.

Learn to code both basic and advanced collision detection. Make simple the math behind 2D rotation, velocity, and collision. Run your game designs at 60 frames per second or better.

Process multi-touch screen input. Implement a multitude of other game features like pickups, firing weapons, HUDs, generating and playing sound FX, scenery, level transition, high scores, and more.

What this book covers

Chapter 1, Player 1 UP, is an introduction to the three cool games that we will build. We will also get the development environment set up.

Chapter 2, Tappy Defender – First Step, is about planning the game project and getting the code for our first game engine up and running. We will implement a main game loop, control the frame rate, and draw to the screen.

Chapter 3, Tappy Defender – Taking Flight, teaches us to add lots of new objects and some features like player controls, enemies, and scrolling stars in the background. In the *Things that go bump – collision detection* section, we will discuss our collision detection options and implement an efficient solution for this game.

Chapter 4, Tappy Defender – Going Home, completes the game, including adding high scores, victory conditions, sound FX, and more.

Chapter 5, Platformer – Upgrading the Game Engine, provides a good understanding of what is needed in a simple game engine. We can quickly learn about and build a more advanced and flexible engine, suitable for a really tough, retro 2D platform game.

Chapter 6, Platformer – Bob, Beeps, and Bumps, uses our new game engine to add a class to manage the sound FX and a class to implement the more complex player controls that are required by a game of this type. We can then make Bob, our playable character, an animated running, jumping hero.

Chapter 7, Platformer – Guns, Life, Money, and the Enemy, continues the subject of the previous two chapters; we add a ton of features in this one. We will add collectible pick-ups and power-ups, a deadly homing enemy, and a patrolling guard. Of course with all this, Bob is going to need a machine gun to defend himself, and he gets one!

Chapter 8, Platformer – Putting It All Together, is where our platform game comes to life. We will add lots of new platform tile types and scenery objects, multiple scrolling parallax backgrounds, collision detection, and a teleporting system so that Bob can travel between the levels of the game. Using our range of tile types, scenery objects, and backgrounds, we will implement four playable levels linked together by the teleporting system.

Chapter 9, Asteroids at 60 FPS with OpenGL ES 2, contains the final project of this book, which is an introduction to 2D games with the super fast OpenGL graphics library. In this chapter, we will quickly learn how to draw with OpenGL ES 2 and integrate the drawing system into our game engine. By the end of the chapter, we will have a working engine that draws an Asteroids-style spaceship to the screen.

Chapter 10, Move and Draw with OpenGL ES 2, is where we will quickly integrate our sound and control systems from the previous project. Then, we can add a game border, twinkling star system, spinning asteroids, a neat HUD, progressively difficult levels, and a rapid fire gun to the player's spaceship.

Chapter 11, Things That Go Bump – Part II, completes the Asteroids game by adding the collision detection. The math required to detect collisions with the irregularly-shaped spinning asteroids is made simple and implemented into the game engine. By the end of this chapter, you will have the third and final fully playable game.

What you need for this book

Any recent and free version of Eclipse or Android Studio running on any of the major operating systems can use the code in this book.

Android Studio is the recommended development tool, and at time of publication, the minimum system requirements are:

For Windows:

- Microsoft Windows 8/7/Vista/2003 (32 or 64-bit)
- 2 GB RAM minimum, 4 GB RAM recommended
- 400 MB hard disk space
- At least 1 GB for Android SDK, emulator system images, and caches
- 1280 x 800 minimum screen resolution
- Java Development Kit (JDK) 7
- Optional for accelerated emulator: Intel processor with support for Intel VT-x, Intel EM64T (Intel 64), and Execute Disable (XD) Bit functionality

For Mac OS X:

- Mac OS X 10.8.5 or higher, up to 10.9 (Mavericks)
- 2 GB RAM minimum, 4 GB RAM recommended
- 400 MB hard disk space
- At least 1 GB for Android SDK, emulator system images, and caches
- 1280 x 800 minimum screen resolution
- Java Runtime Environment (JRE) 6
- Java Development Kit (JDK) 7
- Optional for accelerated emulator: Intel processor with support for Intel VT-x, Intel EM64T (Intel 64), and Execute Disable (XD) Bit functionality

On Mac OS, run Android Studio with Java Runtime Environment (JRE) 6 for optimized font rendering. You can then configure your project to use JDK 6 or JDK 7.

For Linux:

- GNOME or KDE desktop
- GNU C Library (glibc) 2.15 or later
- 2 GB RAM minimum, 4 GB RAM recommended
- 400 MB hard disk space
- At least 1 GB for Android SDK, emulator system images, and caches
- 1280 x 800 minimum screen resolution
- Oracle Java Development Kit (JDK) 7

Tested on Ubuntu 14.04, Trusty Tahr (64-bit distribution capable of running 32-bit applications).

Who this book is for

The book is best suited for existing Android or Java programmers, who want to adapt their skills to make exciting Android games.

The book is also for readers who might have no Android, game programming, or even Java experience, but a good understanding of object-oriented programming is assumed.

Also, a determined programming beginner with at least some OOP experience can follow along and build all the projects, because of the step-by-step approach of the book. This book will also be ideally suited for readers who have completed *Learning Java By Building Android Games*.

Conventions

In this book, you will find a number of text styles that distinguish between different kinds of information. Here are some examples of these styles and an explanation of their meaning.

Code words in text, database table names, folder names, filenames, file extensions, pathnames, dummy URLs, user input, and Twitter handles are shown as follows: "We will first add all the classes, and then update LevelManager in the usual three places."

A block of code is set as follows:

```
if (lm.isPlaying()) {
  // Reset the players location as
  // the world centre of the viewport
  //if game is playing
  vp.setWorldCentre(lm.gameObjects.get(lm.playerIndex)
    .getWorldLocation().x,
    lm.gameObjects.get(lm.playerIndex)
    .getWorldLocation().y);
```

When we wish to draw your attention to a particular part of a code block, the relevant lines or items are set in bold:

```
//Has player fallen out of the map?
if (lm.player.getWorldLocation().x < 0 ||
  lm.player.getWorldLocation().x > lm.mapWidth ||
  lm.player.getWorldLocation().y > lm.mapHeight) {
```

New terms and **important words** are shown in bold. Words that you see on the screen, for example, in menus or dialog boxes, appear in the text like this: "In the **Create New Project** window shown next, we need to enter some basic information about our app."

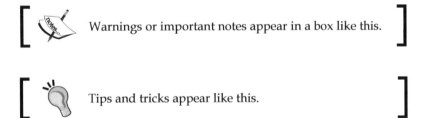

Warnings or important notes appear in a box like this.

Tips and tricks appear like this.

Reader feedback

Feedback from our readers is always welcome. Let us know what you think about this book—what you liked or disliked. Reader feedback is important for us as it helps us develop titles that you will really get the most out of.

To send us general feedback, simply e-mail feedback@packtpub.com, and mention the book's title in the subject of your message.

If there is a topic that you have expertise in and you are interested in either writing or contributing to a book, see our author guide at www.packtpub.com/authors.

Customer support

Now that you are the proud owner of a Packt book, we have a number of things to help you to get the most from your purchase.

Downloading the example code

You can download the example code files from your account at `http://www.packtpub.com` for all the Packt Publishing books you have purchased. If you purchased this book elsewhere, you can visit `http://www.packtpub.com/support` and register to have the files e-mailed directly to you.

Downloading the color images of this book

We also provide you with a PDF file that has color images of the screenshots/ diagrams used in this book. The color images will help you better understand the changes in the output. You can download this file from: `https://www.packtpub.com/sites/default/files/downloads/0122OS_ColoredImages.pdf`.

Errata

Although we have taken every care to ensure the accuracy of our content, mistakes do happen. If you find a mistake in one of our books—maybe a mistake in the text or the code—we would be grateful if you could report this to us. By doing so, you can save other readers from frustration and help us improve subsequent versions of this book. If you find any errata, please report them by visiting `http://www.packtpub.com/submit-errata`, selecting your book, clicking on the **Errata Submission Form** link, and entering the details of your errata. Once your errata are verified, your submission will be accepted and the errata will be uploaded to our website or added to any list of existing errata under the Errata section of that title.

To view the previously submitted errata, go to `https://www.packtpub.com/books/content/support` and enter the name of the book in the search field. The required information will appear under the **Errata** section.

Piracy

Piracy of copyrighted material on the Internet is an ongoing problem across all media. At Packt, we take the protection of our copyright and licenses very seriously. If you come across any illegal copies of our works in any form on the Internet, please provide us with the location address or website name immediately so that we can pursue a remedy.

Please contact us at copyright@packtpub.com with a link to the suspected pirated material.

We appreciate your help in protecting our authors and our ability to bring you valuable content.

Questions

If you have a problem with any aspect of this book, you can contact us at questions@packtpub.com, and we will do our best to address the problem.

1
Player 1 UP

The terminology used by old arcade and pinball machines "1 UP" was a kind of notice to the players that they were playing (up) now. It was also used to indicate earning an extra life. Are you ready to build three great games?

We will build three cool games together. Every line of code for these three games is shown in this book; you will never have to refer to the code files to see what is going on. Also, the entire file set required to build all three games is included in the download bundle that can be obtained from the books page on the Packt website.

All the code, Android manifest files, and the graphical and audio assets are included in the download as well. The three cool games are progressively more challenging to implement.

The first project uses a simple but functional game engine that clearly demonstrates the essentials of a main game loop. The game will be fully working with the home screen, high scores, sound, and animation. But by the end of the project, as we add features and try to balance the game play, we will soon see that we need more flexibility in order to add features.

In the second project, a hard retro platformer, we will see how we can use a simple and flexible design to build a relatively fast and very flexible game engine, which is extendable and reusable. This flexibility will allow us to make quite a complex and well-featured game. This game will have multiple levels, different environments, and more. This in turn will highlight the need for being able to draw graphics more quickly. That leads us on to the third project.

In the third project, we will build an Asteroids-like game called **Asteroids simulator**. Although the game won't have as many features as the previous project, it will feature the super-smooth drawing of hundreds of animated game objects running at over 60 frames per second. We will achieve this by learning about and using the **Open Graphics Library for Embedded Systems (OpenGL ES 2)**.

By the end of this book, you will have a whole repertoire of design ideas, techniques, and code templates that you can use in your future games. By seeing the strengths and weaknesses of the different ways of making games on Android, you will be able to successfully design and build games in the most appropriate way for your next big game.

A closer look at the games

Here is a quick glimpse at the three projects.

Tappy Defender

Fly Flappy Bird-style with one finger to reach your home planet, while avoiding multiple enemies. Features include:

- Basic animation
- Home screen

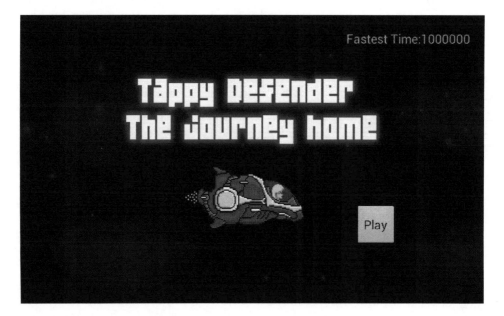

- Collision detection
- High scores
- Simple HUD

- One-finger touch screen controls

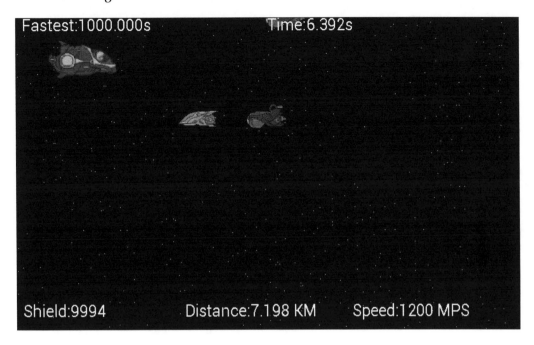

Tough retro platformer

This is a genuinely tough-to-beat retro style platform game. We have to guide Bob from the underground fire caves through the city, forest, and finally to the mountains. It has four challenging levels. Features include:

- A more advanced, flexible game engine
- More advanced "sprite sheet" character animation
- A level builder engine to design your levels in text format
- Multiple scrolling parallax backgrounds
- Transition between levels

- A more advanced HUD

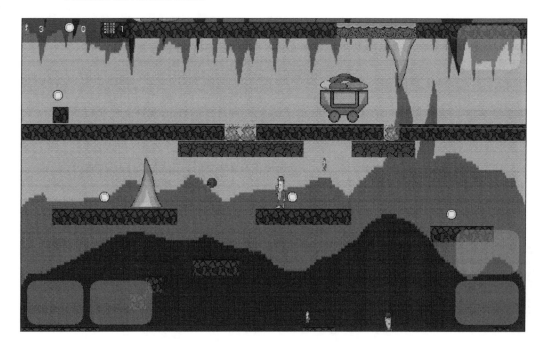

- Add loads of extra diverse levels
- Sound manager to easily manage sound FX
- Pickups
- An upgradeable gun
- Seek-and-destroy enemy drones
- Simple AI scripting for patrolling enemy guards
- Hazards such as fire pits

- Scenery objects to create atmosphere

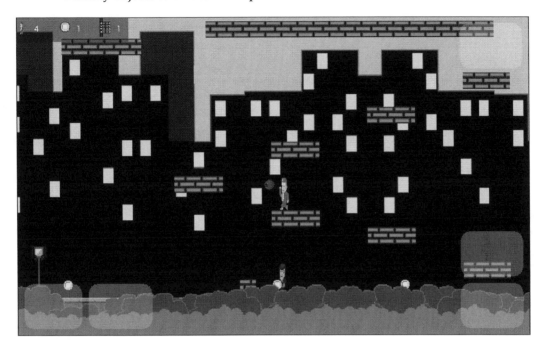

Asteroids simulator

This is a classic shooter with retro vector-graphics style visuals. It involves clearing waves of smoothly animated spinning asteroids with a rapid fire gun. Features include:

- 60 frames per second or better, even on old hardware
- An introduction to OpenGL ES 2
- Shooter with waves of progressive difficulty

- Advanced multiphase collision detection

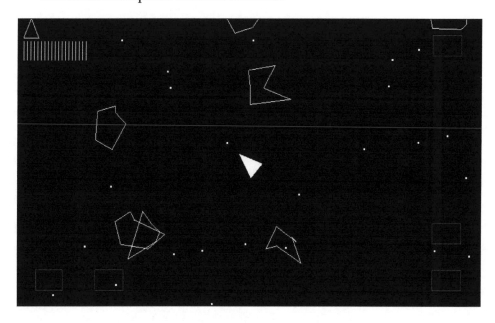

Setting up your development environment

All the code in this book and the download bundle will work in your favorite Android IDE. However, I found the latest version of Android Studio exceptionally friendly to use and the code was written and tested in it as well.

If you don't currently use Android Studio, I encourage you to give it a try. Here is a quick overview of how to get up and running quickly. This guide includes steps to install the Java JDK in case you are completely new to Android development.

 If you already have your preferred development environment ready to go then jump straight to *Chapter 2, Tappy Defender – First Step*.

The first thing we need to do is prepare your PC to develop for Android using Java. Fortunately, this is made quite simple for us.

If you are learning on Mac or Linux everything in this book will still work. The next two tutorials have Windows-specific instructions and screenshots. However, it shouldn't be too difficult to vary the steps slightly to suit Mac or Linux.

All we need to do is:

1. Install the **Java Development Kit (JDK)**, which allows us to develop in Java.

2. Then install Android Studio to make Android development fast and easy. Android Studio uses the JDK and some other Android-specific tools that get automatically installed when we install Android Studio.

Installing the JDK

The first thing we need to do is get the latest version of the JDK. To complete this guide, perform the following instructions:

1. We need to be on the Java website, so visit:
    `http://www.oracle.com/technetwork/java/javase/downloads/index.html`.

2. Find the three buttons shown here and click on the one that says **JDK** that is highlighted in the following image. They are on the right-hand side of the web page. Then, click on the **Download** button under the **JDK** option:

3. You will be taken to a page that has multiple options to download the JDK. In the **Product/File Description** column, you need to click the option that matches your operating system. Windows, Mac, Linux, and some other less common options are all listed.

4. A common question asked here is, do I have 32- or 64-bit windows? To find out, right-click on your **My Computer** icon (**This PC** on Windows 8), click on the **Properties** option, and look under the **System** heading at the **System type** entry:

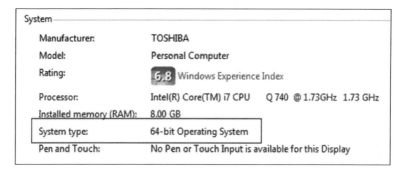

5. Click on the somewhat hidden **Accept License Agreement** checkbox:

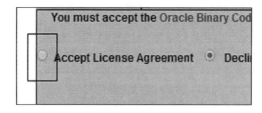

6. Now, click on **download for your OS** and type as previously determined. Wait for the download to finish.

7. In your downloads folder, double-click on the file you just downloaded. The latest version at the time of writing for a 64-bit Windows PC was jdk-8u5-windows-x64. If you are using Mac/Linux or have a 32-bit OS, your filename will vary accordingly.

8. In the first of several install dialogs, click on the **Next** button and you will see the following dialog box:

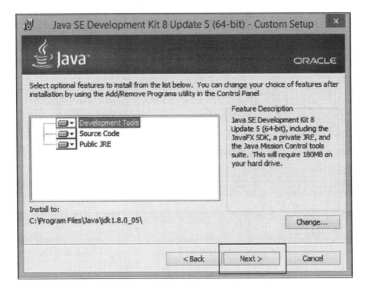

9. Accept the defaults shown in the previous image by clicking on **Next**. In the next dialog box, you can accept the default install location by clicking on **Next**.

10. Next up is the last dialog of the Java installer; for this click on **Close**.

 The JDK is now installed. Next, we will make sure that Android Studio is able to use the JDK.

11. Right-click on your **My Computer** icon (**This PC** on windows 8) and click on **Properties** | **Advanced system settings** | **Environment Variables...** | **New...** (under **System variables**, not under **User variables**). Now, you can see the **New System Variable** dialog box:

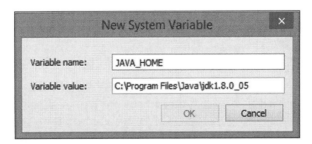

12. Type JAVA_HOME for **Variable name:** and enter C:\Program Files\ Java\jdk1.8.0_05 for the **Variable value:** field. If you installed the JDK somewhere else, then the file path you enter in the **Variable value:** field will need to point to wherever you put it. Your exact file path will likely have a different ending to match the latest version of Java at the time you downloaded it.

13. Click on **OK** to save your new settings.

14. Now under **System variables**, click on **Path** and then click on the **Edit...** button. At the very end of the text in the **Variable value:** field, enter the following text to add our new variable to the file paths that Windows will use, ;JAVA_HOME. Be sure not to miss the semicolon from the beginning.

15. Click on **OK** to save the updated **Path** variable.

16. Now, click on **OK** again to clear the **Advanced system settings** dialog box.

The JDK is now installed on our PC.

Installing Android Studio

Without delay, let's get Android Studio installed, and then we can begin our first game project. Visit:

https://developer.android.com/sdk/index.html

1. Click on the button labeled **DOWNLOAD ANDROID STUDIO FOR WINDOWS** to start the Android Studio download. This will take you to another web page with a very similar looking button to the one you just clicked on.

2. Accept the license by checking the checkbox and commence the download by clicking the button labeled **DOWNLOAD ANDROID STUDIO FOR WINDOWS** and wait for the download to complete.

3. In the folder you just downloaded Android Studio to, right-click on the android-studio-bundle-135.12465-windows.exe file and click on **Run as administrator**. The end of your filename will vary depending on the version of Android Studio and your operating system.

4. When asked if you want to allow the following program from an unknown publisher to make changes to your computer, click on **Yes**. On the next screen, click on **Next**.

5. On the screen pictured here, you can choose which users of your PC can use Android Studio. Choose which is right for you as all options will work, and then click on **Next**:

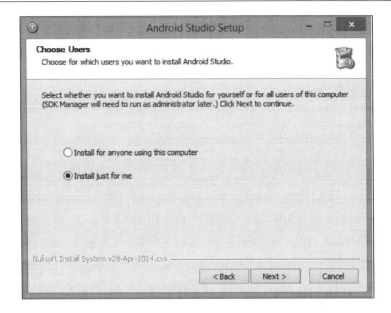

6. In the next dialog, leave the default settings and then click on **Next**.

7. On the **Choose start menu folder** dialog box leave the defaults and click on **Install**.

8. On the Installation complete dialog, click on **Finish** to run Android Studio for the first time.

9. The next dialog is for users who have already used Android Studio, so assuming you are first-time user, select the **I do not have a previous version of Android Studio or I do not want to import my settings** checkbox. Then click on **OK**:

That was the last piece of software we needed. We will begin to use Android Studio straight away in the next chapter.

Summary

This chapter was deliberately kept as short as possible, so we can get on with building some games. We will do this now.

2
Tappy Defender – First Step

Welcome to the first game, which we will learn about in three chapters. In this chapter, we will closely examine the goals for the finished product. It helps a lot when building a game, if we know exactly what we are trying to achieve.

We can then look at the structure of our code, including an approximate design pattern that we will be adhering to. Then, we will put together the code skeleton of our first game engine. Finally, to finish the chapter, we will draw our first real object from the game and animate it on the screen.

We will then be ready for *Chapter 3, Tappy Defender – Taking Flight*, where we can make really fast progress before completing our first game in *Chapter 4, Tappy Defender – Going Home*.

Planning the first game

In this section, we will flesh out exactly what our game will be. The backstory; who is our hero and what are they trying to achieve? The game mechanics; what will the player actually do? What buttons will he press and in what way is that a challenge or fun thing to do? Then, we will look at the rules. What constitutes victory, death, and progress? Finally, we will get technical and start to examine how we will actually build the game.

Backstory

Valerie has been defending the far outposts of humanity since the early '80s. Her brave exploits were originally immortalized in the 1981 arcade classic, Defender. However, after over 30 years on the front line, she is retiring and it is time to begin the journey home. Unfortunately, in a recent skirmish, her ship's engines and navigation systems were severely damaged. Therefore, now she must fly all the way home using only her boost thruster.

This means that she must fly her ship by simultaneously thrusting up and forward, kind of bouncing really, while avoiding enemies who try to crash into her. In a recent communication with Earth, Valerie was heard to claim that it was, "Like trying to fly a lame bird." This is some concept art of Valerie in her damaged ship because it helps to visualize our game as early as possible.

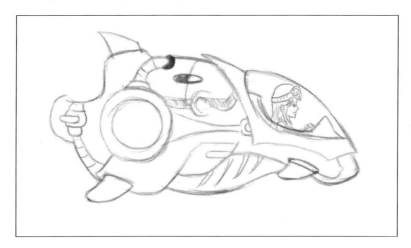

Now that we have learned a little bit about our hero and her predicament, we take a closer look at the mechanics of the game.

The game mechanics

Mechanics are the key actions that a player must make and become good at, to be able to beat the game. When designing a game, you can rely on tried and tested ideas for mechanics or you can invent your own. In Tappy Defender, we will be using a mechanic where the player taps and holds the screen to boost the ship.

This boosting will raise the ship up the screen, but will also make the ship speed up and therefore be more vulnerable. When the player removes their finger, the boost engine will cut out and the ship will fall downward and decelerate, thus making the ship slightly less vulnerable. Therefore, a very fine and masterful balance of boosting and not boosting is required to survive.

Tappy Defender is of course heavily inspired by Flappy Bird and a multitude of similar games that followed its success.

Instead of a how-far-can-I-get scoring system like Flappy Bird, Tappy Defender will have a goal of reaching "home". Then, the player can replay the game multiple times in order to try and beat their fastest time. Of course to go faster, the player must boost more frequently and put Valerie in greater peril.

 In the unlikely event you have never played or seen Flappy Bird, it is well worth spending 5 minutes having a play with this type of game now. You can download one of the many Flappy Bird inspired apps from the Google Play store:

`https://play.google.com/store/search?q=flappy%20 bird&c=apps`

Rules for the game

Here, we will define things which balance the game and make it fair and consistent for the player:

- The player's ship is much tougher than the enemy ships. This is because the player's ship has shields. Each time the player collides with an enemy, the enemy is instantly destroyed, but the player loses a shield. The player has three shields.
- The player will need to fly a set number of kilometers to reach home.
- Every time the player reaches home, they win the game. If their time was the fastest, they also get a new fastest time, like a high score.
- Enemies will spawn at a random height on the far right of the screen and fly toward the player at a random speed.

The player is always positioned on the far left of the screen, but boosting will mean the enemies approach more quickly.

The design

We will use a loose design pattern, where we will separate our code based on a control part, model part, and view. This is how we will separate our code into three areas.

Control

This is the part of our code that will control all other parts. It will decide when to show the view, it will initialize all our game objects from the model, and it will prompt decisions based on the states of data to take place within the model.

Model

The model is our game data and logic. What do the ships look like? Where on the screen are our ships? How fast are they going, and so on. Furthermore, the model part of our code is the intelligence system for each of our game objects. Although our enemies in this game don't have sophisticated AI, they will know and decide for themselves how fast they are going, when to respawn and more.

View

The view is exactly what it sounds like. It is the part of our code that will do the actual drawing based on the state of the models. It will draw when the control part of our code tells it. It will not have any influence over the game objects. For example, the view will not decide where an object is or even what it looks like. It just draws and then hands control back to the control code.

Design pattern reality check

In reality, the separation is not as clear as the discussion suggests. In fact, the code for drawing and control is within the same class. However, you will see that the logic of drawing and controlling is separate within that class.

By separating our game into these three parts, we will see how we simplify the development and avoid getting tied up in messy code that constantly expands as we add new features to our game.

Let's look more closely at where this pattern fits in with our code.

The game code structure

First of all, we must take account of the system we are working within. In this case, it is the Android system. If you have been making Android apps for a while, you may be wondering where this pattern stuff fits in with the Android Activity lifecycle. If you are new to Android, you might ask what the Activity lifecycle is.

The Android Activity lifecycle

The Android Activity lifecycle is the framework we must work within to make any type of Android app. There is a class called `Activity` that we must derive from and is an entry point to our app. In addition, we need to be aware that this class, that our game is an object of, also has some methods we can override. These methods control the lifecycle of our app.

When an app is started by the user, our `Activity` object is created and a number of the methods that we can override are called in sequence. This is what happens.

When the `Activity` object is created, three methods are called in sequence; `onCreate()`, `onStart()`, and `onResume()`. At this point, the app is now running. In addition, when the user quits an app or the app is interrupted, perhaps by a phone call, the `onPause` method is called. The user may decide, perhaps after completing their phone call, to return to the app. If this happens, the `onResume` method is called, following which the app is running again.

Should the user not return to the app or the Android system decides that it wants the system resources for something else, two further methods are called to clean up. First `onStop()`, and then `onDestroy()`. The app is now destroyed and any attempt to return to the game again will result in the Activity lifecycle starting from the beginning.

All we have to do as game programmers is be aware of this lifecycle and observe a few rules of good housekeeping. We will implement and explain the rules of good housekeeping as we proceed.

> The Android Activity lifecycle is much more complex and far more nuanced than I have just explained it. However, we know everything we need to get programming our first game. If you want to know more please have a look at this article on the Android developer's web site at:
>
> http://developer.android.com/reference/android/app/Activity.html

Once we have catered for the Android Activity lifecycle, the core methods of our class representing the control part of the pattern will be as simple as this:

1. Update the state of our game objects.
2. Draw the game objects based on their state.
3. Pause to lock the frame rate.
4. Get player input. Actually because parts 1, 2, and 3 happen in a thread, this part can happen at any time.
5. Repeat.

One last bit of preparation, before we start to build our game for real.

The Android Studio file structure

The Android system is quite particular about where we put our class files, including `Activity` and where in the file hierarchy we place our assets like sound files and graphics.

Here is a really quick overview of where we will be putting everything. You don't need to memorize this, as we will remind ourselves of the correct folder while adding assets. We will step through the activity/class creation process the first few times we need to do it.

As a heads up, here is an annotated diagram of what your Android Studio project explorer will look like by the end of the Tappy Defender project:

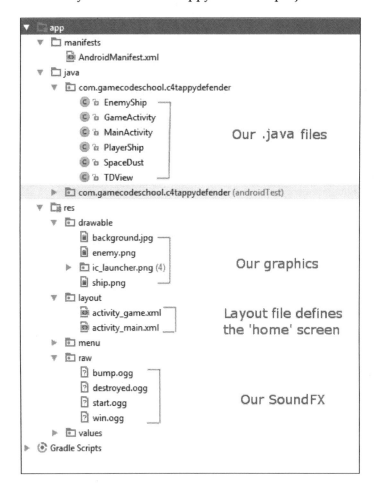

Now, we can actually start building Tappy Defender.

Building the home screen

Since we have done all the planning and preparation, we can get started with the code.

Downloading the example code

You can download the example code files from your account at http://www.packtpub.com for all the Packt Publishing books you have purchased. If you purchased this book elsewhere, you can visit http://www.packtpub.com/support and register to have the files e-mailed directly to you.

To use the code files, you will still need to create an Android Studio project. In addition, you will need to change the package name in the very first line of code of each of the JAVA files. Change the package name to match the package name of the project you created. Finally, you will need to make sure that any assets such as images or sound files are placed into the appropriate folder in the project. All the required assets for each project are supplied in the download bundle.

Creating the project

Fire up Android Studio and create a new project by following these steps. All the files to get the project to where we will be, by the end of this chapter, are in the download bundle in the Chapter2 folder.

1. On the **Welcome to Android Studio** dialog, click on **Start a new Android Studio project**.

2. In the **Create New Project** window shown next, we need to enter some basic information about our app. These bits of information will be used by Android Studio to determine the package name.

In the following image, you can see the **Edit** link where you can customize the package name if required.

3. If you will be copy/pasting the supplied code into your project, then use C1 Tappy Defender for the **Application name** field and gamecodeschool.com in the **Company Domain** field as shown in the following screenshot:

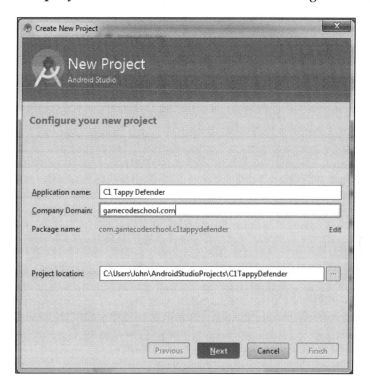

4. Click on the **Next** button when you're ready. When asked to select the form factors, your app will run on, we can accept the default settings (**Phone and Tablet**). So click on **Next** again.

5. On the **Add an activity to mobile** dialog, just click on **Blank Activity** followed by the **Next** button.

6. On the **Customize the Activity** dialog, again we can accept the default settings because MainActivity seems like a good name for our main Activity. So click on the **Finish** button.

What we did

Android Studio has built the project and created a number of files, most of which we will see and edit during the course of building this game. As mentioned earlier, even if you are just copying and pasting the code, you need to go through this step because Android Studio is doing things behind the scenes to make our project work.

Building the home screen UI

The first and simplest part of our Tappy Defender game is the home screen. All we need is a neat picture with a scene about the game, a high score, and a button to start the game. The finished home screen will look a bit like this:

When we built the project, Android Studio opens up two files ready for us to edit. You can see them as tabs in the following Android Studio UI designer. The files (and tabs) are `MainActivity.java` and `activity_main.xml`:

The MainActivity.java file is the entry point to our game, and we will see this in more detail soon. The activity_main.xml file is the UI layout that our home screen will use. Now, we can go ahead and edit the activity_main.xml file, so it actually looks like our home screen should.

1. First of all, your game will be played with the Android device in landscape mode. If we change our UI preview window to landscape, we will see your progress more accurately. Look for the button shown in the next image. It is just preceding the UI preview:

2. Click on the button shown in the preceding screenshot, and your UI preview will switch to landscape like this:

3. Make sure activity_main.xml is open by clicking on its tab.

4. Now, we will set in a background image. You can use your own or mine from Chapter2/drawable/background.jpg in the download bundle. Add your chosen image to the drawable folder of the project in Android Studio.

5. In the **Properties** window of the UI designer, find and click on the **background** property as shown in the next image:

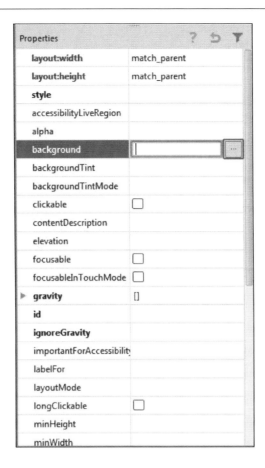

6. Also, in the previous image the button labelled **...** is outlined. It is just to the right of the **background** property. Click on that **...** button and browse to and select the background image file that you will be using.

7. Next, we need a **TextView** widget that we will use to display the high score. Note that there is already a **TextView** widget on the layout. It says **Hello World**. You will modify this and use it for our high score. Left click on it and drag the **TextView** to where you want it. You can copy me if you intend using the supplied background or put it where it looks best with your background.

8. Next, in the **Properties** window, find and click on the **id** property. Enter `textHighScore`. Type it exactly as shown because when we write some Java code in a later tutorial, we will refer to this ID in order to manipulate it, to show the player's fastest time.

9. You can also edit the **text** property to say High Score: 99999 or similar so that the **TextView** looks the part. However, this isn't necessary because your Java code will take care of this later.

10. Now, we will drag a button from the widget palette as shown in the following screenshot:

11. Drag it to where it looks good on your background. You can copy me if using the supplied background or put it where it looks best with your background.

What we did

We now have a cool background with neatly arranged widgets (a **TextView** and a **Button**) for your home screen. We can add functionality via Java code to the **Button** widget next. Revisit the **TextView** for the player's high score in *Chapter 4, Tappy Defender – Going Home*. The important point is that both the widgets have been assigned a unique ID that we can use to reference and manipulate in your Java code.

Coding the functionality

Now, we have a simple layout for our game home screen. Now, we need to add the functionality that will allow the player to click on the **Play** button to start the game.

Click on the tab for the MainActivity.java file. The code that was automatically generated for us is not exactly what we need. Therefore, we will start again as it is simpler and quicker than tinkering with what is already there.

Delete the entire contents of the `MainActivity.java` file except the package name and enter the following code in it. Of course, your package name may be different.

```
package com.gamecodeschool.cltappydefender;

import android.app.Activity;
import android.os.Bundle;

public class MainActivity extends Activity{

    // This is the entry point to our game
    @Override
    protected void onCreate(Bundle savedInstanceState) {
        super.onCreate(savedInstanceState);

        //Here we set our UI layout as the view
        setContentView(R.layout.activity_main);

    }
}
```

The mentioned code is the current contents of our main `MainActivity` class and the entry point of our game, the `onCreate` method. The line of code that begins with `setContentView...` is the line that loads our UI layout from `activity_main.xml` to the players screen. We can run the game now and see our home screen, but let's make some more progress, following which we will look at how we run the game on a real device at the end of the chapter.

Now, let's handle the **Play** button on our home screen. Add the two highlighted lines of the following code into the `onCreate` method just after the call to `setContentView()`. The first new line creates a new `Button` object and gets a reference to `Button` in our UI layout. The second line is the code that listens for clicks on the button.

```
//Here we set our UI layout as the view
setContentView(R.layout.activity_main);

// Get a reference to the button in our layout
final Button buttonPlay =
            (Button)findViewById(R.id.buttonPlay);
// Listen for clicks
buttonPlay.setOnClickListener(this);
```

Note that we have a few errors in our code. We can resolve these errors by holding down the *Alt* keyboard key and then pressing *Enter*. This will add an import directive for the Button class.

We still have one error. We need to implement an interface so that our code listens to the button clicks. Modify the MainActivity class declaration as highlighted:

```
public class MainActivity extends Activity
        implements View.OnClickListener{
```

When we implement the onClickListener interface, we must also implement the onClick method. This is where we will handle what happens when a button is clicked. We can automatically generate the onClick method by right-clicking somewhere after the onCreate method, but within the MainActivity class, and navigating to **Generate | Implement methods | onClick(v:View):void. Or just add the given code.**

We also need to have Android Studio add another import directive for Android. view.View. Use the *Alt | Enter* keyboard combination again.

We can now scroll to near the bottom of the MainActivity class and see that Android Studio has implemented an empty onClick method for us. We should have no errors in your code at this point. Here is the onClick method:

```
@Override
public void onClick(View v) {
  //Our code goes here
}
```

As we only have one Button object and one listener, we can safely assume that any clicks on our home screen are the player pressing our **Play** button.

Android uses the Intent class to switch between activities. As we need to go to a new activity when the **Play** button is clicked, we will create a new Intent object and pass in the name of our future Activity class, GameActivity to its constructor. We can then use the Intent object to switch activities. Add the following code to the body of the onClick method:

```
// must be the Play button.
// Create a new Intent object
Intent i = new Intent(this, GameActivity.class);
// Start our GameActivity class via the Intent
startActivity(i);
// Now shut this activity down
finish();
```

Once again, we have errors in our code because we need to generate a new import directive, this time for the Intent class so use the *Alt | Enter* keyboard combination again. We still have one error in our code. This is because our GameActivity class does not exist yet. We will now solve this problem.

Creating GameActivity

We have seen that when the player clicks on the **Play** button, main activity will close and game activity will begin. Therefore, we need to create a new activity called GameActivity that will be were your game actually executes.

1. From the main menu, navigate to **File | New | Activity | Blank Activity**.

2. In the **Customize the Activity** dialog, change the **Activity Name** field to GameActivity.

3. We can accept all the other default settings from this dialog, so click on **Finish**.

4. As we did with your MainActivity class, we will code this class from scratch. Therefore, delete the entire code content from GameActivity.java.

What we did

Android Studio has generated two more files for us and done some work behind the scenes that we will investigate soon. The new files are GameActivity.java and activity_game.xml. They are both automatically opened for us in two new tabs, in the same place as the other tabs above the UI designer.

We will never need activity_game.xml because we will build a dynamically generated game view, not a static UI. Feel free to close that now or just ignore it. We will come back to the GameActivity.java file, when we start to code our game for real, later in the chapter in the *Coding the game loop* section.

Configuring the AndroidManifest.xml file

We briefly mentioned that when we create a new project or a new activity, Android Studio does more than just creating two files for us. This is why we create new projects/activities the way we do.

One of the things going on behind the scenes is the creation and modification of the AndroidManifest.xml file in the manifests directory.

This file is required for our app to work. Also, it needs to be edited to make our app work the way we want it to. Android Studio has automatically configured the basics for us, but we will now do two more things to this file.

By editing the `AndroidManifest.xml` file, we will force both of our activities to run with a full screen, and we will also lock them to a landscape layout. Let's make these changes here:

1. Open the `manifests` folder now, and double click on the `AndroidManifest.xml` file to open it in the code editor.

2. In the `AndroidManifest.xml` file, find the following line of code:

   `android:name=".MainActivity"`

3. Immediately following it, type or copy and paste these two lines to make `MainActivity` run full screen and lock it in the landscape orientation:

   `android:theme="@android:style/Theme.NoTitleBar.Fullscreen"`
   `android:screenOrientation="landscape"`

4. In the `AndroidManifest.xml` file, find the following line of code:

   `android:name=".GameActivity"`

5. Immediately following it, type or copy and paste these two lines to make `GameActivity` run full screen and lock it in the landscape orientation:

   `android:theme="@android:style/Theme.NoTitleBar.Fullscreen"`
   `android:screenOrientation="landscape"`

What we did

We have now configured both activities from our game to be full screen. This presents a much more pleasing appearance to our player. In addition, we have disabled the player's ability to affect our game by rotating their Android device.

Coding the game loop

We said that we will not be using a UI layout for our game screen, but instead a dynamically drawn view. This is where the view of our pattern comes in. Let's create a new class to represent our view, then we will put in the fundamental building blocks of our Tappy Defender game.

Building the view

We will leave our two activity classes alone for a while so that we can take a look at our class that will represent the view of our game. As we discussed at the start of this chapter, the view and the controller aspects will be part of the same class.

The Android API provides us with an ideal class for our requirements. The `android.view.SurfaceView` class not only provides us a view that is designed for drawing pixels, text, lines, and sprites onto, but also enables us to quickly handle player input as well.

As if this wasn't useful enough, we can also spawn a thread by implementing the runnable interface allowing our main game loop to get player input and other system essentials at the same time. We will deal with the general structure of your new `SurfaceView` implementation now, so we can fill in the details as we progress with the project.

Creating a new class for the view

Without further delay, we can create a new class which extends `SurfaceView`.

1. Right-click the folder containing our `.java` files and select **New | Java Class** then click on **OK**.

2. In the **Create New Class** dialog, name the new class `TDView`, (Tappy Defender view). Now, click on **OK** to have Android Studio autogenerate the class.

3. The new class will open in the code editor. Amend the code to have it extend `SurfaceView` and implement `Runnable` as discussed in the previous section. Edit the highlighted parts of the code that follows:

    ```
    package com.gamecodeschool.c1tappydefender;

    import android.view.SurfaceView;

    public class TDView extends SurfaceView implements
    Runnable{

    }
    ```

4. Use the *Alt | Enter* combination to import the missing classes.

5. Note that we still have an error in our code. This is because we must provide a constructor for our `SurfaceView` implementation. Right-click just below the `TDView` class declaration and navigate to **Generate | Constructor | SurfaceView(Context:context)**. Or you can just type this in as shown in the next block of code. Now click on **OK**.

What we did

We now have a new class called TDView, which extends SurfaceView for our drawing requirements and implements Runnable for our threading needs. We have also generated a constructor, which we will use soon to initialize our new class.

The Context parameter that is passed into our constructor is a reference to the current state of our application within the Android system that is held by our GameActivity class. This Context parameter is useful/essential for a number of things that we will be implementing throughout this project.

So far, our TDView class will look like this:

```
package com.gamecodeschool.c1tappydefender;

import android.content.Context;
import android.view.SurfaceView;

public class TDView extends SurfaceView implements Runnable{

    public TDView(Context context) {
        super(context);
    }
}
```

Structuring the class code

Now that we have our TDView class extended from the SurfaceView class, we can start coding it. To control the game, we need to be able to update all the game data/objects. This implies an update method. In addition, we are obviously going to want to draw all our game data once every frame after they have been updated. Let's keep all of our drawing code together in a method called draw. Furthermore, we need to control the frequency with which this happens. Therefore, a control method seems like it should be part of the class as well.

We also know that everything needs to happen in your thread; so to achieve this, we should wrap the code in the run method. Lastly, we need a way to control when the thread should and shouldn't do its work so we need an infinite loop controlled by a Boolean, perhaps, playing.

Copy the following code into the body of our TDView class to implement what we just discussed:

```
@Override
    public void run() {
        while (playing) {
```

```
        update();
        draw();
        control();
    }
}
```

This is the bare-bones of our game. The `run` method will execute in a thread, but it will only execute the game loop while the Boolean `playing` instance is true. Then, it will update all the game data, draw the screen based on that game data, and control how long it is until the `run` method is called again.

Now, we can quickly build on this code. First of all, we can implement the three methods that we call from the `run` method. Type the following code in the body of our `TDView` class before the closing curly brace of the `run` method:

```
private void update(){

}

private void draw(){

}

private void control(){

}
```

We now need to declare our playing member variable. We can do this using the `volatile` keyword as it will be accessed from outside the thread and from within. Type this code just after the `TDView` class declaration:

```
volatile boolean playing;
```

Now, we know that we can control the execution of code within the run method with the infinite loop and the `playing` variable. We also need to start and stop the actual thread itself. Not just when we decide, but when the player unexpectedly quits the game. What if he gets a phone call or just taps the home button on his device.

To handle these events, we need the `TDView` class and `GameActivity` to work together. Now, in the `TDView` class, we can implement a `pause` method and a `resume` method. Within them, we put the code to stop and start our thread. Implement these two methods within the body of the `TDView` class:

```
// Clean up our thread if the game is interrupted or the player
quits
public void pause() {
```

```
        playing = false;
        try {
            gameThread.join();
        } catch (InterruptedException e) {

        }
    }


    // Make a new thread and start it
    // Execution moves to our R
    public void resume() {
            playing = true;
            gameThread = new Thread(this);
            gameThread.start();
    }
```

Now, we need an instance of a `Thread` class called `gameThread`. We can declare it as a member variable of `TDView` just after the class declaration, right after our Boolean `playing` parameter. Like this:

```
volatile boolean playing;
Thread gameThread = null;
```

Note that the `onPause` and `onResume` methods are public. We can now add code to our `GameActivity` class to call these methods at the appropriate time. Remember that `GameActivity` extends `Activity`. Therefore, use the overridden `Activity` lifecycle methods.

By overriding the `onPause` method, whenever the activity is paused, we can shut down the thread. This avoids potentially embarrassing the player and having to explain to his caller, why they can hear sound FX in the background.

By overriding `onResume()`, we can have our thread start up in the last phase of the Android lifecycle before the app is actually running.

 Note the distinction between the `pause` and `resume` methods of the `TDView` class and the overridden `onPause` and `onResume` methods of the `GameActivity` class.

The game activity

Before you implement/override this method, note that all they will do is call the parent version of their respective methods followed by the public methods in the `TDView` class to which they correspond.

You might remember back to the section when we created our new `GameActivity` class, we deleted the entire code contents? With that in mind, here is the outline of the code we will need in `GameActivity.java` including the implementation of the overridden methods within the body of the `GameActivity` class that we discussed in the previous section. Type this code in `GameActivity.java`:

```
package com.gamecodeschool.c1tappydefender;

import android.app.Activity;
import android.os.Bundle;

public class GameActivity extends Activity {

    // This is where the "Play" button from HomeActivity sends us
    @Override
    protected void onCreate(Bundle savedInstanceState) {
        super.onCreate(savedInstanceState);


    }

    // If the Activity is paused make sure to pause our thread
    @Override
    protected void onPause() {
        super.onPause();
        gameView.pause();
    }

    // If the Activity is resumed make sure to resume our thread
    @Override
    protected void onResume() {
        super.onResume();
        gameView.resume();
    }


}
```

Finally, let's go ahead and declare an object of the `TDView` class. Do this just after the `GameActivity` class declaration:

```
// Our object to handle the View
private TDView gameView;
```

Now, within the onCreate method, we need to instantiate your object, keeping in mind that your constructor in TDView.java takes a Context object as an argument. Then, we use the newly instantiated object in a call to setContentView(). Remember when we built our home screen, we called setContentView() and passed in our UI design. This time, we are setting the player's view to be the object of our TDView class. Copy the following code into the onCreate method of the GameActivity class:

```
// Create an instance of our Tappy Defender View (TDView)
// Also passing in "this" which is the Context of our app
gameView = new TDView(this);

// Make our gameView the view for the Activity
setContentView(gameView);
```

At this point, we can actually run our game and click on the **Play** button to proceed to the GameView activity, which will use TDView as its view and start our thread. Obviously, there is nothing to see yet, so let's work on the model of our design pattern and build the basic outline of our first game object. At the end of the chapter, we will see how to run the game on an Android device.

The PlayerShip object

We need to keep the model part of our code as separate as possible from the rest. We can do this by creating a class for our player's spaceship. Let's call our new class PlayerShip.

Go ahead and add a new class to the project, and call it PlayerShip. Here are a few quick steps on how to do that. Now, right-click the folder with our .java files in it and navigate to **New | Java Class**, then enter PlayerShip as the name and click on **OK**.

What do we need our PlayerShip class to be able to know about itself? As a bare minimum it needs to:

- Know where it is on the screen
- What it looks like
- How fast it is flying

These requirements suggest a few member variables we can declare. Enter the code just after the class declaration that we generated:

```
private Bitmap bitmap;
private int x, y;
private int speed = 0;
```

As usual, use the *Alt | Enter* keyboard combination to import any missing classes. In the previous block of code, we see that we have declared an object of type `Bitmap` that we will use to hold the graphic which represents our ship.

We have also declared three `int` type variables; x and y to hold the spaceship's screen coordinates and another `int` type variable, `speed` to hold a value for how fast our spaceship is traveling.

Now, let's consider what our `PlayerShip` class needs to do. Again as a bare minimum it needs to:

- Prepare itself
- Update itself
- Share it's state with our view

A constructor seems to be the ideal place to prepare itself. We can initialize its x and y coordinate variables and set a starting speed with the `speed` variable.

The other thing the constructor will need to do is to load the bitmap graphic, which represents its appearance. To load bitmaps, we require an Android `Context` object. This implies that the constructor that we write will need to receive a `Context` object from our view.

With all this in mind, here is our `PlayerShip` constructor to implement point one from our to-do list:

```
// Constructor
public PlayerShip(Context context) {
        x = 50;
        y = 50;
        speed = 1;
        bitmap = BitmapFactory.decodeResource
        (context.getResources(), R.drawable.ship);


    }
```

As usual, we need to import some new classes using the *Alt | Enter* combination. After importing all the new classes required by the line which initializes our bitmap object, we can see we still have an error; `Cannot resolve symbol ship`.

Let's dissect the line that loads the ship bitmap as we will be seeing this quite a lot throughout the book.

The `BitmapFactory` class is using its static method `decodeResource()` to attempt to load our graphic of the player ship. It requires two parameters. The first is the `getResources` method supplied by the `Context` object that was passed from the view.

The second parameter `R.drawable.ship` is requesting a graphic called `ship` from the (R)esource folder named `drawable`. All we have to do to resolve this error is to copy our graphic, named `ship.png`, into the `drawable` folder of our project.

Simply drag and drop/copy and paste the `ship.png` graphic contained in the `Chapter2/drawable` folder from the download bundle into the `res/drawable` folder in the Android Studio project explorer window. The following is a `ship.png` image:

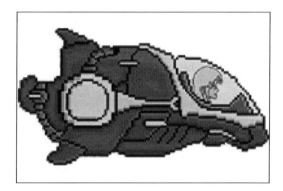

Number two on our list of things that `PlayerShip` needs to do is, to update itself. Let's implement a public `update` method that can be called from our `TDView` class. The method will simply increment the ship's *x* value by 1 each time it is called. Clearly, we need to get more advanced than this. For now implement the method in the `PlayerShip` class like this:

```
public void update() {
    x++;
}
```

Number three on the to-do list is to share its state with the view. We can do this by providing a bunch of getter methods like this:

```
//Getters
public Bitmap getBitmap() {
    return bitmap;
}

public int getSpeed() {
    return speed;
```

```
  }

  public int getX() {
    return x;
  }

  public int getY() {
    return y;
  }
```

Now your `TDView` class can be instantiated, and find out what it likes about any `PlayerShip` objects. However, only the `PlayerShip` class itself can decide how it should look, what properties it has, and how it behaves.

We can see how we will draw our player's ship to the screen and animate it as well.

Drawing the scene

As we will see, drawing a bitmap is really trivial. But the coordinate system that we use to draw our graphics onto needs a brief explanation.

Plotting and drawing

When we draw a `Bitmap` object to the screen, we pass in the coordinates we want to draw the object at. The available coordinates of a given Android device depend on the resolution of its screen.

For example, the Samsung Galaxy S4 phone has a screen resolution of 1920 pixels (across) by 1080 pixels (down) when held in a landscape view.

The numbering system of these coordinates starts in the top-left hand corner at 0,0 and proceeds down and to the right until the bottom right corner is pixel 1919, 1079. The apparent 1 pixel disparity between 1920/ 1919 and 1080/ 1079 is because the numbering starts at 0.

Therefore, when we draw a bitmap or any other drawable to the screen, we must specify *x*, *y* coordinates.

Furthermore, a bitmap is, of course, comprised of many pixels. So which pixel of a given bitmap is drawn at the *x*, *y* screen coordinate that we will be specifying?

The answer is the top-left pixel of the `Bitmap` object. Take a look at the next image, which should clarify the screen coordinates using the Samsung Galaxy S4 as an example.

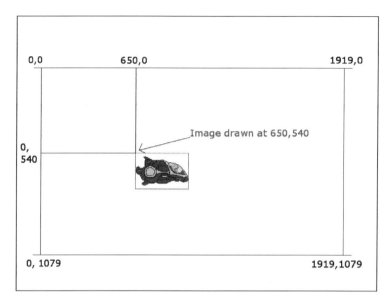

For now, when drawing just a single ship at an arbitrary location, this information is of little consequence. It will become more important in the next chapter, when we start constraining our graphics to the visible screen and respawning them when they disappear.

So let's just bare this in mind and get on with drawing our ship to the screen.

Drawing PlayerShip

Now that we know all this, we can add some code to our `TDView` class, so we can see our `PlayerShip` class in action. First, we need a new `PlayerShip` object with class scope. The following code is the `TDView` class declaration:

```
//Game objects
private PlayerShip player;
```

We also need a bunch of objects that we haven't seen yet to help us actually do some drawing. We need a canvas and some paint.

The Canvas and Paint objects

The aptly named `Canvas` class provides just what you will expect—a virtual canvas to draw our graphics upon.

We can make a virtual canvas using the `Canvas` class and project it onto our `SurfaceView` object which is the view of your `GameActivity` class. We can actually add `Bitmap` objects and even manipulate individual pixels on our `Canvas` object using methods from our `Paint` object. In addition, we also need an object of the `SurfaceHolder` class. This allows us to lock your `Canvas` object while we are manipulating it and unlock it when we are ready to draw the frame.

We will see in more detail how these classes work as we proceed. Type this code immediately following the previous line of code we typed:

```
// For drawing
private Paint paint;
private Canvas canvas;
private SurfaceHolder ourHolder;
```

As usual, we need to use the *Alt | Enter* keyboard combination to import some new classes for the two lines of code that follow. From this point on, we will save digital link and just assume that you know to do this each time you add a new class.

Next, we need to set up to prepare for drawing. The best place to do this is in the `TDView()`, constructor. Type the following code to prepare our `Paint` and `SurfaceHolder` objects for action:

```
// Initialize our drawing objects
ourHolder = getHolder();
paint = new Paint();
```

Immediately after the previous line of code, we can at last call `new()` to initialize our `PlayerShip` object:

```
// Initialize our player ship
player = new PlayerShip(context);
```

Now, we can jump to our `TDView` class's `update` method and do this:

```
// Update the player
player.update();
```

That's it. The `PlayerShip` class (part of the model) knows what to do, and we can add all kinds of artificial intelligence into our `PlayerShip` class. The `TDView` class (the controller) just says when it is time to update. You can easily imagine that all we need to do is create lots of different game objects with different properties and behaviors and call their `update` methods once per frame.

Now, jump to the `TDView` class's `draw` method. Let's draw our `player` object by performing the following:

1. Check that our `SurfaceHolder` class is valid.
2. Lock the `Canvas` object.
3. Clear the screen with a call to `drawColor()`.
4. Splash some virtual paint on it by calling `drawBitmap()` and passing in the `PlayerShip` bitmap and an *x, y* coordinate.
5. Finally, unlock the `Canvas` object and draw the scene.

To achieve these things, type this code in the `draw` method:

```
if (ourHolder.getSurface().isValid()) {

    //First we lock the area of memory we will be drawing to
    canvas = ourHolder.lockCanvas();

    // Rub out the last frame
    canvas.drawColor(Color.argb(255, 0, 0, 0));

    // Draw the player
    canvas.drawBitmap(
        player.getBitmap(),
        player.getX(),
        player.getY(),
        paint);

    // Unlock and draw the scene
    ourHolder.unlockCanvasAndPost(canvas);
}
```

At this point, we can actually run the game. If our eyesight is fast enough or our Android device slow enough, we will just about see our player spaceship fly across the screen with immense speed.

There is just one more thing to do before we deploy our game so far.

Controlling the frame rate

The reason we can barely see anything is that even though we only move our ship at one pixel per frame along the *x* axis (in the `PlayerShip` class's `update` method), our thread is calling the `run` method in an unrestricted manner. This is probably happening hundreds of times per second. What we need to do is control this rate.

Sixty frames per second (FPS) is a reasonable goal. This goal implies the need for timing. The Android system measures time in milliseconds (thousandths of a second). Therefore, we can add the following code to the `control` method:

```
try {
    gameThread.sleep(17);
    } catch (InterruptedException e) {

    }
```

In the preceding code, we paused the thread for 17 milliseconds (*1000(milliseconds)/60(FPS)*) by calling `gameThread.sleep` with `17` as the argument to the method. We wrap the code within a `try`/`catch` block.

Deploying the game

Now, we can run our game to see our spaceship floating through space (starting at 50 pixels on the *x* axis and 50 pixels on the *y* axis).

Android Studio enables us to fairly quickly create emulators, on which we can test our games on a development PC. However, even the most simple of games will not run well on an emulator. When we start testing things like player input, the experience is so awful that it is best to avoid using emulators completely.

The solution is to carry out debugging on a real Android device. It is very easy to prepare for this.

Debugging on an Android device

The first thing to do is to visit your device manufacturer's website and obtain and install any drivers that are required for your device and operating system.

The next few steps will setup the Android device for debugging. Note that different manufacturers structure the menu options slightly differently than others. The following sequence is probably very close, if not exact to enable debugging on most devices.

1. Tap the **Settings** menu option or the **Settings** app.
2. Tap **Developer** options.
3. Tap the checkbox for **USB Debugging**.
4. Connect your Android device to the USB port of your development system. The next image shows on the Android tab. At the bottom of the Android Studio UI, you can see that **Samsung GT-I9100 Android 4.1.2 (API 16)** has been detected:

5. Click on the **Play** icon from the Android Studio toolbar:

6. When prompted, click on **OK** to run the game on your chosen device.

The game will now run on the device. Any output or errors can be seen in the **logcat** window, also on the **Android** tab:

```
logcat
02-02 13:14:54.860  10308-10308/com.gamecodeschool.cltappydefender D/libEGL:  loaded /system/lib/egl/libEGL_mali.so
02-02 13:14:54.900  10308-10308/com.gamecodeschool.cltappydefender D/libEGL:  loaded /system/lib/egl/libGLESv1_CM_mali.so
02-02 13:14:54.900  10308-10308/com.gamecodeschool.cltappydefender D/libEGL:  loaded /system/lib/egl/libGLESv2_mali.so
02-02 13:14:54.905  10308-10308/com.gamecodeschool.cltappydefender D/:  Device driver API match
        Device driver API version: 10
        User space API version: 10
02-02 13:14:54.905  10308-10308/com.gamecodeschool.cltappydefender D/:  mali: REVISION=Linux-r2p4-02rel0 BUILD_DATE=Thu Oct 25 08:43:05 KST 2012
02-02 13:14:54.945  10308-10308/com.gamecodeschool.cltappydefender D/OpenGLRenderer:  Enabling debug mode 0
```

Watch with awe as our player's spaceship moves slowly from left to right.

Summary

In this chapter, we spent a lot of time setting up the structure, game loop, and thread. We also spent time handling the Android Activity lifecycle.

Now, we have all this in place, and we can easily start adding more game objects to make Tappy Defender quickly feel more like a real game in the next chapter.

3

Tappy Defender – Taking Flight

We are now ready to quickly add a lot of new objects and some features as well. By the end of this chapter, we will be really close to a playable game. We will detect the player touching the screen, so he can control the spaceship. We will add virtual boosters to our `SpaceShip` class to move the ship up and down and increase the speed.

We will then detect the resolution of the Android device and use it to do things like prevent the player boosting off the screen, and to detect when our enemies need to respawn.

We will create a new `EnemyShip` class, which will represent the suicidal enemies. We will also see how we can easily spawn and then control them without changing any of the logic from the control part of our code.

We will add a scrolling effect by adding a `SpaceDust` class and spawning dozens of them to make it look like the player is whizzing through space.

Finally, we will learn about, and implement, collision detection so we know when our player has been hit by an enemy, as well as look at a graphical trick to help us with debugging our collision detection code.

Controlling the spaceship

We have our player's spaceship floating aimlessly on the screen starting 50 pixels from the left and 50 pixels from the top and drifting slowly to the right. Now, we can give the player the power to control the spaceship.

Remember the design for the controls is a one finger tap and hold to boost, release to quit boosting and decelerate.

Detecting touches

The `SurfaceView` class that we extended for our view is perfect for handling screen touches.

All we need to do is override the `onTouchEvent` method within our `TDView` class. Let's see the code in full, and then we can examine it more closely to make sure we understand what is going on. Enter this method in the `TDView` class and import the necessary classes in the usual way. I have highlighted the parts of the code that we will be customizing later:

```
// SurfaceView allows us to handle the onTouchEvent
@Override
public boolean onTouchEvent(MotionEvent motionEvent) {

    // There are many different events in MotionEvent
    // We care about just 2 - for now.
    switch (motionEvent.getAction() & MotionEvent.ACTION_MASK) {

        // Has the player lifted their finger up?
        case MotionEvent.ACTION_UP:
            // Do something here
            break;

        // Has the player touched the screen?
        case MotionEvent.ACTION_DOWN:
            // Do something here
            break;
    }
    return true;
}
```

This is how the `onTouchEvent` method works so far. The player touches the screen; this can be any kind of contact at all. It could be a swipe, a pinch, multiple fingers, and so on. A detailed message is sent to the `onTouchEvent` method.

The details of the event are contained in the `MotionEvent` class parameter, as we can see in our code. The `MotionEvent` class holds lots of data. It knows how many fingers were placed on the screen, the coordinates of each, and if any gestures were made as well.

As we are implementing a simple tap and hold to boost, release to stop boosting control scheme; we can simply switch using the `motionEvent.getAction()` & `MotionEvent.ACTION_MASK` condition and cater for just two of many possible different cases.

The case `MotionEvent.ACTION_UP:` will, as the name suggests, tell us when the player removes a finger from the screen. Then, perhaps unsurprisingly, case `MotionEvent.ACTION_DOWN:` tells us if the player places a finger on the screen.

> What we can find out through the `MotionEvent` class is quite vast. Why not take a look at the full scope of its potential here: `http://developer.android.com/reference/android/view/MotionEvent.html`. We will also explore this class further in the next project that we start to build in *Chapter 5, Platformer – Upgrading the Game Engine.*

Adding boosters to the spaceship

Now, all we need to do is think about how we will use these events to control the spaceship. First of all, the spaceship needs to know if it is boosting or not boosting. This suggests a Boolean member variable. Add this code just after the class declaration in the `PlayerShip` class:

```
private boolean boosting;
```

We then need to initialize it when a `PlayerShip` object is created. So add this to the `PlayerShip` constructor:

```
boosting = false;
```

Now, we need to let the `onTouchEvent` method toggle `boosting` between true and false, boosting and not boosting. Add these methods to the `PlayerShip` class:

```
public void setBoosting() {
  boosting = true;
}

public void stopBoosting() {
  boosting = false;
}
```

Now, we can call these public methods from our `onTouchEvent` method to control the state of whether the spaceship is boosting or not. Add this new code in the `onTouchEvent` method:

```
// Has the player lifted there finger up?
case MotionEvent.ACTION_UP:
  player.stopBoosting();
  break;

// Has the player touched the screen?
case MotionEvent.ACTION_DOWN:
  player.setBoosting();
  break;
```

Now, our view is talking to our model; all we need to do is make the boosting variable do something depending on which state it is in. The logical place for this code will be the `PlayerShip` class's `update` method.

We will change the `speed` variable of our spaceship based on whether the ship is currently boosting. At first this seems simple, but there are a few minor issues with just increasing the speed based on whether the ship is boosting:

- One problem is that the `update` method is called 60 times every second. So, it wouldn't take much boosting to have the ship flying at ridiculous speeds. We need to constrain the ship's speed.

- Another problem is that our spaceship will rise up the screen when boosting, and there is nothing to stop it whizzing straight off the top of the screen, never to be seen again. We need to constrain the ship's *x* and *y* coordinates within the screen.

- When the ship is not boosting and the speed steadily returns to zero, what will bring the ship back down again? We will need a simple gravity physics simulation.

To solve these three problems, we can add code to our `PlayerShip` class. However, before we do this, a quick word about gameplay balance. The code which we will see very soon uses different integer values, for example, we initialize `GRAVITY` to `-12` and `MAX_SPEED` to `20`. These numbers have no bearing in reality!

They are simply the arbitrary numbers that make the gameplay balanced. Feel free to play with all these arbitrary figures to make the game harder, easier, or even impossible. At the end of *Chapter 4, Tappy Defender – Going Home*, we will look more closely at game iteration and look again at difficulty and balance.

With three of our previously stated problems in mind, add the following member variables just after the class declaration in the `PlayerShip` class:

```
private final int GRAVITY = -12;

// Stop ship leaving the screen
private int maxY;
private int minY;

//Limit the bounds of the ship's speed
private final int MIN_SPEED = 1;
private final int MAX_SPEED = 20;
```

Now, we made a start to solve our three problems, we can add code to our `PlayerShip` class's `update` method. We will delete the one line of code, we put in there in the previous chapter. That was just there to take a quick look at our ship in action. Enter the new code of our `PlayerShip` class's `update` method. We will take a closer look afterward:

```
public void update() {

  // Are we boosting?
  if (boosting) {
    // Speed up
    speed += 2;
  } else {
    // Slow down
    speed -= 5;
  }

  // Constrain top speed
  if (speed > MAX_SPEED) {
    speed = MAX_SPEED;
  }

  // Never stop completely
  if (speed < MIN_SPEED) {
    speed = MIN_SPEED;
  }

  // move the ship up or down
  y -= speed + GRAVITY;

  // But don't let ship stray off screen
  if (y < minY) {
```

```
        y = minY;
    }

    if (y > maxY) {
       y = maxY;
    }


}
```

In order from the top of the previous block of code, we are increasing and decreasing the speed variable by apparently arbitrary amounts, each frame of the game, based on if the ship is boosting or not.

We then constrain the speed of the ship to a maximum of 20 and a minimum of 1, as specified by the variables we added earlier. With the line `y -= speed + GRAVITY`, we move the graphic on screen either up or down based on speed and gravity. The apparently arbitrary values for `GRAVITY` and `MAX_SPEED` work nicely to allow the player to awkwardly and precariously bounce along through space.

Finally, we stop the ship from ever disappearing off the screen by making sure the ship graphic is never drawn beyond `maxY` and `minY`. You have probably noticed that, as of yet, we haven't initialized `maxY` and `minY`. Furthermore, what will we initialize them to anyway as many Android devices have vastly different screen resolutions?

What we need to do is discover the resolution of the Android device at run time and use the information to initialize `MaxY` and `minY`.

Detecting the screen resolution

We know that we need the maximum *y* coordinate of the player's screen. Later in the project when we start adding backgrounds and enemy ships, we will realize that we also need the maximum *x* coordinate as well. With this in mind, let's see how we can get this information and make it available to the `PlayerShip` class.

The most expedient time to detect the screen resolution is as the app is starting, and before our view and the model have been instantiated. This implies that our `GameActivity` class is a good place to do it. We will now add code to the `onCreate` method of the `GameActivity` class. Add this new code to the `onCreate` class, before the call to `new...` that creates our `TDView` object:

```
// Get a Display object to access screen details
Display display = getWindowManager().getDefaultDisplay();
// Load the resolution into a Point object
Point size = new Point();
display.getSize(size);
```

The previous code declares and initializes an object of the `Display` type using `getWindowManager().getDefaultDisplay();`. Then we create a new object of type `Point`. The `Point` object can hold two coordinates and we then pass it as an argument into the `getSize` method of our new `Display` object.

We now have the resolution of the Android device our game is running on, neatly stored in `size`. Now pass this on to the parts of our code which require it. First, we will change the arguments we pass in the call to `new`, which initializes our `TDView` object. Change the call to `new` as shown next to pass in the screen resolution to the `TDView` constructor:

```
// Create an instance of our Tappy Defender View
// Also passing in this.
// Also passing in the screen resolution to the constructor
gameView = new TDView(this, size.x, size.y);
```

Then, of course, we need to update the `TDView` constructor itself. In the `TDView.java` file, amend the `TDView` constructor's signature so that the declaration now looks like this:

```
TDView(Context context, int x, int y) {
```

Now, still in the constructor, change the way we initialize the player of our `PlayerShip` object:

```
player = new PlayerShip(context, x, y);
```

Of course, we must now amend the constructor declaration within the `PlayerShip` class itself, to this:

```
public PlayerShip(Context context, int screenX, int screenY) {
```

In addition, we can now initialize our `maxY` and `minY` variables within the `PlayerShip` constructor. Before we see the code, we need to consider exactly how this will work.

The coordinates of the bitmap that holds our spaceship graphic is drawn with the top-left corner at the *x = 0* and *y = 0* coordinates passed in to `drawBitmap()` in the `TDView` class's `draw` method. This means that there are pixels off to the right and after the coordinates at which we begin to draw the ship. Take a look at this next image to visualize this:

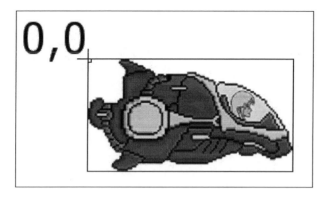

Therefore, we must set our `minY` and `maxY` values with this in mind. As the image illustrates, the top pixel of the bitmap is indeed drawn exactly at the ships *y*. We can then be confident that `minY` should be zero.

The bottom of the ship, however, is drawn at *y + the height of the bitmap*.

We can now add two lines of code to our constructor to initialize these variables:

```
maxY = screenY - bitmap.getHeight();
minY = 0;
```

You can now run the game and test out your boosters!

Building the enemies

Now that we have the tap controls implemented, it is time to add some enemies that the player can boost to avoid.

This is going to be much easier than when we added our player's spaceship because most of what we need is in place already. All we have to do is code a class to represent our enemy, instantiate as many enemy objects as we need, call their `update` methods, and then draw them.

As we will see, the `update` method for our enemy will be quite different to that of `PlayerShip`. It will need to handle things like simple AI to fly toward the player. It will also need to handle respawning when it leaves the screen.

Designing the enemy

To begin with, create a new Java class and call it EnemyShip. Add these member variables inside the class so your new class will look like this:

```
public class EnemyShip{
    private Bitmap bitmap;
    private int x, y;
    private int speed = 1;

    // Detect enemies leaving the screen
    private int maxX;
    private int minX;

    // Spawn enemies within screen bounds
    private int maxY;
    private int minY;
}
```

Now, add some getter and setter methods so that the draw method can access what it needs to draw, and where it needs to draw it. There is nothing new or unusual here:

```
//Getters and Setters
public Bitmap getBitmap(){
   return bitmap;
}

public int getX() {
   return x;
}

public int getY() {
   return y;
}
```

Spawning the enemy

Let's implement the EnemyShip constructor in full. Enter the code now, and we will then take a closer look:

```
// Constructor
public EnemyShip(Context context, int screenX, int screenY){
    bitmap = BitmapFactory.decodeResource
    (context.getResources(), R.drawable.enemy);
```

```
    maxX = screenX;
    maxY = screenY;
    minX = 0;
    minY = 0;

    Random generator = new Random();
    speed = generator.nextInt(6)+10;

    x = screenX;
    y = generator.nextInt(maxY) - bitmap.getHeight();
}
```

The constructors' signature is exactly that of the PlayerShip class. A Context class for manipulating your Bitmap object and screenX and screenY that hold the resolution of the screen.

Just as we did with the PlayerShip class, we load up an image into Bitmap. Of course, we once again need to add an image file named enemy.png to the drawable folder of our project. There is a neat enemy graphic in the Chapter3/drawable folder of the download bundle or you can design your own. Any size between roughly 32 x 32 and 256 x 256 will suffice for the purposes of this game. Also, like those supplied, your graphics do not need to be square. We will see that our game engine is imperfect when it comes to how it looks on different screen sizes, and we will address this in the next project:

Next, we initialize maxX, maxY, minX, and minY. Although the enemies only move horizontally, we need the maxY and minY coordinates to make sure that we spawn them at a sensible height. The maxX coordinate will enable us to spawn them just off-screen horizontally.

We create a new object of type `Random` and generate a random number between the values of 10 and 15. These are the maximum and minimum speeds our enemies can travel at. These values are fairly arbitrary, and we might adjust them when we do some play-testing in *Chapter 4, Tappy Defender – Going Home.*

If you are wondering how `generator.nextInt(6)+10;` comes up with a number between 10 and 15, it is because the 6 argument causes `nextInt()` to return a number between 0 and 5.

We then set the enemy ship's *x* coordinate to screen, which spawns it on the far left of the screen. Actually, this spawns it off screen. However, that is fine because it will then emerge in to the player's view rather than just appearing all at once.

We now generate another random number based on `maxY` — the height of the enemy ship bitmap (`bitmap.getHeight()`) — to create a random but sensible *y* coordinate for our enemy ship to spawn at.

What we need to do now is to give our enemies life by coding their update method.

Making the enemy think

Now, we can handle the `EnemyShip` class's `update` method. For now, we just need to handle two things. First, fly the enemy toward the player's end of the screen. We need to take account of the enemy's speed and the player's speed to simulate this accurately. The reason we need to do this is because when the player boosts, he expects his speed to increase, and objects to rush toward him more quickly. However, the spaceship graphic is horizontally static.

We can increase the rate of travel of an enemy in proportion to both the enemy's static and randomly generated speed at the same time as the player's dynamically set speed (through boosting). This will give the player a sense of speeding up even though the ship graphic never moves forward.

The other issue is that the enemy ship will eventually fly off the screen, on the left-hand side. We need to detect when this happens and respawn it on the right-hand side with a new random *y* coordinate and a new random speed. This is just like we did in the constructor.

Finally before we get to the actual code, let's consider something. If the enemy is going to take note of and use the player's speed, it will need to be able to get it. Note that in the next block of code, the `EnemyShip` class's `update` method declaration has a parameter to receive the player's speed.

We will see how this is passed in when we add code to the TDView class's update method soon. Enter the following code for the EnemyShip class's update method to implement what we have just discussed:

```
public void update(int playerSpeed){

  // Move to the left
  x -= playerSpeed;
  x -= speed;

  //respawn when off screen
  if(x < minX-bitmap.getWidth()){
    Random generator = new Random();
    speed = generator.nextInt(10)+10;
    x = maxX;
    y = generator.nextInt(maxY) - bitmap.getHeight();
  }
}
```

As you can see, we first decreased the enemy's *x* coordinate by the player's speed then by the enemy's speed. As the player boosts, the enemy will fly at the player faster. However, if the player is not boosting then the enemy will attack at the speed that was previously and randomly generated.

```
// Move to the left
x -= playerSpeed;
x -= speed;
```

After this, we simply detected if the right-hand edge of the enemy bitmap has disappeared from the left-hand side of the screen. This is done by detecting if the EnemyShip class's *x* coordinate is the width of the bitmap off screen.

```
if(x < minX-bitmap.getWidth()){
```

Then we respawn the very same object to come at the player again. This appears to the player as if it is an entirely new enemy.

The last three things we must do are create a new object from EnemyShip by declaring and then initializing an object. Actually, let's make three.

Here, were we declared our player's ship in our TDView.java file, declare three enemy ships like this:

```
// Game objects
private PlayerShip player;
public EnemyShip enemy1;
```

```
public EnemyShip enemy2;
public EnemyShip enemy3;
```

Now, in the constructor of our TDView class, initialize our three new enemies:

```
// Initialize our player ship
player = new PlayerShip(context, x, y);
enemy1 = new EnemyShip(context, x, y);
enemy2 = new EnemyShip(context, x, y);
enemy3 = new EnemyShip(context, x, y);
```

In the update method of our TDView class, we call each of the new object's update methods in turn. Here, we also see how we pass in the player's speed to each of our enemies so they can use it in their update methods to adjust speed accordingly.

```
// Update the player
player.update();
// Update the enemies
enemy1.update(player.getSpeed());
enemy2.update(player.getSpeed());
enemy3.update(player.getSpeed());
```

Finally, in the TDView class's draw method, we draw our new enemies to the screen.

```
// Draw the player
canvas.drawBitmap
    (player.getBitmap(), player.getX(), player.getY(), paint);

canvas.drawBitmap
    (enemy1.getBitmap(),
    enemy1.getX(),
    enemy1.getY(), paint);

canvas.drawBitmap
    (enemy2.getBitmap(),
    enemy2.getX(),
    enemy2.getY(), paint);

canvas.drawBitmap
    (enemy3.getBitmap(),
    enemy3.getX(),
    enemy3.getY(), paint);
```

You can run the game and give this a try now.

The first and most obvious problem is that the player and the enemies fly right through each other. We will solve this problem later in this chapter, in the *Things that go bump – collision detection* section. But right now, we can make our player's sense of immersion better by drawing a star/space dust field as a background.

The thrill of flight – scrolling the background

Implementing our space dust is going to be really quick and easy. All we will do is create a SpaceDust class with very similar properties to our other game objects. Spawn them into the game at a random location, move them toward the player at a random speed, and respawn them on the far right of the screen, again with a random speed and *y* coordinate.

Then in our TDView class, we can declare a whole array of these objects, update, and draw them each frame.

Create a new class and call it SpaceDust. Now enter this code:

```java
public class SpaceDust {

    private int x, y;
    private int speed;

    // Detect dust leaving the screen
    private int maxX;
    private int maxY;
    private int minX;
    private int minY;

    // Constructor
    public SpaceDust(int screenX, int screenY){

        maxX = screenX;
        maxY = screenY;
        minX = 0;
        minY = 0;

        // Set a speed between  0 and 9
        Random generator = new Random();
        speed = generator.nextInt(10);
```

```java
        //  Set the starting coordinates
        x = generator.nextInt(maxX);
        y = generator.nextInt(maxY);
    }

    public void update(int playerSpeed){
        // Speed up when the player does
        x -= playerSpeed;
        x -= speed;

        //respawn space dust
        if(x < 0){
            x = maxX;
            Random generator = new Random();
            y = generator.nextInt(maxY);
            speed = generator.nextInt(15);
        }
    }

    // Getters and Setters
    public int getX() {

        return x;
    }

    public int getY() {

        return y;
    }
}
```

Here is what is happening in the SpaceDust class. At the top of the previous block of code, we declare our usual speed and maximum and minimum variables. They will allow us to detect when the SpaceDust object leaves the left of the screen and needs respawning on the right, and provide sensible bounds for the height at which we respawn the object.

Then inside the SpaceDust constructor, we initialize the speed, x, and y variables with random values, but within the bounds set by the maximum and minimum variables we just initialized.

Then we implement the SpaceDust class's update method, which moves the object to the left based on the speed of the object and the player, then checks if the object has flown of the left-hand edge of the screen and respawns it with random but appropriate values if it has.

At the bottom, we provide two getter methods so that our `draw` method knows where to draw each speck of dust.

Now, we can create an `ArrayList` object to hold all our `SpaceDust` objects. Declare it just under the declaration of the other game objects near the top of the `TDView` class:

```
// Make some random space dust
public ArrayList<SpaceDust> dustList = new
    ArrayList<SpaceDust>();
```

In the `TDView` constructor, we can initialize a whole bunch of the `SpaceDust` objects using a `for` loop and then stash them into the `ArrayList` object:

```
int numSpecs = 40;

for (int i = 0; i < numSpecs; i++) {
  // Where will the dust spawn?
  SpaceDust spec = new SpaceDust(x, y);
  dustList.add(spec);
}
```

We create forty specks of dust in total. Each time through the loop, we create a new speck of dust and the `SpaceDust` constructor assigns it a random location and a random speed. We then put the `SpaceDust` object into our `ArrayList` object with `dustList.add(spec);`

Next, we jump to our `TDView` class's `update` method and use an enhanced `for` loop to call `update()` on each of our `SpaceDust` objects:

```
for (SpaceDust sd : dustList) {
  sd.update(player.getSpeed());
}
```

Remember that we passed in the player speed so that the dust increases and decreases its speed relative to the player's speed.

Now to draw all our space dust, we loop through our `ArrayList` object and draw a speck at a time. Of course, we add the code to our `TDView` class's `draw` method, but we must make sure to draw the space dust first so it appears behind the other game objects. In addition, we have an extra line to switch pixel color to white before using the `drawPoint` method of our `Canvas` object to plot a single pixel for each `SpaceDust` object.

In the `draw` method of the `TDView` class, add this code to draw our dust:

```
// White specs of dust
paint.setColor(Color.argb(255, 255, 255, 255));

//Draw the dust from our arrayList
for (SpaceDust sd : dustList) {
    canvas.drawPoint(sd.getX(), sd.getY(), paint);

    // Draw the player
    // ...
}
```

The only new thing here is the `canvas.drawpoint...` line of code. Apart from drawing bitmaps to the screen, the `Canvas` class allows us to draw primitives, like points and lines, as well as things like text and shapes. We will use these features when drawing a HUD for our game in *Chapter 4, Tappy Defender – Going Home.*

Why not run the app and check out how much neat stuff we have implemented? In this screenshot, I have temporarily increased the number of the `SpaceDust` objects to `200`, just for fun. You can also see that we have enemies drawn, attacking at a random *y* coordinate with random speed:

Things that go bump – collision detection

Collision detection is quite a broad subject. Throughout the three projects in this book, we will use a whole range of different ways to detect when things collide.

So, here is a quick look at our options for collision detection, and in which circumstances different methods may be appropriate.

Essentially, we just need to know when certain objects from our game touch other objects. We can then respond to that event by exploding, reducing shields, playing a sound, or whatever is appropriate. We need a broad understanding of our different options so we can make the right decisions in any particular game.

Collision detection options

First of all, here are a few of the different mathematical calculations we can utilize and when they may be useful.

Rectangle intersection

This type of collision detection is really straightforward. We draw an imaginary rectangle; we can call it a hitbox or bounding rectangle, around the objects we want to test for collision. Then, test to see if they intersect. If they do, we have a collision:

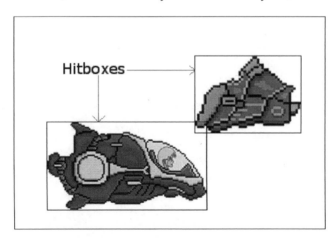

Where the hitboxes intersect, we have a collision. As we can see from the previous image, this is far from perfect. However, in some situations, it is sufficient. To implement this method, all we need to do is test for the intersection using the x and y coordinates of both objects.

Don't use the following code. It is for demonstration purposes only.

```
if(ship.getHitbox().right > enemy.getHitbox().left
    && ship.getHitbox().left < enemy.getHitbox().right ){
    // Ship is intersecting enemy on x axis
    //But they could be at different heights

    if(ship.getHitbox().top < enemy.getHitbox().bottom
        && ship.getHitbox().bottom > enemy.getHitbox().top ){
        // Ship is intersecting enemy on y axis as well
        // Crash
    }
}
```

The preceding code assumes we have a `getHitbox` method that returns the left and right *x* coordinates as well as the top and bottom *y* coordinates of the given object. In the aforementioned code, we first check to see if the *x* axes overlap. If they don't, then there is no point going any further. If they do, then check the *y* axes. If they don't, it could have been an enemy whizzing by above or below. If they overlap on the *y* axis as well, then we have a collision.

Note that we can check the *x* and *y* axis in either order as long as we check them both.

Radius overlapping

This method is also checking to see if two hitboxes intersect with each other, but as the title suggests, it does so using circles instead. There are obvious advantages and disadvantages. Mainly that this works well with shapes more circular in nature and less well with elongated shapes.

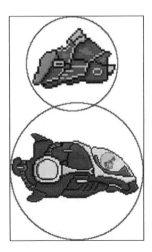

From the previous image, it is easy to see how the radius overlapping method is inaccurate for these particular objects and not hard to imagine how for a circular object like a ball it would be perfect.

Here is how we can implement this method.

 The following code is for demonstration purposes only.

```
// Get the distance of the two objects from
// the edges of the circles on the x axis
distanceX = (ship.getHitBox.centerX + ship.getHitBox.radius) -
   (enemy.getHitBox.centerX + enemy.getHitBox.radius;

// Get the distance of the two objects from
// the edges of the circles on the y axis
distanceY = (ship.getHitBox.centerY + ship.getHitBox.radius) -
   (enemy.getHitBox.centerY + enemy.getHitBox.radius;

// Calculate the distance between the center of each circle
double distance = Math.sqrt
    (distanceX * distanceX + distanceY * distanceY);

// Finally see if the two circles overlap
if (distance < ship.getHitBox.radius + enemy.getHitBox.radius) {
    // bump
}
```

The code again makes some assumptions. Like we have a `getHitBox` method that can return the radius as well as the center *x* and *y* coordinates. Furthermore, because the static `Math.sqrt` method takes and returns a variable of type `double`, we will need to start working with different types in our `SpaceShip` and `EnemyShip` classes.

 If the way we initialize distance: `Math.sqrt(distanceX * distanceX + distanceY * distanceY);` looks a little confusing, it is simply using Pythagoras' theorem to get the length of the hypotenuse of a triangle which is equal in length to a straight line drawn between the centers of the two circles. In the last line of our solution, we test if `distance < ship.getHitBox.radius + enemy.getHitBox.radius`, then we can be certain that we must have a collision. That is because if the center points of two circles are closer than the combined length of their radii, they must be overlapping.

The crossing number algorithm

This method is mathematically more complicated. However, as we will see in our third and final project, it is perfect for detecting when a point intersects a convex polygon:

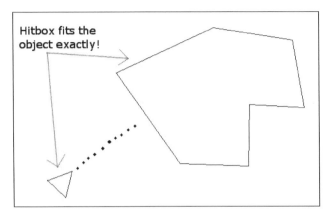

This is perfect for an Asteroids clone, and we will explore this method more as well as see it in action in our final project.

Optimizations

As we have seen, the different collision detection methods can have at least two problems depending on which method you use in which situation. The problems are lack of accuracy and drain on CPU cycles.

Multiple hitboxes

The first problem, a lack of accuracy, can be solved by having multiple hitboxes per object.

We simply add the required number of hitboxes to our game object to most effectively *wrap* it, and then perform the same rectangle intersection code on each in turn.

Neighbor checking

This method allows us to only check objects that are in the approximate same area as each other. It can be achieved by checking which neighborhood of our game a given two objects are in, and then only performing the more CPU intensive collision detection if there is a realistic chance that a collision could occur.

Suppose we have 10 objects that each need to be checked against each other, then we need to perform 10 squared (100) collision checks. If we do neighbor checking first, we can significantly reduce this number. In the very hypothetical situation in the diagram, we would only need to do an absolute maximum of 11 collision checks, instead of 100, for our 10 objects, if we first check to see if objects share the same sector.

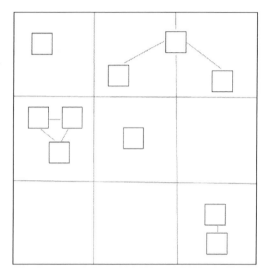

Implementing this in code can be as simple as having a sector member variable for each game object, then looping through the list of objects and just checking if they are in the same sector.

 We will use all these options and optimizations over the course of our three game projects.

Best options for Tappy Defender

Now that we know our collision detection options, we can decide the best course of action in our current game. All our ships are approximately rectangular (or square), there are few or no extremities on any of them, and we only have one object were we really care about a collision (with all the others).

This tends to suggest that we can use a single rectangular hitbox for the player and the enemy and perform purely corner aligned, global collision detection. If you're disappointed that we are going for the easy option, then you will be pleased to hear we will be getting into all the fancier techniques over the next two projects.

To make life even easier, the Android API has a handy the `Rect` class that can not only represent our hitboxes, but also has a neat `intersects` method that basically does the same thing as rectangle intersection collision detection. Let's think about how to add collision detection to our game.

First, all of our enemies and our player ship are going to need a hitbox. Add this code to declare a new `Rect` member called `hitbox`. Do this in both the `PlayerShip` and `EnemyShip` class:

```
// A hit box for collision detection
private Rect hitBox;
```

> **Important!**
> Be sure to do the previous step and the next three blocks of code for both the `EnemyShip` class as well as the `PlayerShip` class. I will remind you each time but just thought it worth mentioning beforehand as well.

Now, we need to add a getter method to the `PlayerShip` class and the `EnemyShip` class. Add this code to both classes:

```
public Rect getHitbox(){
  return hitBox;
}
```

And next, we need to make sure we initialize our hitboxes in both constructors. Make sure to enter the code right at the end of the constructor:

```
// Initialize the hit box
hitBox = new Rect(x, y, bitmap.getWidth(), bitmap.getHeight());
```

Now we need to make sure the hitboxes are kept up-to-date with the coordinates of our enemies and our player. The best place to do this is the `update` method of the enemy/player ships. The next block of code will update the hitboxes with the ship's current coordinates. Be sure to add this block of code at the very end of the `update()` methods so that the hitbox is updated with the coordinates after the `update` methods have done their adjustments. Again, add it to both `PlayerShip` and `EnemyShip`:

```
// Refresh hit box location
hitBox.left = x;
hitBox.top = y;
hitBox.right = x + bitmap.getWidth();
hitBox.bottom = y + bitmap.getHeight();
```

Our hitboxes have the coordinates that represent the outline of our bitmaps. This situation is nearly perfect, apart from the transparent bits around the edges.

Now, we can use our hitboxes from the TDView class's update method to detect collisions. But first, we need to decide what we are going to do when a collision occurs.

We need to refer to the rules of our game. We discussed them back at the beginning of *Chapter 2, Tappy Defender – First Step*. We know that the player has three shields but an enemy blows up after one hit. It makes sense to leave things like shields to a later part of the chapter, but we need some way to see our collision detection in action and make sure it is working.

Probably, the simplest way to acknowledge a collision at this stage, will be to make the enemy ship disappear and respawn as normal, as if it is a totally new enemy. We already have a mechanism in place for this. We know that when an enemy moves off the left of the screen it respawns as if it is a new enemy on the right. All we need to do is instantly transport the enemy to a location off of the left of the screen and the EnemyShip class will do the rest.

We need to be able to change the EnemyShip object's *x* coordinate. Let's add a setter method to the EnemyShip class so we can manipulate the *x* coordinate of all our enemy spaceships. Like this:

```
// This is used by the TDView update() method to
// Make an enemy out of bounds and force a re-spawn
public void setX(int x) {
   this.x = x;
}
```

Now, we can carry out collision detection and respond when we get a hit. The next block of code uses the static method Rect.intersects() to detect a hit by comparing the player ship's hitbox with each of the enemy hitboxes in turn. If a hit is detected, the appropriate enemy is moved off screen, ready to be respawned by its own update method in the next frame. Enter this code at the very top of the TDView class's update method:

```
// Collision detection on new positions
// Before move because we are testing last frames
// position which has just been drawn

// If you are using images in excess of 100 pixels
// wide then increase the -100 value accordingly
if(Rect.intersects
   (player.getHitbox(), enemy1.getHitbox())){
      enemy1.setX(-100);
```

```
}

if(Rect.intersects
  (player.getHitbox(), enemy2.getHitbox())){
    enemy2.setX(-100);
}

if(Rect.intersects
  (player.getHitbox(), enemy3.getHitbox())){
    enemy3.setX(-100);
}
```

That's it, our collisions will now work. It may be nice to be able to really see what is going on. For the purposes of debugging, let's draw a rectangle around all our spaceships, so we can see the hitboxes. We will use the `drawRect` method of the `Paint` class and pass the properties of our hitboxes in as arguments to define the area to draw. As you will expect, this code goes in the `draw` method. Note that it should go before the code that draws our ships so that the rectangles are drawn behind them, but after we clear the screen, as shown by the highlighted code:

```
// Rub out the last frame
canvas.drawColor(Color.argb(255, 0, 0, 0));

// For debugging
// Switch to white pixels
paint.setColor(Color.argb(255, 255, 255, 255));

// Draw Hit boxes
canvas.drawRect(player.getHitbox().left,
  player.getHitbox().top,
  player.getHitbox().right,
  player.getHitbox().bottom,
  paint);

canvas.drawRect(enemy1.getHitbox().left,
  enemy1.getHitbox().top,
  enemy1.getHitbox().right,
  enemy1.getHitbox().bottom,
  paint);

canvas.drawRect(enemy2.getHitbox().left,
  enemy2.getHitbox().top,
  enemy2.getHitbox().right,
  enemy2.getHitbox().bottom,
```

```
    paint);

canvas.drawRect(enemy3.getHitbox().left,
  enemy3.getHitbox().top,
  enemy3.getHitbox().right,
  enemy3.getHitbox().bottom,
  paint);
```

We can now run Tappy Defender and see the game in action complete with debugging mode hitboxes enabled:

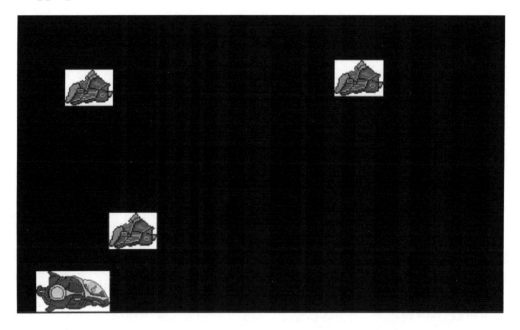

We can comment out this debugging code when we are done with it and then uncomment it should we need it again later.

Summary

We now have all the game objects that we need for a complete game. They all think and represent themselves internally in the model part of our design pattern. Furthermore, our player can at last control his spaceship, and we can detect when he crashes.

In the next chapter, we will put the finishing touches to our game including adding a HUD (Heads Up Display), implementing the game rules, adding some extra features, and play-testing our game to get everything in balance.

4
Tappy Defender – Going Home

We are on the home straight of our first game. In this chapter, we will draw a HUD to show the player in-game information, and implement the rules of the game so that the player can win, lose, and get fastest times.

After that, we will make a pause screen so the player can admire their achievements (or not) after they win or lose.

In this chapter, we will also generate our own sound FX and then add them to the game. Following that, we will enable the player to save their fastest time, and finally we will add a whole bunch of minor improvements, including a bit of difficulty balancing based on the screen resolution of the player's Android device.

Displaying a HUD

We need to start making our game a bit more rounded. Games have a score or, in our case, a time, and other rules as well. For the player to keep check on their progress we need to display the stats of the game.

Here, we will quickly set up a HUD that will show the player everything they need to know on screen while he is dodging enemies. We will also declare and initialize the variables required to supply data to the HUD. In the next section, *Implementing the rules*, we can begin to manipulate variables such as, shields, time, fastest time, and so on.

We can start by adding some member variables to the TDView class. We use a float value for the distanceRemaining variable because we will be using pseudo-kilometers and fractions of kilometers to represent the distance remaining until our hero makes it to her home planet. For the timeTaken, timeStarted, and fastestTime variables, we will use the **long** type because time is represented in milliseconds and the values get really big. Add this code after the TDView class declaration:

```
private float distanceRemaining;
private long timeTaken;
private long timeStarted;
private long fastestTime;
```

For now, we will just leave these variables with their default values and concentrate on displaying them in our HUD. We will make them useful and meaningful in the next section, *Implementing the rules*.

Now, we can go ahead and draw our HUD to display all the data the player may want to know while playing. As so often, we will be using our versatile Paint class object paint to do the bulk of the work. This time, we use the drawText method to add text to the screen, the setTextAlign method to justify our text, and setTextSize to scale the size of the text.

We can now add this code to our TDView class's draw method. Add it as the last thing to draw, just before the call to unlockCanvasAndPost(), as shown by the highlighted code:

```
// Draw the hud
paint.setTextAlign(Paint.Align.LEFT);
paint.setColor(Color.argb(255, 255, 255, 255));
paint.setTextSize(25);
canvas.drawText("Fastest:"+ fastestTime + "s", 10, 20, paint);
canvas.drawText("Time:" + timeTaken + "s", screenX / 2, 20,
paint);
canvas.drawText("Distance:" +
  distanceRemaining / 1000 +
  " KM", screenX / 3, screenY - 20, paint);

canvas.drawText("Shield:" +
  player.getShieldStrength(), 10, screenY - 20, paint);

canvas.drawText("Speed:" +
```

```
    player.getSpeed() * 60 +
    " MPS", (screenX /3 ) * 2, screenY - 20, paint);
```

```
// Unlock and draw the scene
ourHolder.unlockCanvasAndPost(canvas);
```

After entering this code, we have some errors and probably some questions.

First, we will deal with the questions. We will look more closely at what we are doing to `fastestTime`, `timeTaken`, `distanceRemaining`, and the value returned by `getSpeed` in the next section, *Implementing the rules*. Simply put, they are representations of distance and time that serve to give the player a sense of how they are doing. They are not real simulations of distance, although the time is accurate.

The first error we will deal with is caused by a call to a nonexistent method `player.getShieldStrength`. Add a member variable `shieldStrength` to the `PlayerShip` class:

```
private int shieldStrength;
```

Initialize it to 2 in the `PlayerShip` constructor:

```
shieldStrength = 2;
```

Implement your missing getter method in the `PlayerShip` class:

```
public int getShieldStrength() {
    return shieldStrength;
}
```

The final errors are caused by the undeclared variables `screenX` and `screenY`. It is now apparent that we need the screen resolution in this part of our code. The fastest way to deal with this is to make some new class variables called `screenX` and `screenY`. Declare these now just after the `TDView` class declaration:

```
private int screenX;
private int screenY;
```

As we will see, knowing the screen coordinates is useful in a number of places, so it makes sense to do this.

Now, in the `TDView` constructor, initialize `screenX` and `screenY` with the resolution passed in by the `GameActivity` class. Do this at the start of the constructor:

```
screenX = x;
screenY = y;
```

We can now run the game and see our HUD. The only parts of our HUD with meaningful data are the **Shield** and **Speed** labels. The speed is a pseudo-measurement of MPS (meters per second). Of course it has no bearing on reality, but it is relative to the speed of the whizzing stars, approaching enemies and soon, to the decreasing distance from the player's goal, home:

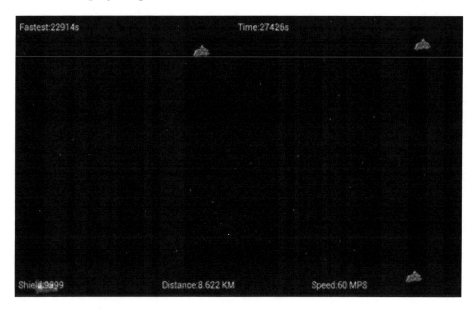

Implementing the rules

Now, we should pause and think about what we need to do later in the project because it will affect what we do while implementing our rules. When the player's ship is destroyed or when player reaches their goal, the game will end. This implies that the game will need to be restarted. We don't want to quit back to the home screen each time, so we need a way to restart the game from within the TDView class.

To facilitate this, we are going to implement a startGame method in our TDView class. The constructor will be able to call it and our game loop will also be able to call it when necessary as well.

It will also be necessary to pass some of the tasks that the constructor currently performs onto the new startGame method so that it can properly do its job. Also, we will use startGame to initialize some of the variables that our game rules and HUD require.

In order to accomplish what we discussed, `startGame()` will need a copy of the application's `Context` object. So, like we did with `startX` and `startY`, we will now make `context` a member of `TDView`. Declare it after the `TDView` class declaration:

```
private Context context;
```

Initialize it in the constructor right after the call to `super()`, like this:

```
super(context);
this.context  = context;
```

We can now implement the new `startGame` method. Most of the code is just moved from the constructor. Note that the subtle but important differences, like using the class version of the screen coordinates `screenX` and `screenY` instead of the constructor parameters *x* and *y*. Also, we initialize `distanceRemaining`, `timeTaken`, and `timeStarted`.

```
private void startGame(){
    //Initialize game objects
        player = new PlayerShip(context, screenX, screenY);
        enemy1 = new EnemyShip(context, screenX, screenY);
        enemy2 = new EnemyShip(context, screenX, screenY);
        enemy3 = new EnemyShip(context, screenX, screenY);

        int numSpecs = 40;
        for (int i = 0; i < numSpecs; i++) {
            // Where will the dust spawn?
            SpaceDust spec = new SpaceDust(screenX, screenY);
            dustList.add(spec);
        }

        // Reset time and distance
        distanceRemaining = 10000;// 10 km
        timeTaken = 0;

        // Get start time
        timeStarted = System.currentTimeMillis();
}
```

Are you are wondering what is going on with the `timeStarted` initialization? We initialized `startTime` using a method of the `System` class, `currentTimeMillis`. Now, `startTime` holds the number of milliseconds since January 1, 1970. We will see how this is used in the upcoming section, *Ending the game*. The `System` class has many uses. Here, we use it to get the number of milliseconds since January 1, 1970. This is a common system for measuring time in a computer. It is called Unix time and the moment before the 1st millisecond of January 1, 1970 is known as the Unix Epoch.

Now, comment out or delete the now unnecessary code from the `TDView` constructor but add the call to `startGame()` in its place:

```
// Initialize our player ship
//player = new PlayerShip(context, x, y);
//enemy1 = new EnemyShip(context, x, y);
//enemy2 = new EnemyShip(context, x, y);
//enemy3 = new EnemyShip(context, x, y);

//int numSpecs = 40;

//for (int i = 0; i < numSpecs; i++) {
      // Where will the dust spawn?
      //SpaceDust spec = new SpaceDust(x, y);
      //dustList.add(spec);
//}
```

```
startGame();
```

Next, we want to create a method to decrement the `PlayerShip` shield strength. This is so that when we detect a collision, we can reduce it by one each time. Add this simple method to the `PlayerShip` class:

```
public void reduceShieldStrength(){
   shieldStrength --;
}
```

Now, we can jump to the `TDView` class's `update` method and add code to implement our game rules a bit further. We will add a Boolean variable `hitDetected` just before we do all our collision detection. Inside each of the `if` blocks which detects a hit, we can set `hitDetected` to `true`.

Then, after all the collision detection code, we can see if a hit has been detected and reduce the player's shield strength accordingly. Here is the top part of the TDView class's update method with the new lines of code highlighted:

```
// Collision detection on new positions
// Before move because we are testing last frames
// position which has just been drawn
boolean hitDetected = false;
if(Rect.intersects(player.getHitbox(), enemy1.getHitbox())){
    hitDetected = true;
    enemy1.setX(-100);
}

if(Rect.intersects(player.getHitbox(), enemy2.getHitbox())){
    hitDetected = true;
    enemy2.setX(-100);
}

if(Rect.intersects(player.getHitbox(), enemy3.getHitbox())){
    hitDetected = true;
    enemy3.setX(-100);
}

if(hitDetected) {
    player.reduceShieldStrength();
        if (player.getShieldStrength() < 0) {
            //game over so do something
    }
}
```

Note the nested if statement after the call to player.reduceShieldStrength. This detects when the player has lost all their shields and failed. We will deal with what happens here soon.

We are really close to finishing off our game rules. We just need to decrease the distanceRemaining relative to the player's speed. This is so that we know when the player has succeeded. We also need to update the timeTaken variable so that the HUD is updated each time our draw method is called. This may not seem important, but thinking ahead a little, we can foresee a time when the game has ended, either because the player has failed or because the player has won. Let's talk about the end of the game.

Ending the game

If the game is not ended, the game is playing, and if the player has just died or won, the game is ended. We need to know when the game is ended and when it is playing. Let's make a new member variable `gameEnded` and declare it after the `TDView` class declaration:

```
private boolean gameEnded;
```

Now, we can initialize `gameEnded` in the `startGame` method. Enter this code as the very last line in the method.

```
gameEnded = false;
```

Now, we can finish the last few lines of our game rules logic, but wrap them in a test to see if the game has ended or not. Add the following code to conditionally update our game rules logic, right at the end of the `TDView` class's `update` method:

```
if(!gameEnded) {
        //subtract distance to home planet based on current speed
        distanceRemaining -= player.getSpeed();

        //How long has the player been flying
        timeTaken = System.currentTimeMillis() - timeStarted;
}
```

Our HUD will now have accurate data to keep the player informed of exactly how they are doing. We can also detect when the player arrives home and wins because `distanceRemaining` will pass zero. In addition, when distance remaining is less than zero, we can test to see if `timeTaken` is less than `fastestTime` and update `fastestTime` if it is. We can also set `gameEnded` to `true`. Add this code directly after the last block of code in the `TDView` class's `update` method:

```
//Completed the game!
if(distanceRemaining < 0){
  //check for new fastest time
  if(timeTaken < fastestTime) {
    fastestTime = timeTaken;
  }

  // avoid ugly negative numbers
  // in the HUD
  distanceRemaining = 0;

  // Now end the game
```

```
    gameEnded = true;
}
```

We ended the game when the player won; now, add this next line of code to end the
game when the player loses all their shields. Update this code in the TDView class's
update method. The new line of code is highlighted:

```
if(hitDetected) {
  player.reduceShieldStrength();
  if (player.getShieldStrength() < 0) {
    gameEnded = true;
  }
}
```

Now, we just need to make something actually happen when gameEnded is set to true.

One way to do this is to alternate how we draw the HUD based on whether the
gameEnded Boolean is true or false. Identify the HUD drawing code in the draw
method, shown again here for easy reference:

```
// Draw the HUD
paint.setTextAlign(Paint.Align.LEFT);
paint.setColor(Color.argb(255, 255, 255, 255));
paint.setTextSize(25);
canvas.drawText("Fastest:"+ fastestTime + "s", 10, 20, paint);
canvas.drawText("Time:" + timeTaken + "s", screenX / 2, 20, paint);

canvas.drawText("Distance:" +
  distanceRemaining / 1000 +
  " KM", screenX / 3, screenY - 20, paint);

canvas.drawText("Shield:" +
  player.getShieldStrength(), 10, screenY - 20, paint);

canvas.drawText("Speed:" +
  player.getSpeed() * 60 +
  " MPS", (screenX /3 ) * 2, screenY - 20, paint);
```

We want to wrap that code in an if-else block. If the game is not ended, draw the
normal HUD else draw an alternative. Wrap the HUD drawing code like this:

```
if(!gameEnded){
  // Draw the hud
  paint.setTextAlign(Paint.Align.LEFT);
  paint.setColor(Color.argb(255, 255, 255, 255));
```

```
        paint.setTextSize(25);
        canvas.drawText("Fastest:"+ fastestTime + "s", 10, 20, paint);

        canvas.drawText("Time:" +
          timeTaken +
          "s", screenX / 2, 20,   paint);

        canvas.drawText("Distance:" +
          distanceRemaining / 1000 +
          " KM", screenX / 3, screenY - 20, paint);

        canvas.drawText("Shield:" +
          player.getShieldStrength(), 10, screenY - 20, paint);

        canvas.drawText("Speed:" +
          player.getSpeed() * 60 +
          " MPS", (screenX /3 ) * 2, screenY - 20, paint);

    }else{
      //this happens when the game is ended
    }
```

Now, let's deal with the `else` block, which we will execute when the game is ended. What we will do is draw a big **Game Over**, and show the end game stats from the HUD. The thread continues on but the HUD stops updating. Enter this code in the `else` block:

```
// Show pause screen
paint.setTextSize(80);
paint.setTextAlign(Paint.Align.CENTER);
canvas.drawText("Game Over", screenX/2, 100, paint);
paint.setTextSize(25);
canvas.drawText("Fastest:"+
  fastestTime + "s", screenX/2, 160, paint);

canvas.drawText("Time:" + timeTaken +
  "s", screenX / 2, 200, paint);

canvas.drawText("Distance remaining:" +
  distanceRemaining/1000 + " KM",screenX/2, 240, paint);

paint.setTextSize(80);
canvas.drawText("Tap to replay!", screenX/2, 350, paint);
```

Note that we switch text sizes using `setTextSize()`, and we align all the text in the center of the screen using `setTextAlign()`. This is what it looks like when you run the game. We just need a way to restart the game after it has ended:

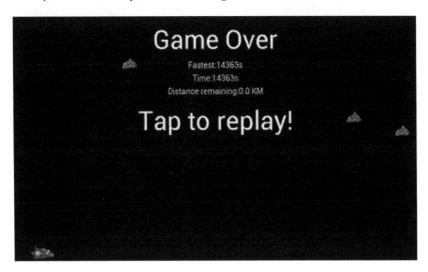

Restarting the game

To allow the player to restart after the game has ended, we just need to listen for a touch and call `startGame()`. Lets edit our `onTouchListener()` code to achieve this. The case `MotionEvent.ACTION_DOWN:` is the case we are interested in amending. We can simply add conditions here that if the screen is touched while the game is ended, restart. The new code to add to case `MotionEvent.ACTION_DOWN:` is highlighted:

```
// Has the player touched the screen?
case MotionEvent.ACTION_DOWN:
    player.setBoosting();
    // If we are currently on the pause screen, start a new game
    if(gameEnded){
        startGame();
    }
    break;
```

Try it out. You can now restart the game from the pause menu by tapping the screen. Is it just me or is it a bit quiet round here?

Adding sound FX

Adding sound effects in Android is really straightforward. First, let's look at where we can get our sound FX from. If you just want to get on with the coding, you can use my sound FX in the `Chapter4/assets` folder.

Generating the FX

We require four sound FX for our Tappy Defender game:

- The sound for when our player crashes into an alien, which we will call `bump.ogg`.
- The sound for when the player is destroyed, which we will call `destroyed.ogg`.
- A fun sound for when the game first begins, which we will call `start.ogg`.
- Finally, a victory whoop-type sound, which we will call `win.ogg`.

Here is a very quick guide to make these sound FX using BFXR. Grab a free copy of BFXR from `www.bfxr.net`.

Follow the simple instructions on the website to set it up. Try out a few of these things to make our cool sound FX.

 This is a very condensed tutorial. You can do so much with BFXR. To learn more read the tips on the website at the previous URL.

1. Run `bfxr.exe`.

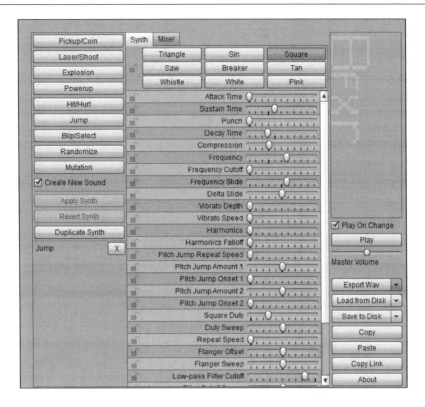

2. Try out all the preset types, which generate a random sound of the type you are working on. When you have a sound that is close to what you want, move to the next step:

3. Use the sliders to fine-tune the pitch, duration, and other aspects of your new sound:

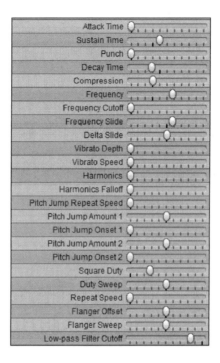

4. Save your sound by clicking on the **Export Wav** button. Despite the name of this button, as we will see we can save in formats other than `.wav` too.

5. Android likes to work with sounds in the OGG format, so when asked to name your file use the `.ogg` extension at the end of the filename. Remember we need to create `bump.ogg`, `destroyed.ogg`, `start.ogg`, and `win.ogg`.

6. Repeat steps 2 to 5 and create the four sound FX that we discussed.

7. Right-click the `app` folder in Android Studio. From the pop-up menu, navigate to **New | Android resource directory**.

8. In the **Directory name** field, type `assets`. Click on **OK** to create the `assets` folder.

9. Use your operating system's file manager to add a folder called `assets` to the main folder of the project, then add the four sound files to the new assets folder in your project.

The SoundPool class

To play our sounds, we will use the SoundPool class. We are using the deprecated version of the SoundPool constructor because the new version needs API 21 or newer and it is likely that lots of readers will be using an earlier version of Android. We can dynamically get the Android version and provide a different version of the code for pre- and post-API level 21, but the older constructor meets our needs.

Coding the sound FX

Declare a SoundPool object and some integers to represent the individual sounds. Add this code just after the TDView class declaration:

```
private SoundPool soundPool;
    int start = -1;
    int bump = -1;
    int destroyed = -1;
    int win = -1;
```

Next, we can initialize our SoundPool object and our integer sound IDs. We wrap the code in a try-catch block as required.

Note that the call to load() starts a process of converting our .ogg files to raw sound data. If the process is not finished when a call to playSound() is made, the sound won't play. The calls to load() are in the likely order of them being used to minimize this possibility. Enter this code in the constructor of our TDView class as shown. The new code is highlighted:

```
TDView(Context context, int x, int y) {
  super(context);
  this.context  = context;

  // This SoundPool is deprecated but don't worry
  soundPool = new SoundPool(10, AudioManager.STREAM_MUSIC,0);
  try{
    //Create objects of the 2 required classes
    AssetManager assetManager = context.getAssets();
    AssetFileDescriptor descriptor;

    //create our three fx in memory ready for use
    descriptor = assetManager.openFd("start.ogg");
    start = soundPool.load(descriptor, 0);

    descriptor = assetManager.openFd("win.ogg");
```

```
    win = soundPool.load(descriptor, 0);

    descriptor = assetManager.openFd("bump.ogg");
    bump = soundPool.load(descriptor, 0);

    descriptor = assetManager.openFd("destroyed.ogg");
    destroyed = soundPool.load(descriptor, 0);


}catch(IOException e){
    //Print an error message to the console
    Log.e("error", "failed to load sound files");
}
```

Add a call to playSound() using the appropriate reference at the points in our code which represent the appropriate event in our game. We have four sounds, so four calls to playSound() will be made.

The first goes at the very end of the startGame() method:

```
soundPool.play(start, 1, 1, 0, 0, 1);
```

The next two are highlighted in the if(hitDetected) block:

```
if(hitDetected) {
  soundPool.play(bump, 1, 1, 0, 0, 1);
  player.reduceShieldStrength();
  if (player.getShieldStrength() < 0) {
      soundPool.play(destroyed, 1, 1, 0, 0, 1);
      paused = true;
  }
}
```

The last one is in the if(distanceRemaining < 0) block, as highlighted:

```
//Completed the game!
if(distanceRemaining < 0){
    soundPool.play(win, 1, 1, 0, 0, 1);
    //check for new fastest time
    if(timeTaken < fastestTime) {
        fastestTime = timeTaken;
    }

    // avoid ugly negative numbers
    // in the HUD
```

```
    distanceRemaining = 0;

    // Now end the game
    gameEnded = true;
}
```

It's time to run Tappy Defender now and hear the sound in action.

We will see how to save our player's high score by saving it to a file when they achieve it and loading it back up again when Tappy Defender starts.

Adding persistence

You may have noticed that the current fastest time is zero and can therefore never be beaten. The other problem is that every time the player quits the game the high score is lost. Now, we will load a default high score from a file. When a new high score is achieved, save it to the file. It doesn't matter if the player quits the game or even switches off their phone; their high score will remain.

First we need two new objects. Declare them as members of the TDView class after the TDView class declaration. The first is a SharedPreferences object and the second is an Editor object, which actually writes to the file for us:

```
private SharedPreferences prefs;
private SharedPreferences.Editor editor;
```

We use prefs first as we just want to attempt to load a high score if one exists. We will also initialize editor ready for when we save our high score. We do this in the TDView constructor:

```
// Get a reference to a file called HiScores.
// If id doesn't exist one is created
prefs = context.getSharedPreferences("HiScores",
  context.MODE_PRIVATE);

// Initialize the editor ready
editor = prefs.edit();

// Load fastest time from a entry in the file
//  labeled "fastestTime"
// if not available highscore = 1000000
fastestTime = prefs.getLong("fastestTime", 1000000);
```

Let's use our `Editor` object to write any new fastest times to the `HiScores` file when appropriate. Add the extra highlighted lines shown to add the proposed changes to our file, first into a buffer and then commit the changes:

```
//Completed the game!
if(distanceRemaining < 0){
    soundPool.play(win, 1, 1, 0, 0, 1);
    //check for new fastest time
    if(timeTaken < fastestTime) {
        // Save high score
        editor.putLong("fastestTime", timeTaken);
        editor.commit();
        fastestTime = timeTaken;
    }

    // avoid ugly negative numbers
    // in the HUD
    distanceRemaining = 0;

    // Now end the game
    gameEnded = true;
}
```

The last thing we need to do is get the home screen to load up the fastest time and display it to the player. We will load the fastest time in exactly the same way as we did in our `TDView` constructor. We will also get a reference to our `TextView` through its ID `textHighScore`, which we assigned way back at the beginning of *Chapter 2, Tappy Defender – First Step*. We then use the `setText` method to display it to the player.

Open up `MainActivity.java` and add the highlighted code to the `onCreate` method to achieve what we just discussed:

```
// This is the entry point to our game
@Override
protected void onCreate(Bundle savedInstanceState) {
  super.onCreate(savedInstanceState);

  //Here we set our UI layout as the view
  setContentView(R.layout.activity_main);

  // Prepare to load fastest time
  SharedPreferences prefs;
  SharedPreferences.Editor editor;
```

```
prefs = getSharedPreferences("HiScores", MODE_PRIVATE);


// Get a reference to the button in our layout
final Button buttonPlay =
  (Button)findViewById(R.id.buttonPlay);

// Get a reference to the TextView in our layout
final TextView textFastestTime =
  (TextView)findViewById(R.id.textHighScore);

// Listen for clicks
buttonPlay.setOnClickListener(this);

// Load fastest time
// if not available our high score = 1000000
long fastestTime = prefs.getLong("fastestTime", 1000000);

// Put the high score in our TextView
textFastestTime.setText("Fastest Time:" + fastestTime);

}
```

Now, we have a complete working game. However, it is not really finished yet. To make a game that is genuinely playable and fun, we have to improve, refine, test, and iterate.

Iteration

How can we make our game better and more playable? Let's look at a number of possibilities and then go ahead and implement them.

Multiple different enemy graphics

Let's make the enemies a bit more interesting by adding a few more graphics to the game. First, we need to add the extra graphics to the project. Copy and paste enemy2.png and enemy3.png from the Chapter4/drawables folder of the download bundle into the drawables folder in Android Studio.

enemy2 and enemy3

Now, we just need to amend the `EnemyShip` constructor. This code generates a random number between 0 and 2, and then switches to load a different enemy bitmap accordingly. Our completed constructor now looks like this:

```
// Constructor
public EnemyShip(Context context, int screenX, int screenY){
    Random generator = new Random();
    int whichBitmap = generator.nextInt(3);
    switch (whichBitmap){
        case 0:
            bitmap = BitmapFactory.decodeResource
            (context.getResources(), R.drawable.enemy3);
            break;

        case 1:
            bitmap = BitmapFactory.decodeResource
            (context.getResources(), R.drawable.enemy2);
            break;

        case 2:
            bitmap = BitmapFactory.decodeResource
            (context.getResources(), R.drawable.enemy);
            break;
    }

    maxX = screenX;
    maxY = screenY;
    minX = 0;
    minY = 0;

    speed = generator.nextInt(6)+10;
    x = screenX;
    y = generator.nextInt(maxY) - bitmap.getHeight();

    // Initialize the hit box
    hitBox = new Rect(x, y, bitmap.getWidth(), bitmap.getHeight());

}
```

Note that we just need to move the `Random generator = new Random();` line of code to the top of the constructor, so we can use it to choose a bitmap as well as generate a random height later in the constructor, as usual.

An exercise in balance

Probably the biggest playability issue in the game is the difference in difficulty when playing on a medium/high resolution screen as opposed to a low resolution screen. For example, one of my testing devices is a Samsung Galaxy S2. It is a few years old now, and the screen resolution is 800 x 480 pixels when held in the landscape position. For comparison, I tested the game on a Samsung Galaxy S4 that has 1920 x 1080 pixels in landscape mode. This is more than double the resolution of the S2.

On the S4, the player seems to effortlessly glide in between the almost insignificant enemies, while on the S2, the player is faced with an almost impenetrable wall of alien steel.

The real solution to this problem is to draw game objects at pseudo-real-world coordinates, and then map these coordinates back to the device at the same scale, regardless of resolution. This way, the game will look and play the same on both an S2 and an S4. In the next project, we will build a more advanced game engine that does this.

Of course, we will still have the consideration of the actual physical screen size, making the player's experience varied, but this is a much more accepted situation by gamers.

As a quick and dirty solution, we will vary the size of the ships and the number of enemies. So on lower resolutions, we will have three enemies, but we will shrink their size. On higher resolutions, we will increase the number of enemies gradually.

In the `EnemyShip` class, just after the `switch` block that loads our enemy graphics into our `Bitmap` object, add the line shown highlighted to call a new method that we will write soon, `scaleBitmap()`:

```
switch (whichBitmap){
    case 0:
            bitmap = BitmapFactory.decodeResource(context.
              getResources(),
            R.drawable.enemy3);
            break;

    case 1:
            bitmap = BitmapFactory.decodeResource(context.
              getResources(),
            R.drawable.enemy2);
            break;
```

```
        case 2:
                bitmap = BitmapFactory.decodeResource(context.
                  getResources(),
                R.drawable.enemy);
                break;
    }


    scaleBitmap(screenX);
```

Now, we will write our new `scaleBitmap` method. This simple helper method takes a single argument, which as we have seen is the horizontal resolution of the screen. We then use the resolution and the static `createScaledBitmap` method to reduce our `Bitmap` objects on a scale of 2 or 3 depending on the resolution of the screen. Add the new `scaleBitmap` method to the `EnemyShip` class:

```
public void scaleBitmap(int x){

   if(x < 1000) {
        bitmap = Bitmap.createScaledBitmap(bitmap,
        bitmap.getWidth() / 3,
        bitmap.getHeight() / 3,
        false);
   }else if(x < 1200){
        bitmap = Bitmap.createScaledBitmap(bitmap,
        bitmap.getWidth() / 2,
        bitmap.getHeight() / 2,
        false);
    }
}
```

The enemies will be scaled down in size on lower resolution screens. Now, let's increase the number of enemies for the higher resolutions.

For this, we will add code to the `TDView` class to add extra enemies to higher resolution screens.

> Warning! This code sucks, but it works and it shows us where we can make improvements in our next project. When planning a game, there is always a trade-off between good design and simplicity. By keeping things organized from the start, we can get away with a bit of hacking near the end. Yes, we can redesign the way we spawn and store our game objects, and if Tappy Defender was an ongoing project then this would be worthwhile.

Add two more enemy ship objects after the first three, as shown:

```
// Game objects
private PlayerShip player;
public EnemyShip enemy1;
public EnemyShip enemy2;
public EnemyShip enemy3;
public EnemyShip enemy4;
public EnemyShip enemy5;
```

Now, add code to conditionally initialize these two new objects in the startGame method:

```
enemy1 = new EnemyShip(context, screenX, screenY);
enemy2 = new EnemyShip(context, screenX, screenY);
enemy3 = new EnemyShip(context, screenX, screenY);

if(screenX > 1000){
   enemy4 = new EnemyShip(context, screenX, screenY);
}

if(screenX > 1200){
   enemy5 = new EnemyShip(context, screenX, screenY);
}
```

Add code in the update method to update our fourth and fifth enemies and check for collisions:

```
// Collision detection on new positions
// Before move because we are testing last frames
// position which has just been drawn
boolean hitDetected = false;
if(Rect.intersects(player.getHitbox(), enemy1.getHitbox())){
   hitDetected = true;
   enemy1.setX(-100);
}


if(Rect.intersects(player.getHitbox(), enemy2.getHitbox())){
   hitDetected = true;
   enemy2.setX(-100);
```

```
    }


    if(Rect.intersects(player.getHitbox(), enemy3.getHitbox())){
      hitDetected = true;
      enemy3.setX(-100);
    }


    if(screenX > 1000){
      if(Rect.intersects(player.getHitbox(), enemy4.getHitbox())){
          hitDetected = true;
          enemy4.setX(-100);
      }
    }


    if(screenX > 1200){
      if(Rect.intersects(player.getHitbox(), enemy5.getHitbox())){
          hitDetected = true;
          enemy5.setX(-100);
      }
    }

    if(hitDetected) {
    soundPool.play(bump, 1, 1, 0, 0, 1);
                player.reduceShieldStrength();
                if (player.getShieldStrength() < 0) {
                    soundPool.play(destroyed, 1, 1, 0, 0, 1);
                    gameEnded = true;
                }
    }


    // Update the player
    player.update();
    // Update the enemies
    enemy1.update(player.getSpeed());
```

```
enemy2.update(player.getSpeed());
enemy3.update(player.getSpeed());

if(screenX > 1000) {
  enemy4.update(player.getSpeed());
}
if(screenX > 1200) {
  enemy5.update(player.getSpeed());
}
```

Finally, in the `draw` method, draw our extra enemies when appropriate:

```
// Draw the player
canvas.drawBitmap(player.getBitmap(), player.getX(),
player.getY(), paint);
canvas.drawBitmap(enemy1.getBitmap(),
  enemy1.getX(), enemy1.getY(), paint);
canvas.drawBitmap(enemy2.getBitmap(),
  enemy2.getX(), enemy2.getY(), paint);
canvas.drawBitmap(enemy3.getBitmap(),
  enemy3.getX(), enemy3.getY(), paint);

if(screenX > 1000) {
  canvas.drawBitmap(enemy4.getBitmap(),
  enemy4.getX(), enemy4.getY(), paint);
}
if(screenX > 1200) {
  canvas.drawBitmap(enemy5.getBitmap(),
  enemy5.getX(), enemy5.getY(), paint);
}
```

Of course, we now realize that we may like to scale the player as well. This makes it plain that perhaps we need a `Ship` class, from which we can derive `PlayerShip` and `EnemyShip`.

Add to this the cumbersome manner in which we added the extra enemies for higher resolution screens and a much more polymorphic solution is probably worthwhile. We will see how we can seriously improve this and virtually every other aspect of our game engine in the next project.

Format time

Look at how time is formatted in the player's HUD:

`Time:10407s`

Yuck! Let's write a simple helper method to make this look a whole lot nicer. We will add a new method to the TDView class called formatTime(). The method uses the number of elapsed milliseconds in this game (timeTaken) and reorganizes them into seconds and fractions of a second. It pads the fractions with zeros where appropriate and returns the result as a String ready to be drawn in the TDView class's draw method. The reason the method takes an argument rather than just using the member variable timeTaken is so we can reuse this code in a minute.

```
private String formatTime(long time){
    long seconds = (time) / 1000;
    long thousandths = (time) - (seconds * 1000);
    String strThousandths = "" + thousandths;
    if (thousandths < 100){strThousandths = "0" + thousandths;}
    if (thousandths < 10){strThousandths = "0" + strThousandths;}
    String stringTime = "" + seconds + "." + strThousandths;
    return stringTime;
}
```

We amend the line that draws the time in the player's HUD. For context, in the next piece of code, I have commented out the entirety of the original line and provided the new line, which includes our call to formatTime(), and highlighted it:

```
//canvas.drawText("Time:" + timeTaken + "s", screenX / 2, 20,
paint);
canvas.drawText("Time:" +
  formatTime(timeTaken) +
  "s", screenX / 2, 20, paint);
```

In addition, with one minor change, we can use this formatting on the **Fastest:** label in the HUD as well. Again, the old line is commented out and the new one is highlighted. Find and amend the code in the TDView class's draw method:

```
//canvas.drawText("Fastest:" + fastestTime + "s", 10, 20, paint);
canvas.drawText("Fastest:" +
  formatTime(fastestTime) +
  "s", 10, 20, paint);
```

We should also update the time formatting on the pause screen. The lines to change are commented out and the new lines to add are highlighted:

```
// Show pause screen
paint.setTextSize(80);
paint.setTextAlign(Paint.Align.CENTER);
canvas.drawText("Game Over", screenX/2, 100, paint);
paint.setTextSize(25);

// canvas.drawText("Fastest:"
  + fastestTime + "s", screenX/2, 160, paint);
canvas.drawText("Fastest:"+
  formatTime(fastestTime) + "s", screenX/2, 160, paint);

// canvas.drawText("Time:" +
  timeTaken + "s", screenX / 2, 200, paint);
canvas.drawText("Time:"
  + formatTime(timeTaken) + "s", screenX / 2, 200, paint);

canvas.drawText("Distance remaining:" +
  distanceRemaining/1000 + " KM",screenX/2, 240, paint);
paint.setTextSize(80);
canvas.drawText("Tap to replay!", screenX/2, 350, paint);
```

Fastest: is now formatted in the same way as **Time:** on both the in-game HUD and the pause screen HUD. Take a look at our neatly formatted time now:

Fastest:14.363s   Time:23.265s

Handle the back button

We will quickly add a small block of code to handle what happens when the player presses the back button on their Android device. Add this new method to both the GameActivity and MainActivity classes. We simply check if the back button was pressed, and if it was, call finish() to let the operating system know we are done with this activity.

```
// If the player hits the back button, quit the app
public boolean onKeyDown(int keyCode, KeyEvent event) {
  if (keyCode == KeyEvent.KEYCODE_BACK) {
      finish();
      return true;
  }
  return false;
}
```

The finished game

Finally, in case you are following along for the theory and not the practical, here is the finished `GameActivity` on a high resolution screen with a few hundred extra stars and shields:

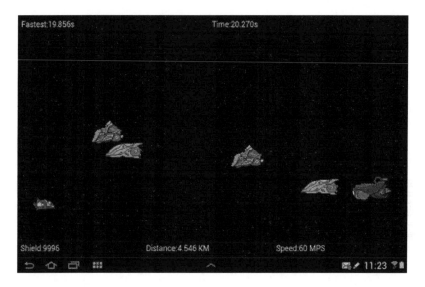

Summary

We have implemented the component parts of a basic game engine. We can do so much more. Of course, a modern mobile game will have a lot more going on than in ours. How will we handle collisions when there are lots more game objects? Couldn't we tighten up our class hierarchy a bit, as there were lots of similarities between our `PlayerShip` and `EnemyShip` classes? How can we add complex internal character animations without confusing the structure of our code, and what if we want smart enemies, enemies who can actually think?

We need realistic backgrounds, side objectives, power-ups, and pick-ups. We want a game world with real-world coordinates that map back accurately regardless of the resolution of the screen.

We need a smarter game loop that runs the game at the same speed regardless of the CPU it is being processed on. Most of all, what we really need, more than any of these things, is a dirty big machine gun. Let's build a classic platform game.

5
Platformer – Upgrading the Game Engine

Welcome to the second project of this book. Here, we will build a really tough retro platform game. It is not tough to build, but tough to beat when you play it. At the end of the project, we will also discuss ways to make the game play a little less punishing should you wish.

This chapter will focus entirely on our game engine and essentially lead to an upgraded version of the Tappy Defender code.

First, we will discuss what we want to achieve with this game: the backstory, game mechanics, and rules.

Then, we will quickly create an activity that instantiates a view that will do all the work.

After that, we will flesh out the basic structure of our PlatformView class, which will have some subtle, but important differences to our TDView class. Most notably, PlatformView will have a simple but effective way of managing the timing of all the events of our game.

We will then start the iterative process of building our GameObject class, from which almost every entity of the game world will be derived.

Next, we will discuss the concept of a viewport through which the game world is viewed by the player. We will no longer be designing our game objects to operate at the level of the screen resolution, but they will now exist in a world with their own x and y coordinates that we can think of as virtual meters. There is also a simple system of depth on the z axis as well. This will be handled by our new Viewport class.

After this, we will look at how we design and layout the content of our game. This is done via a class that is used as a level designer and can be used in a nonprogrammatic way to map out the jumps, enemies, rewards, and goals that constitute the layout of a level.

To manage the level designs and load them into our game engine, we will need another class. We will call it `LevelManager`.

Finally in this chapter, we will look at our enhanced `update` and `draw` methods within the `PlatformView` class so that we can actually run our new game and see the first output on the screen.

With so much to do, we better get started.

The game

The game we will build is based on the game play of some of the brutally hard platform games of the '80s, such as Bounty Bob Strikes Back and Impossible Mission. These games featured difficult jumps and required insanely precise timing at the same time as giving the player an unforgiving number of lives/chances. This style of game works well for us because we can actually build a multilevel playable game in just four chapters.

The design of the classes will make it really easy for you to add your own extra features, and game objects or make it slightly less challenging to play should you want to.

The backstory

Our hero Bob, having just returned from a secret mission to destroy an evil scientist at the center of the Earth, finds he is deep underground. Worse, it seems that although he has defeated the evil scientist, it was not in time to save the planet from the powerful guards and deadly flying robot drones that he unleashed.

Bob must make his way from the deep underground fiery cave, through the heavily guarded city, and forest, high in the mountains, where he hopes to live, free from the terrifying new order that has taken over the planet.

On his journey through these four levels, he must avoid guards, destroy drones, collect lots of money, and upgrade his initially puny machine gun.

The game mechanics

The game will be about executing precise jumps, planning the best route through a level to collect the loot and escape. Bob will be able to stand precariously on ledges with whole pixels of his feet overhanging, to be able to make seemingly impossible jumps. Bob will be able to control the distance he travels while jumping, meaning that sometimes he will often need to make sure he doesn't over jump.

Bob will need to collect machine gun upgrades before attempting to escape via heavily guarded areas.

Bob will only have three lives, but may be able to find some more on his journey.

Rules for the game

When Bob loses a life by being caught by a drone/guard, touching fire, or falling out of the game world, he will respawn at the start of the current level. Drones can fly, and will home in on Bob as soon as he comes into view. Bob will need to make sure he has enough firepower to handle the drones. Guards will patrol predetermined parts of the level, but they are tough and can only be knocked back by Bob's machine gun. Usually, Bob will need to execute a precisely timed jump to progress past a guard.

The environment will also be tough. Bob will need to completely master each level, as one wrong jump will send him plummeting back to the start, straight into the clutches of an enemy or even to his fiery death.

Upgrading the game engine

All the talk of guards, drones, fire, collectibles, guns, and the implied much larger game world suggests a much more complex system to manage. One of the goals of our game engine will be to make this complexity easily manageable. The other goal will be to separate the level design from the coding. When our game is done, you will be able to sit back and design the most evil, yet rewarding levels, in multiple different environments without touching the code.

The platform activity

First we start off with our `Activity` class, which is the entry point into our game. There is not much new here, so let's go ahead and get it built quickly. Create a new project, and in the **Application Name** field, enter `C5 Platform Game`. Choose **Phones and tablets**, then **Blank Activity** when prompted. In the **Activity Name** field, type `PlatformActivity`.

Obviously you don't have to follow my exact naming choices, but just remember to make minor alterations in the code to reflect your own naming choices.

You can delete `activity_platform.xml` from the `layout` folder. You can also delete all the code within the `PlatformActivity.java` file. Just leave the package declaration. Now, we have an entirely blank canvas ready for us to start coding. Here is the entirety of our project so far:

```
package com.gamecodeschool.c5platformgame;
```

Let's start building our engine. Just like in our Tappy Defender project, we will build a class to handle the view aspect of our game. Perhaps unsurprisingly, we will call the class `PlatformView`. Therefore, our `PlatformActivity` class needs to instantiate a `PlatformView` object and set it as the main view of the app, just like in the previous project.

We will be making some significant upgrades to our engine, but this will mainly happen in the view. In the code for the `PlatformActivity` class that we will look at next, we do much the same as in the previous project. First, declare the `PlatformView` object and set it as the main view in the overridden `onCreate` method; however, before we do this, we also capture and pass in the resolution of the device's screen.

We do this using the `Display` class and chaining the `getWindowManager()` and `getDefaultDisplay()` methods to get the properties of the physical display hardware that our game will be running on. Then, we create an object of type `Point` called resolution and store the resolution of the display into our `Point` object by calling `display.getSize(size)`.

This stores the horizontal and vertical number of pixels of the screen into `size.x` and `size.y`, respectively. We can then go ahead and instantiate a new `PlatformView` object by calling its constructor and passing in the values stored in `size.x` and `size.y`. As before, we also pass in the application, `Context` object (`this`) that like in the previous project, we will find many uses for.

We can then set `platformView` as the view by calling `setContentView()` in the usual way. As earlier, we override the `Activity` class's lifecycle methods `onPause()` and `onResume()` to have them call their respective methods in our soon-to-be-written `PlatformView` class. These two methods can then start and stop our `Thread` class.

Here is the entirety of the code for the `PlatformActivity` class that we have just discussed, with no significant new aspects. Type or copy and paste the code into your project. The code for this chapter can be found within the download bundle from the book's page on the Packt Publishing website. All the code and assets from this chapter can be found in the `Chapter5` folder. This file is called `PlatformActivity.java`.

 Remember to import all the new classes when prompted to do so, or by pressing the *Alt | Enter* keyboard combination while hovering the cursor over the error when a missing class causes this error.

```java
import android.app.Activity;
import android.graphics.Point;
import android.os.Bundle;
import android.view.Display;

public class PlatformActivity extends Activity {

    // Our object to handle the View
    private PlatformView platformView;

    @Override
    protected void onCreate(Bundle savedInstanceState) {
        super.onCreate(savedInstanceState);

        // Get a Display object to access screen details
        Display display = getWindowManager().getDefaultDisplay();

        // Load the resolution into a Point object
        Point resolution = new Point();
        display.getSize(resolution);

        // And finally set the view for our game
        // Also passing in the screen resolution
        platformView = new PlatformView
        (this, resolution.x, resolution.y);

        // Make our platformView the view for the Activity
        setContentView(platformView);

    }
}
```

```
// If the Activity is paused make sure to pause our thread
@Override
protected void onPause() {
    super.onPause();
    platformView.pause();
}

// If the Activity is resumed make sure to resume our thread
@Override
protected void onResume() {
    super.onResume();
    platformView.resume();
}
}
```

 Obviously, until we create our `PlatformView` class, there will be errors in our `PlatformActivity` class's code.

Locking the layout to landscape

Just as we did for the last project, we will make sure the game runs in the landscape mode only. We will make our `AndroidManifest.xml` file force our `PlatformActivity` class to run with a full screen, and we will also lock it to a landscape layout. Let's make these changes:

1. Open the `manifests` folder now and double-click the `AndroidManifest.xml` file to open it in the code editor.

2. In the `AndroidManifest.xml` file, find the following line of code:

   ```
   android:name=".PlatformActivity"
   ```

3. Immediately after it, type or copy and paste these two lines to make `PlatformActivity` run full screen and lock it in the landscape orientation.

   ```
   android:theme="@android:style/Theme.NoTitleBar.Fullscreen"
   android:screenOrientation="landscape"
   ```

Now, we can move on to the real guts of our game and see how we can implement all these improvements we talked about.

The PlatformView class

This class, by the time it is completed, will be dependent on many other classes. I don't want to just present each class in turn, as this would be quite hard to follow and exactly what code implements which feature will become confusing. Instead, we will look at, and code, each feature in turn, as we require them, and then revisit many of the classes multiple times to add more features. This will keep the focus on the specific purpose of each part of the code.

Having said this, great care has been taken so that although we will revisit many of these classes multiple times, we won't be constantly deleting code, just adding to it. When we add to it, the code will be presented in its proper context with the new parts highlighted among the existing code.

With regard to the structure of the classes, they are designed to be as minimal as possible, while at the same time, not restricting your potential to easily add features and extend the code.

This is not a lesson in game engine design, but more a lesson in seeing how many different features we can learn to implement and cram into four chapters, without the code becoming unmanageable.

If you plan to build very large-scale games, especially when working as a team, then a more robust design will be necessary. This more robust design will also mean a whole lot of extra classes, interfaces, packages, and so on.

> If this type of discussion interests you, I highly recommend the book, *Beginning Android Games* by Mario Zechner, published by APRESS. Mario is the founder/creator of the LibGDX cross-platform game library, and his book goes into great detail about the design patterns required to build a highly extensible and reusable code base for games. The only downside to the great design detail that this book has, is that it would take around 600 pages to build a simple retro Snake game.

First, let's create the class. Right-click on the package name in the Android Studio project explorer and navigate to **New | Java Class**. Call the new class `PlatformView`. Delete the autogenerated contents of the class, as we will add our own code soon.

We will continue to add code to this class over the entirety of the project. The full extent of the code that we add to the class in this chapter can be found in the download bundle at `Chapter5/PlatformView.java`.

We need a class that can manage our level. Let's call it `LevelManager`.

We also need a class that can hold the data for our level, as we can then extend it each time we create a new/different level design. Let's call the parent class LevelData, and our first real level for Bob to escape from, LevelCave.

Furthermore, as this game is going to have many enemies, props, and terrain types, we are going to need a cleaner system of managing them all. We need a fairly generic GameObject class, which all the different game objects can extend. We can then manage them really easily in our update and draw methods.

We will also, as a matter of necessity, build a slightly more complicated method of detecting the players input. We will create an InputController class to delegate all of the code from PlatformView. However, the details of this class we will not see, until we have fully fleshed out our Player object to represent the player in the next chapter.

We can quickly code our basic PlatformView class with very similar code to the first project, but with a few notable exceptions that we will discuss.

The basic structure of PlatformView

Here are the necessary imports and our member variables to get us started. We will add to these a fair bit as the project continues.

Note that we also declare three new object types, lm that will be our LevelManager class, vp that will be our Viewport class, and ic that is our InputController class. We will begin working on some of these in this chapter. These declarations will of course show an error until we implement their respective classes.

```
import android.content.Context;
import android.graphics.Canvas;
import android.graphics.Color;
import android.graphics.Paint;
import android.graphics.Rect;
import android.util.Log;
import android.view.SurfaceHolder;
import android.view.SurfaceView;

public class PlatformView extends SurfaceView
    implements Runnable {

    private boolean debugging = true;
    private volatile boolean running;
    private Thread gameThread = null;

    // For drawing
```

```
private Paint paint;
// Canvas could initially be local.
// But later we will use it outside of draw()
private Canvas canvas;
private SurfaceHolder ourHolder;

Context context;
long startFrameTime;
long timeThisFrame;
long fps;

// Our new engine classes
private LevelManager lm;
private Viewport vp;
InputController ic;
```

Here, we have our `PlatformView` constructor. At this stage, it does nothing new, in fact, it has less code than our `TDView` constructor but it will soon be enhanced. For now, enter the code as shown:

```
PlatformView(Context context, int screenWidth,
    int screenHeight) {

    super(context);
    this.context = context;

    // Initialize our drawing objects
    ourHolder = getHolder();
    paint = new Paint();
}
```

Here is our thread's `run` method. Note that before the call to `update()`, we get the current time in milliseconds and put it in the `startFrameTime` long variable. Then after `draw()` has completed, we make another call to get the system time and measure how many milliseconds have elapsed since the frame started. We then carry out the calculation `fps = 1000 / thisFrameTime`, which gives us the number of frames per second our game ran at, in that last frame. This value is stored in the `fps` variable. We will be using this all over the place as we proceed with the game. Code the `run` method that we have just discussed, like this:

```
@Override
public void run() {

    while (running) {
```

```
        startFrameTime = System.currentTimeMillis();

        update();
        draw();

        // Calculate the fps this frame
        // We can then use the result to
        // time animations and movement.
        timeThisFrame = System.currentTimeMillis() - startFrameTime;
            if (timeThisFrame >= 1) {
                fps = 1000 / timeThisFrame;
            }
        }
    }
```

Later in the chapter, we will see how we manage the extra complexity of multiple object types and update them when necessary. For now, just add an empty `update` method to the `PlatformView` class like this:

```
private void update() {
  // Our new update() code will go here
}
```

Here, we see the familiar parts of our `draw` method. Later in this chapter, we will see some of the new code. For now, add the basics of the `draw` method as shown next as this will remain unchanged:

```
private void draw() {

        if (ourHolder.getSurface().isValid()){
        //First we lock the area of memory we will be drawing to
        canvas = ourHolder.lockCanvas();

        // Rub out the last frame with arbitrary color
        paint.setColor(Color.argb(255, 0, 0, 255));
        canvas.drawColor(Color.argb(255, 0, 0, 255));

        // New drawing code will go here

        // Unlock and draw the scene
        ourHolder.unlockCanvasAndPost(canvas);
    }
}
```

The last parts of the first phase of putting together our view is the pause and resume methods, which are called by PlatformActivity when the corresponding Activity lifecycle methods are called by the operating system. They are unchanged from the previous project, but here they are again for the sake of completeness and being able to follow along easily. Add these methods to the PlatformView class:

```
// Clean up our thread if the game is interrupted
public void pause() {
  running = false;
  try {
      gameThread.join();
  } catch (InterruptedException e) {
      Log.e("error", "failed to pause thread");
  }
}


// Make a new thread and start it
// Execution moves to our run method
public void resume() {
    running = true;
    gameThread = new Thread(this);
    gameThread.start();

}

}// End of PlatformView
```

Now, we have the basic outline of our view coded and ready. Let's take our first look at the GameObject class.

The GameObject class

We know that we need a parent class to hold the vast majority of our game objects as we want to improve on the inflexibility and code duplication of the last project. From the previous project, we also know many of the properties and methods it will require.

First, we need a simple class to represent the world location of all our future
GameObject classes. This class will hold a detailed location on both the *x* and *y*
axis. Note that these are totally independent to the coordinates of the pixels of the
device on which our game will run. We can think of the *z* coordinate as a layer
number. The lower numbers get drawn first. Therefore, create a new Java class, call it
Vector2Point5D, and enter this code:

```
public class Vector2Point5D {

    float x;
    float y;
    int z;
}
```

Now, let's have a look at, and code the basic working outline of, the GameObject
class, and then throughout the project, we can come back and add extra features.
Create a new Java class and call it GameObject. Let's look at the code we need to start
to make this class useful. First, we import the classes we need.

```
import android.content.Context;
import android.graphics.Bitmap;
import android.graphics.BitmapFactory;
```

When we code GameObject itself, note that the class does not provide a constructor
as this will be handled differently, depending on the specific GameObject that we
are implementing.

The first variable you will notice in the code is worldLocation, which, as you may
expect, is of type Vector2Point5D. We then have two float members, which will
hold the width and height of the GameObject class. Next up, we have the Boolean
variables active and visible which will be used, perhaps to label an object when
it is active, visible, or otherwise. We will begin to see later in the chapter how this is
of benefit.

We will also need to know how many frames of internal animation any given object
has. The default will be 1, so animFrameCount is initialized accordingly.

We then have a char class called type. This type variable will determine exactly
what any particular GameObject might be. It will be used extensively. The last
member variable for now is bitmapName. We will see that it will become useful
to know the name of the graphic, which represents the appearance of each of our
individual objects. Add the member variables we have just discussed:

```
public abstract class GameObject {

    private Vector2Point5D worldLocation;
```

```
private float width;
private float height;

private boolean active = true;
private boolean visible = true;
private int animFrameCount = 1;
private char type;

private String bitmapName;
```

Now, we can look at the first part of the functionality of `GameObject`. We have the abstract method `update()`. The plan was that all objects will need to update themselves. Turns out that this was over ambitious in just four chapters, and some of our objects (mainly the platforms and scenery) will just provide an empty `update()` implementation. However, there is nothing to stop you making the scenery more interactive than we have time for now, or make the platforms more dynamic and adventurous once we see how things work. Add the abstract `update` method:

```
public abstract void update(long fps, float gravity);
```

We handle our methods that manage our graphics. We have a getter to retrieve `bitmapName`. Then, we have `prepareBitmap()`, which uses the string `bitmapName` to make an Android resource ID from a `.png` image file. This file must be present in the `drawable` folder of the project. A bitmap is created as we have seen before.

Now our `prepareBitmap` method does something new. It uses the `createScaledBitmap` method to change the size of the bitmap we just created. It not only uses the `animFrameCount`, which we already discussed, but also the `pixelsPerMetre` variable, which is a parameter of the method.

The idea being, that each device has a `pixelsPerMetre` value that is appropriate for the device, which will help us create an identical view of the game across devices with different resolutions. We will see exactly where we get this `pixelsPerMetre` value from, when we discuss the `Viewport` class. Enter the following methods in the `GameObject` class:

```
public String getBitmapName() {
        return bitmapName;
}

public Bitmap prepareBitmap(Context context,
    String bitmapName,
    int pixelsPerMetre) {
```

```
    // Make a resource id from the bitmapName
    int resID = context.getResources().
        getIdentifier(bitmapName,
        "drawable", context.getPackageName());


    // Create the bitmap
    Bitmap bitmap = BitmapFactory.
        decodeResource(context.getResources(),
        resID);

    // Scale the bitmap based on the number of pixels per metre
    // Multiply by the number of frames in the image
    // Default 1 frame
    bitmap = Bitmap.createScaledBitmap(bitmap,
                (int) (width * animFrameCount * pixelsPerMetre),
                (int) (height * pixelsPerMetre),
                false);

    return bitmap;
}
```

We also want to be able to know where in the world each `GameObject` is and, of course, to set where in the world it is. Here are a getter and a setter, which do just that.

```
    public Vector2Point5D getWorldLocation() {
        return worldLocation;
    }

    public void setWorldLocation(float x, float y, int z) {
        this.worldLocation = new Vector2Point5D();
        this.worldLocation.x = x;
        this.worldLocation.y = y;
        this.worldLocation.z = z;
    }
```

We also want to be able to both, get and set many of the member variables we have already discussed. These getters and setters will do that.

```
    public void setBitmapName(String bitmapName){
        this.bitmapName = bitmapName;
    }


    public float getWidth() {
        return width;
```

```
    }

    public void setWidth(float width) {
        this.width = width;
    }

    public float getHeight() {
        return height;
    }

    public void setHeight(float height) {
        this.height = height;
    }
```

Furthermore, we will want to check and change the status of our active and visible variables as well.

```
    public boolean isActive() {
        return active;
    }

    public boolean isVisible() {
        return visible;
    }

    public void setVisible(boolean visible) {
        this.visible = visible;
    }
```

Set and get type of each GameObject.

```
    public char getType() {
        return type;
    }

    public void setType(char type) {
        this.type = type;
    }



    }// End of GameObject
```

Now, we will create our first of many child classes from `GameObject`. Right-click on the package name in the Android Studio explorer and create a class called `Grass`. This will be our first basic tile type that the player can walk about on.

This straightforward code uses the constructor to initialize height, width, type, and its location in the game world. Note that all this information is passed in as parameters to the constructor. The only thing the `Grass` class "knows", and one of the few things that will differentiate it from some of the other simple `GameObject` child classes, is the value used for `bitmapName`, which in this case is `turf`.

As discussed previously, we also provide an empty implementation of the `update` method:

```
public class Grass extends GameObject {

    Grass(float worldStartX, float worldStartY, char type) {
        final float HEIGHT = 1;
        final float WIDTH = 1;

        setHeight(HEIGHT); // 1 metre tall
        setWidth(WIDTH); // 1 metre wide

        setType(type);


        // Choose a Bitmap
        setBitmapName("turf");

        // Where does the tile start
        // X and y locations from constructor parameters
        setWorldLocation(worldStartX, worldStartY, 0);
    }

    public void update(long fps, float gravity) {}
}
```

Now, add the `turf.png` graphic from the `Chapter5/drawable` folder in the download bundle to the `drawable` folder in Android Studio.

Finally, we will do an absolute barebones implementation of our `Player` class that will also extend `GameObject`. We will not be putting any functionality into this class just an *x* and *y* world location. This is so that the `Viewport` class, which we will implement next, knows where to focus.

Here is the `Player` class, which will represent Bob our hero. The class at this stage is as simple and straightforward as, and nearly identical to the `Grass` class. This will change and evolve substantially as we progress. Note that we set the type to `p`.

```
import android.content.Context;

public class Player extends GameObject {

    Player(Context context, float worldStartX,
        float worldStartY, int pixelsPerMetre) {

        final float HEIGHT = 2;
        final float WIDTH = 1;

        setHeight(HEIGHT); // 2 metre tall
        setWidth(WIDTH); // 1 metre wide

        setType('p');

        // Choose a Bitmap
        // This is a sprite sheet with multiple frames
        // of animation. So it will look silly until we animate it
        // In chapter 6.

        setBitmapName("player");

        // X and y locations from constructor parameters

        setWorldLocation(worldStartX, worldStartY, 0);

    }

    public void update(long fps, float gravity) {

    }
}
```

Add the `player.png` graphic from the `drawable` folder in the download bundle to the `drawable` folder in Android Studio. The graphic is a multiframe sprite sheet, so it won't display nicely until we animate it in *Chapter 6, Platformer – Bob, Beeps, and Bumps* , but it will serve its purpose as a placeholder for now.

As we will see next, the view of the game world that the player sees, will focus on Bob, as you will probably expect.

The view through a viewport

A viewport can be thought of as the movie camera that follows the action of our game. It defines the area of the game world that is to be shown to the player. Typically, it will center on Bob.

It also serves the combined function of making our draw method more efficient by determining which objects are inside and outside the player's field of vision. There is no point drawing or processing a bunch of enemies, if they are not relevant at any given moment.

This will significantly speed up tasks like collision detection by implementing a first phase of detection by removing objects off screen from the list of objects to check for collisions, and it is surprisingly simple to do.

Furthermore, our `Viewport` class will have the task of translating game world coordinates into appropriate pixel coordinates for drawing on the screen. We will also see how this class calculates the `pixelsPerMetre` value that our `GameObject` class used in the `prepareBitmap` method.

The `Viewport` class really is an all singing and dancing thing. So let's get coding.

First, we will declare a whole bunch of useful variables. We have another `Vector2Point5D`, which will just be used to represent whatever point in the world is currently the central focus in the viewport. Then, we have separate integer values for `pixelsPerMetreX` and `pixelsPerMetreY`.

 Actually, in this implementation, there is no distinction between `pixelsPerMetrX` and `pixelsPerMetreY`. However, the `Viewport` class can be upgraded to take into account different ratios of width to height of the device, based on screen size, rather than just resolution. We don't do so in this implementation.

Next, we simply have the resolution of the screen in both axes: `screenXResolution` and `screenYResolution`. We then have `screenCentreX` and `screenCentreY`, which are basically the two previous variables divided by two to find the middle.

In our list of declared variables, we have `metresToShowX` and `metresToShowY` that will be the number of meters we will squash into our viewport. Changing these values will show more or less of the game world on screen.

The last member, we will declare at this point, is the `int numClipped`. This we will use to output debugging text to see what effect our `Viewport` class is having with regard to making drawing, updates, and multiphase collision detection, more efficient.

Create a new class called `Viewport` and declare the variables we have just discussed:

```
import android.graphics.Rect;

public class Viewport {
    private Vector2Point5D currentViewportWorldCentre;
    private Rect convertedRect;
    private int pixelsPerMetreX;
    private int pixelsPerMetreY;
    private int screenXResolution;
    private int screenYResolution;
    private int screenCentreX;
    private int screenCentreY;
    private int metresToShowX;
    private int metresToShowY;
    private int numClipped;
```

Now, let's look at the constructor. The constructor just needs to know the resolution of the screen. This is obtained in parameters *x* and *y*, which, of course, we assign to `screenXResolution` and `screenYResolution`, respectively.

Then, as previously suggested, we divide those two previous variables by two and assign the results to `screenCentreX` and `screenCentreY`, respectively.

The `pixelsPerMetreX` and `pixelsPerMetreY` are calculated by dividing by 32 and 18 (again, respectively), so a device with a resolution of 840 x 400 pixels will have pixels per meter *x/y* of 32/22. Now, we have variables that refer to the number of pixels of screen real estate on the current device that represents a meter of our game world. We will see a number of times in our code, where this will be useful.

We will actually draw a slightly wider area than this, to make sure we don't have any unsightly gaps/lines around the edge of the screen and assign 34 to `metresToShowX` and 20 to `metresToShowY`. Now, we have variables that refer to the amount of our game world that we will draw each frame.

 Once we have some screen output, you can experiment with these values to create a more or less zoomed-in or zoomed-out experience for the player.

Nearing the end of the constructor, we create a new Rect object called convertedRect that we will see in action soon. We call new() on currentViewportWorldCentre, so it is ready for action shortly.

```
Viewport(int x, int y){

        screenXResolution = x;
        screenYResolution = y;

        screenCentreX = screenXResolution / 2;
        screenCentreY = screenYResolution / 2;

        pixelsPerMetreX = screenXResolution / 32;
        pixelsPerMetreY = screenYResolution / 18;

        metresToShowX = 34;
        metresToShowY = 20;

        convertedRect = new Rect();
        currentViewportWorldCentre = new Vector2Point5D();


}
```

If some of the screenshots throughout this project look slightly different to the results you get, it is because some images have been taken using different viewport settings to highlight different aspects of the game world.

The first method we write for the Viewport class is setWorldCentre(). It receives an *x* and a *y* parameter, which is promptly assigned as the currentWorldCentre. We need this method because of course the player will be moving around in the world, and we need to let the Viewport class know where Bob is. Also, as we will see in *Chapter 8, Putting It All together*, we will also have a situation where we don't want Bob as the center of attention.

```
void setWorldCentre(float x, float y){
  currentViewportWorldCentre.x  = x;
  currentViewportWorldCentre.y  = y;
}
```

Now, a few simple getters and setters that will be useful to us as we progress.

```
public int getScreenWidth(){
  return  screenXResolution;
```

```
}

public int getScreenHeight(){
   return   screenYResolution;
}

public int getPixelsPerMetreX(){
   return   pixelsPerMetreX;
}
```

We fulfil one of the primary roles of the `Viewport` class with the `worldToScreen()` method. As the name suggests, this is the method that converts the locations of all the objects currently in the visible viewport from world coordinates to pixel coordinates that can actually be drawn to the screen. It returns our previously prepared `rectToDraw` object as the result.

This is how `worldToScreen()` works. It receives the *x* and *y* world locations of an object along with that object's width and height. With these values, each in turn, subtracts the objects world coordinate multiplied by the pixels per meter for the current screen, from the appropriate current world viewport center (*x* or *y*). Then, for the left and top coordinates of the object, the result is subtracted from the pixel screen center value and for the bottom and right coordinates, it is added.

These values are then packed into the left, top, right, and bottom values of `convertedRect` and returned to the `draw` method of `PlatformView`. Add the `worldToScreen` method to the `Viewport` class:

```
public Rect worldToScreen(
   float objectX,
   float objectY,
   float objectWidth,
   float objectHeight){

  int left = (int) (screenCentreX -
   ((currentViewportWorldCentre.x - objectX)
   * pixelsPerMetreX));

   int top =   (int) (screenCentreY -
   ((currentViewportWorldCentre.y - objectY)
   * pixelsPerMetreY));

  int right = (int) (left +
   (objectWidth *
   pixelsPerMetreX));
```

```
    int bottom = (int) (top +
      (objectHeight *
      pixelsPerMetreY));

    convertedRect.set(left, top, right, bottom);

    return convertedRect;
}
```

Now, we implement the second primary function of the `Viewport` class, removing objects that are currently of no interest to us. We call this clipping, and the method we will call; `clipObjects()`.

Once again, we receive as parameters the x, y, `width`, and `height` of an object. The test starts by assuming that we want to clip the current object and we assign `true` to clipped.

Then, the four nested `if` statements test whether each and every point of the object is within the bounds of the related side of the viewport. If it is, we set `clipped` to `false`. Some of the levels we will design have in excess of a thousand objects, but we will see that we rarely need to process (update, collision detection, and draw) more than a quarter of them in any given frame. Enter the code for the `clipObjects` method:

```
public boolean clipObjects(float objectX,
    float objectY,
    float objectWidth,
    float objectHeight) {

  boolean clipped = true;

  if (objectX - objectWidth <
    currentViewportWorldCentre.x + (metresToShowX / 2)) {

    if (objectX + objectWidth >
      currentViewportWorldCentre.x - (metresToShowX / 2)) {

      if (objectY - objectHeight <
        currentViewportWorldCentre.y +
        (metresToShowY / 2)) {

        if (objectY + objectHeight >
          currentViewportWorldCentre.y -
          (metresToShowY / 2)){
```

```
                    clipped = false;
            }
        }

      }

  }

  // For debugging
  if(clipped){
      numClipped++;
  }

  return clipped;
}
```

Now, we provide access to the `numClipped` variable so that it can be read and reset to zero each frame.

```
public int getNumClipped(){
  return numClipped;
}

public void resetNumClipped(){
  numClipped = 0;
}

}// End of Viewport
```

Let's declare and initialize our `Viewport` object. Add this code right after we initialize our `Paint` object in the `PlatformView` constructor. The new code is shown highlighted here:

```
// Initialize our drawing objects
ourHolder = getHolder();
paint = new Paint();

// Initialize the viewport
vp = new Viewport(screenWidth, screenHeight);

}// End of constructor
```

We can now describe and position objects in our game world and focus on the precise parts of the world we are interested in. Let's see how we will actually get our objects into that world, so we can then update and draw them as we have done before. We will also look at the concept of a level.

Creating the levels

Here, we will see how to build our `LevelManager`, `LevelData`, and our first real level, `LevelCave`.

The `LevelManager` class will eventually need a copy of our `InputController` class. Therefore, in order to try and keep to our intentions of not having to delete any code, we will include a parameter for `InputController` in our `LevelManager` constructor.

Let's quickly create a blank template for our `InputController` class. Create a new class in the usual way and call it `InputController`. Add this code:

```
public class InputController {
    InputController(int screenWidth, int screenHeight) {
    }
}
```

Now, let's look at our, initially, very simple `LevelData` class. Create a new class, call it `LevelData`, and add this code. At this stage, it holds just an `ArrayList` object for `Strings`.

```
import java.util.ArrayList;

public class LevelData {
    ArrayList<String> tiles;

    // This class will evolve along with the project

    // Tile types
    // . = no tile
    // 1 = Grass

}
```

Next, we can start on what will eventually become our first playable level. Create a new class, call it `LevelCave`, and add this code:

```
import java.util.ArrayList;

public class LevelCave extends LevelData{
```

```
LevelCave() {
tiles = new ArrayList<String>();
this.tiles.add("p.............................................");
this.tiles.add(".............................................");
this.tiles.add("......................111111.................");
this.tiles.add(".............................................");
this.tiles.add("............111111............................");
this.tiles.add(".............................................");
this.tiles.add(".........1111111.............................");
this.tiles.add(".............................................");
this.tiles.add(".............................................");
this.tiles.add(".............................................");
this.tiles.add("............................11111111.........");
this.tiles.add(".............................................");
}
}
```

 The position of p for player in the `LevelCave` file is arbitrary. As long as it is on there, the `Player` object will be initialized. The actual spawn location of the player character is determined by the call to a `loadLevel` method, as we will soon see. I usually put the p for player as the first element on the first line of the map, then it is less likely to be forgotten.

Now, let's talk about how this level design is going to work. We will enter alpha-numeric characters in the `LevelCave` class within the `tiles.add("...")` parts of the code. We will enter a different alpha-numeric character depending on which `GameObject` we want to place into the level. At the moment, we just have p to represent the `Player` object, a 1 to represent a `Grass` object, and a period (.) to represent an empty space of one game world meter square.

 This implies that the positioning of the `Grass` objects with the 1 character in the previous block of code can be arranged exactly how you like. This is the case, and whenever we look at the code for our `LevelCave` class please feel free to improvise and experiment as you like.

As the project continues, we will add more than twenty different GameObject child classes. Some will be inanimate like Grass, others will be thinking, aggressive enemies. All will be placeable within our level design.

Now, we can implement the class to manage our levels. Create a new Java class and call it LevelManager. Enter the code for the LevelManager class as we go through, and discuss it a block at a time.

First, a few import directives.

```
import android.content.Context;
import android.graphics.Bitmap;
import android.graphics.Rect;
import java.util.ArrayList;
```

Now, the constructor is where we have a String level to hold the name of the level, mapWidth and mapHeight to store the width and height in game world meters of the current level, a Player object because we know we will always have one of them, and an int type called playerIndex.

Soon, we will have an ArrayList object of many GameObject classes, and it will be handy to always have the index of the Player object.

Moving on, we have the Boolean playing because we will need to know when the game is being played or being paused and a float called gravity.

 In the context of this project, gravity will not be used to its full potential, but it can easily be manipulated so that different levels have a different gravity. This is why it is in the LevelManager class.

Finally, we declare an object of type LevelData, an ArrayList object to hold all our GameObject objects, an ArrayList object to hold representations of the players control buttons and a regular array to hold the majority of all the Bitmap objects we will need.

```
public class LevelManager {

    private String level;
```

```
    int mapWidth;
    int mapHeight;

    Player player;
    int playerIndex;

    private boolean playing;
    float gravity;

    LevelData levelData;
    ArrayList<GameObject> gameObjects;

    ArrayList<Rect> currentButtons;
    Bitmap[] bitmapsArray;
```

Then, in the constructor, we examine the signature and see that it receives a `Context` object, `pixelsPerMetre` that will have been determined when the `Viewport` class was constructed, `screenWidth` again direct from the `Viewport` class, a copy of our `InputController` class, and then the name of the level to load. The `int` parameters, `px` and `py`, are the starting coordinates for the player.

We assign the level parameter to our member level, then we switch to determine which class will be our current level. Of course, at the moment, we only have `LevelCave`.

Then, we initialize our `gameObject ArrayList` and our `bitmapsArray`. We then call `loadMapData()`, which is a method we will write shortly. After this, we set `playing` to `true`, and finally we have a getter method to find out what the state of `playing` is. Enter the code we have just discussed in the `LevelManager` class:

```
public LevelManager(Context context,
    int pixelsPerMetre, int screenWidth,
    InputController ic,
    String level,
    float px, float py) {

    this.level = level;

    switch (level) {
        case "LevelCave":
        levelData = new LevelCave();
        break;

        // We can add extra levels here
```

```
        }

        // To hold all our GameObjects
        gameObjects = new ArrayList<>();

        // To hold 1 of every Bitmap
        bitmapsArray = new Bitmap[25];

        // Load all the GameObjects and Bitmaps
        loadMapData(context, pixelsPerMetre, px, py);

        // Ready to play
        playing = true;
    }


    public boolean isPlaying() {
        return playing;
    }
}
```

Now, we have a really simple method which will enable us to get any `Bitmap` object based on the type of `GameObject` we are currently dealing with. This way, each `GameObject` does not have to hold its own `Bitmap` object. For example, we can design a level with hundreds of `Grass` objects. This can easily use up the memory of even a modern tablet.

Our `getBitmap` method takes an `int` value as an index and returns a `Bitmap` object. We will see how we access the appropriate value for `index` in the next method:

```
        // Each index Corresponds to a bitmap
        public Bitmap getBitmap(char blockType) {

            int index;
            switch (blockType) {
                case '.':
                    index = 0;
                    break;

                case '1':
                    index = 1;
                    break;

                case 'p':
                    index = 2;
                    break;
```

```
            default:
                index = 0;
                break;
        }// End switch


        return bitmapsArray[index];

    }// End getBitmap
```

This next method will enable us to get the `index` with which to call the `getBitmap` method. As long as the `char` cases correspond with the `type` values held by the various `GameObject` child classes we create, and the index returned by this method matches the index of the appropriate `Bitmap` held in the `bitmapsArray`, we will only ever need one copy of each `Bitmap` object.

```
    // This method allows each GameObject which 'knows'
    // its type to get the correct index to its Bitmap
    // in the Bitmap array.
    public int getBitmapIndex(char blockType) {

        int index;
        switch (blockType) {
            case '.':
                index = 0;
                break;

            case '1':
                index = 1;
                break;

            case 'p':
                index = 2;
                break;

            default:
                index = 0;
                break;

        }// End switch

        return index;
    }// End getBitmapIndex()
```

Now, we do the real work with the `LevelManager` class, and load our level from our design. The method needs the `pixelsPerMetre` and the `Player` objects coordinates in order to do its work. As this is a large method, the explanations and the code have been split into a few sections.

In this first part, we simply declare an `int` type called `index` and set it to `-1`. As we loop through our level design, it will help us keep track of where we are up to.

Then, we calculate the height and width of the map using the size of `ArrayList` and the length of the first element of `ArrayList`, respectively.

```
// For now we just load all the grass tiles
// and the player. Soon we will have many GameObjects
private void loadMapData(Context context,
   int pixelsPerMetre,
   float px, float py) {

   char c;

   //Keep track of where we load our game objects
   int currentIndex = -1;

   // how wide and high is the map? Viewport needs to know
   mapHeight = levelData.tiles.size();
   mapWidth = levelData.tiles.get(0).length();
```

We enter a nested `for` loop starting with the first element of the first string in our `ArrayList` object. We work from left to right across the first string before moving on to the second string.

We check to see if an object other than an empty space (.) is present at the current location, and if it is, we enter a switch block to create the appropriate object at the designated location.

If we encounter a `1`, then we add a new `Grass` object to `ArrayList`, and if we encounter a `p`, we initialize the `Player` object at the location passed in to the constructor of this `LevelManager` class. When a new `Player` object is created, we also initialize our `playerIndex` and `player` object ready for future use.

```
for (int i = 0; i < levelData.tiles.size(); i++) {
        for (int j = 0; j <
            levelData.tiles.get(i).length(); j++) {

        c = levelData.tiles.get(i).charAt(j);
```

```
                    // Don't want to load the empty spaces
                    if (c != '.'){
                      currentIndex++;
                      switch (c) {

                        case '1':
                            // Add grass to the gameObjects
                            gameObjects.add(new Grass(j, i, c));
                            break;

                        case 'p':
                            // Add a player to the gameObjects
                            gameObjects.add(new Player
                                (context, px, py,
                                 pixelsPerMetre));

                            // We want the index of the player
                            playerIndex = currentIndex;
                            // We want a reference to the player
                            player = (Player)
                            gameObjects.get(playerIndex);

                            break;



                    }// End switch
```

If a new object has been added to gameObjects ArrayList, we need to check if
the corresponding bitmap has been added to the bitmapsArray. If it hasn't, we
add one using the prepareBitmap method of the current GameObject class under
consideration. Here is the code to perform this check and prepare the bitmap, if
necessary:

```
// If the bitmap isn't prepared yet
if (bitmapsArray[getBitmapIndex(c)] == null) {

    // Prepare it now and put it in the bitmapsArrayList
    bitmapsArray[getBitmapIndex(c)] =
        gameObjects.get(currentIndex).
        prepareBitmap(context,
        gameObjects.get(currentIndex).
        getBitmapName(),
        pixelsPerMetre);

}// End if
```

```
}// End if (c != '.'){

}// End for j

}// End for i

}// End loadMapData()


}// End LevelManager
```

Back in the `PlatformView` class, to put all our level objects to use, we call `loadLevel()` just after where we initialized our `Viewport` class in the `PlatformView` constructor. The new code has been highlighted, and the existing code is provided for context:

```
// Initialize the viewport
vp = new Viewport(screenWidth, screenHeight);

// Load the first level
loadLevel("LevelCave", 15, 2);

}
```

Of course, now we need to implement the `loadLevel` method within the `PlatformView` class.

The `loadLevel` method needs to know which level to load, so the `switch` statement in the `LevelManager` constructor can do its work, and it also needs the coordinates to spawn our hero Bob.

We initialize our `LevelManager` object by calling its constructor with the viewport data retrieved from `vp` and the level/player data we have just discussed.

We then create a new `InputController` class, again passing in some data from `vp`. We will see exactly what we do with this data when we build our `InputController` class in *Chapter 6, Bob, Beeps, and Bumps*. Finally, we call `vp.setWorldCentre()` and pass it in the player's location as the coordinates. This centers the screen on Bob.

```
public void loadLevel(String level, float px, float py) {


    lm = null;

    // Create a new LevelManager
    // Pass in a Context, screen details, level name
```

```
    // and player location
    lm = new LevelManager(context,
        vp.getPixelsPerMetreX(),
        vp.getScreenWidth(),
        ic, level, px, py);

    ic = new InputController(vp.getScreenWidth(),
        vp.getScreenHeight());

    // Set the players location as the world centre
    vp.setWorldCentre(lm.gameObjects.get(lm.playerIndex)
        .getWorldLocation().x,
        lm.gameObjects.get(lm.playerIndex)
        .getWorldLocation().y);
}
```

We can add some code to our `update` method that will be first to utilize a primary function of our new `Viewport` class.

The enhanced update method

At last, we can use our handy `ArrayList` of game objects and our `Viewport` functionality to flesh out our enhanced `update` method. In the code that follows, we simply use an enhanced `for` loop to go through each `GameObject`. We check if it `isActive()`, and then send the object's location and dimensions to `clipObjects()` wrapped in an `if` statement. If `clipObjects()` returns `false`, then the object is not clipped and the object is flagged as visible by calling `go.setVisible(true)`. Otherwise, it is flagged as not visible calling `go.setVisible(false)`. This is the only aspect of any object that is updated at the moment. We will see when we run the game, at the end of the chapter, that it is already useful. Enter the new code in the `update` method:

```
for (GameObject go : lm.gameObjects) {
    if (go.isActive()) {
        // Clip anything off-screen
        if (!vp.clipObjects(go.getWorldLocation().x,
            go.getWorldLocation().y,
            go.getWidth(),
            go.getHeight())) {

            // Set visible flag to true
            go.setVisible(true);

        } else {
```

```
                    // Set visible flag to false
                    go.setVisible(false);
                    // Now draw() can ignore them


                }
            }


        }
    }
```

The enhanced draw method

Now, we can be more precise about which objects we need to draw. First, we declare and initialize a new `Rect` object called `toScreen2d`.

Then, we loop through our `gameObjects` `ArrayList` once for each layer starting with the lowest layer. This isn't strictly necessary at this stage because all our objects are, by default, currently on layer zero. We will add objects on layer -1 and 1 before the end of the project, and we don't want to have to rewrite code if we can help it.

Next, we check if the object is visible and on the current layer. If it is, we pass the current object's location and dimensions to the `worldToScreen` method, which returns the result to our previously prepared `toScreen2d` `Rect` object. Then, we call `drawBitmap()` using our `bitmapArray` to provide the appropriate bitmap, and pass in the coordinates of `toScreen2d`. Update the `draw` method as highlighted:

```
    private void draw() {

        if (ourHolder.getSurface().isValid()) {
            //First we lock the area of memory we will be drawing to
            canvas = ourHolder.lockCanvas();

            // Rub out the last frame with arbitrary color
            paint.setColor(Color.argb(255, 0, 0, 255));
            canvas.drawColor(Color.argb(255, 0, 0, 255));
            // Draw all the GameObjects
              Rect toScreen2d = new Rect();

            // Draw a layer at a time
            for (int layer = -1; layer <= 1; layer++){
            for (GameObject go : lm.gameObjects) {
                //Only draw if visible and this layer
                if (go.isVisible() && go.getWorldLocation().z
                  == layer) {
```

```
            toScreen2d.set(vp.worldToScreen
            (go.getWorldLocation().x,
            go.getWorldLocation().y,
            go.getWidth(),
            go.getHeight()));

        // Draw the appropriate bitmap
        canvas.drawBitmap(
            lm.bitmapsArray
            [lm.getBitmapIndex(go.getType())],
            toScreen2d.left,
            toScreen2d.top, paint);
        }
    }
}
```

Now, still in the draw method, we print debugging info to the screen, including the size of our gameObjects ArrayList compared to the number of objects that were clipped this frame.

Then, we finish the draw method by the usual call to unlockCanvasAndPost(). Note that at the end of the if (debugging) block, we call vp.resetNumClipped to set the numClipped variable back to zero ready for the next frame. Add this code straight after the previous block of code in the draw method:

```
// Text for debugging
if (debugging) {
    paint.setTextSize(16);
    paint.setTextAlign(Paint.Align.LEFT);
    paint.setColor(Color.argb(255, 255, 255, 255));
    canvas.drawText("fps:" + fps, 10, 60, paint);

    canvas.drawText("num objects:" +
        lm.gameObjects.size(), 10, 80, paint);

    canvas.drawText("num clipped:" +
        vp.getNumClipped(), 10, 100, paint);

    canvas.drawText("playerX:" +
        lm.gameObjects.get(lm.playerIndex).
        getWorldLocation().x,
        10, 120, paint);

    canvas.drawText("playerY:" +
        lm.gameObjects.get(lm.playerIndex).
```

```
        getWorldLocation().y,
        10, 140, paint);

        //for reset the number of clipped objects each frame
        vp.resetNumClipped();

}// End if(debugging)

// Unlock and draw the scene
ourHolder.unlockCanvasAndPost(canvas);

}// End (ourHolder.getSurface().isValid())
}// End draw()
```

For the first time in this project, we can actually run our game and see some results:

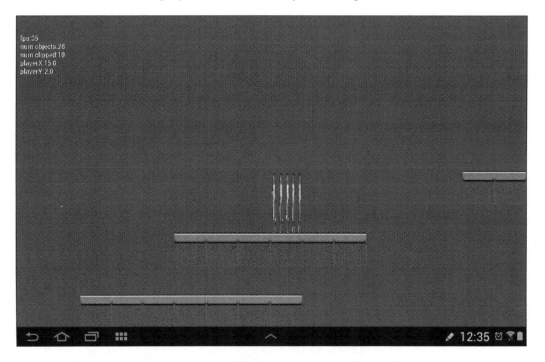

Note in the image the precise layout of the grass from our LevelCave design. You can also see our squashed Bob sprite sheet and the fact that there are 28 objects, but 10 of them have been clipped. As our levels get bigger, the ratio of clipped to unclipped will dramatically increase in favor of the vast majority being clipped.

Summary

We have covered a lot of ground in this chapter, and now have a well fleshed-out game engine.

As we have done much of the setup work, from now on, most of the code we add will also have a visible (or audible) result and be much more satisfying, as we will be able to regularly run our game to see the improvements.

In the next chapter, we will add sound effects and input detection, thus bringing Bob to life. Then, we will see how dangerous his world can be, and will promptly add collision detection so that he can stand on a platform.

6
Platformer – Bob, Beeps, and Bumps

Now that our basic game engine is set up, we can start making some fast progress. In this chapter, we will quickly add a SoundManager class that we will use to make a noise wherever and whenever we please. After that, we will put some meat on the bones of Bob and implement the core functionality we require in the Player class. Then, we can handle the second phase (after clipping) of our multiphase collision detection and give Bob the useful skill of being able to stand on a platform.

After we have achieved this significant feat, we will hand over control of Bob to the player by implementing the InputController class. Bob will at last be able to run around and jump. At the end of this chapter, we will animate Bob's sprite sheet so he actually appears to run, rather than slide everywhere.

The SoundManager class

Throughout the next few chapters, we will be adding sound effects for various events. Sometimes these sounds will be triggered directly in the main PlatformView class, but other times, they will need to be triggered in more remote corners of your code like the InputController class and even within the GameObject class themselves. We will quickly make a simple SoundManager class that can be passed around and used as needed when a beep is required.

Create a new Java class and call it `SoundManager`. This class has three main parts. In the first part, we simply declare a `SoundPool` object and a bunch of `int` variables to hold a reference to each sound effect. Enter the first part of the code, the declaration, and members:

```
import android.content.Context;
import android.content.res.AssetFileDescriptor;
import android.content.res.AssetManager;
import android.media.AudioManager;
import android.media.SoundPool;
import android.util.Log;

import java.io.IOException;

public class SoundManager {
    private SoundPool soundPool;
    int shoot = -1;
    int jump = -1;
    int teleport = -1;
    int coin_pickup = -1;
    int gun_upgrade = -1;
    int player_burn = -1;
    int ricochet = -1;
    int hit_guard = -1;
    int explode = -1;
    int extra_life = -1;
```

The second part of the class is the `loadSound` method, which unsurprisingly loads all the sounds into memory ready for playing. We will call this once we have initialized a `SoundManager` object in the `PlatformView` constructor. Enter this code next:

```
public void loadSound(Context context){
    soundPool = new SoundPool(10, AudioManager.STREAM_MUSIC,0);
    try{
        //Create objects of the 2 required classes
        AssetManager assetManager = context.getAssets();
        AssetFileDescriptor descriptor;

        //create our fx
        descriptor = assetManager.openFd("shoot.ogg");
        shoot = soundPool.load(descriptor, 0);

        descriptor = assetManager.openFd("jump.ogg");
        jump = soundPool.load(descriptor, 0);
```

```
            descriptor = assetManager.openFd("teleport.ogg");
            teleport = soundPool.load(descriptor, 0);

            descriptor = assetManager.openFd("coin_pickup.ogg");
            coin_pickup = soundPool.load(descriptor, 0);

            descriptor = assetManager.openFd("gun_upgrade.ogg");
            gun_upgrade = soundPool.load(descriptor, 0);

            descriptor = assetManager.openFd("player_burn.ogg");
            player_burn = soundPool.load(descriptor, 0);

            descriptor = assetManager.openFd("ricochet.ogg");
            ricochet = soundPool.load(descriptor, 0);

            descriptor = assetManager.openFd("hit_guard.ogg");
            hit_guard = soundPool.load(descriptor, 0);

            descriptor = assetManager.openFd("explode.ogg");
            explode = soundPool.load(descriptor, 0);

            descriptor = assetManager.openFd("extra_life.ogg");
            extra_life = soundPool.load(descriptor, 0);

    }catch(IOException e){
        //Print an error message to the console
        Log.e("error", "failed to load sound files");

    }

}
```

Finally for our `SoundManager` class, we need to be able to play any sound we like. This `playSound` method simply switches on a string passed in as a parameter. When we have a `SoundManager` object, we can just call `playSound()` with an appropriate string argument:

```
public void playSound(String sound){
        switch (sound){
            case "shoot":
                soundPool.play(shoot, 1, 1, 0, 0, 1);
                break;

            case "jump":
                soundPool.play(jump, 1, 1, 0, 0, 1);
```

```
            break;

        case "teleport":
            soundPool.play(teleport, 1, 1, 0, 0, 1);
            break;

        case "coin_pickup":
            soundPool.play(coin_pickup, 1, 1, 0, 0, 1);
            break;

        case "gun_upgrade":
            soundPool.play(gun_upgrade, 1, 1, 0, 0, 1);
            break;

        case "player_burn":
            soundPool.play(player_burn, 1, 1, 0, 0, 1);
            break;

        case "ricochet":
            soundPool.play(ricochet, 1, 1, 0, 0, 1);
            break;

        case "hit_guard":
            soundPool.play(hit_guard, 1, 1, 0, 0, 1);
            break;

        case "explode":
            soundPool.play(explode, 1, 1, 0, 0, 1);
            break;

        case "extra_life":
            soundPool.play(extra_life, 1, 1, 0, 0, 1);
            break;

    }

}
}// End SoundManager
```

Declare a new object of type `SoundManager` after the `PlatformView` class declaration after your new game engine classes from the previous chapter.

```
// Our new engine classes
private LevelManager lm;
private Viewport vp;
```

```
InputController ic;
SoundManager sm;
```

Next, initialize the `SoundManager` object and call `loadSound()` in the `PlatformView` constructor as shown:

```
// Initialize the viewport
vp = new Viewport(screenWidth, screenHeight);

sm = new SoundManager();
sm.loadSound(context);

loadLevel("LevelCave", 15, 2);
```

You can create all your own sounds using BFXR or just copy mine from the `Chapter6/assets` folder. Copy all the sounds to the `assets` folder in your Android Studio project. Create an `assets` folder in the `src/main` folder of your project in order to achieve this if the folder doesn't exist already.

Now, we can play sound effects wherever we like. It's time to bring our hero Bob to life.

Introducing Bob

Here, we can add the meat to the bones of your `Player` class. However, this section won't be the last time we revisit the `Player` class. Now, we will add the necessary functionality to allow Bob to move. Immediately after we have done this, we will add the code to allow the player to use the forthcoming collision detection code and the `Animation` class.

First of all, we need to add some members to the `Player` class. The `Player` class will need to know how fast it can move, when the player is pressing the left or right controls, and if it is falling or jumping. In addition, the `Player` class needs to know how long it has been jumping and how long it should jump for.

The next block of code provides variables for us to monitor all these things. We will very soon see, how we use them to make Bob do what we want.

Now, we know what the variables are for. We can add this code right after the class declaration as shown:

```
public class Player extends GameObject {

    final float MAX_X_VELOCITY = 10;
    boolean isPressingRight = false;
```

```
boolean isPressingLeft = false;


public boolean isFalling;
private boolean isJumping;
private long jumpTime;
private long maxJumpTime = 700;// jump 7 10ths of second
```

Furthermore, there are some other movement-related conditions we will need to track, but they will be useful in other classes as well. Therefore, we will add them as members to the GameObject class. We will track the current horizontal and vertical speed, the direction the object is facing, and whether the object can move at all with the following variables. Add these to the GameObject class:

```
private float xVelocity;
private float yVelocity;
final int LEFT = -1;
final int RIGHT = 1;
private int facing;
private boolean moves = false;
```

Now, in the GameObject class, we will add a move method. This method simply checks that the velocity on either of the axes is not zero and if it is, it moves the object by changing its worldLocation object. This method uses the velocity (either xVelocity or yVelocity) divided by the current frames per second to calculate the distance to move each frame. This ensures that the movement will be exactly correct, regardless of the current frames per second. It doesn't matter if our game executes smoothly or fluctuates a bit, or how powerful or puny the CPU in the Android device is. We will very soon call this move method from within the update method of the Player class. Later in the project, we will call it from other classes as well.

```
void move(long fps){
        if(xVelocity != 0) {
            this.worldLocation.x += xVelocity / fps;
        }

        if(yVelocity != 0) {
            this.worldLocation.y += yVelocity / fps;
        }
    }
```

Next, in the `GameObject` class, we have a bunch of getters and setters for the new variables we added previously. The only part to note is that the setters for the two velocity variables (`setxVelocity` and `setyVelocity`) check `if(moves)` before actually assigning a value. Add these new getters and setters to the `GameObject` class.

```
public int getFacing() {
  return facing;
}

public void setFacing(int facing) {
  this.facing = facing;
}

public float getxVelocity() {
  return xVelocity;
}

public void setxVelocity(float xVelocity) {
  // Only allow for objects that can move
  if(moves) {
    this.xVelocity = xVelocity;
  }
}

public float getyVelocity() {
  return yVelocity;
}

public void setyVelocity(float yVelocity) {
  // Only allow for objects that can move
  if(moves) {
    this.yVelocity = yVelocity;
  }
}

public boolean isMoves() {
  return moves;
}

public void setMoves(boolean moves) {
  this.moves = moves;
}

public void setActive(boolean active) {
  this.active = active;
}
```

Now, back in the `Player` class constructor, we can use some of these new methods to set up the object at creation time. Add the highlighted code to the `Player` constructor:

```
setHeight(HEIGHT); // 2 metre tall
setWidth(WIDTH); // 1 metre wide

// Standing still to start with
setxVelocity(0);
setyVelocity(0);
setFacing(LEFT);
isFalling = false;

// Now for the player's other attributes
// Our game engine will use these
setMoves(true);
setActive(true);
setVisible(true);
//...
```

At last, we can make practical use of all this new code in the `Player` class's `update` method.

First, we handle what happens when `isPressingRight` or `isPressingLeft` is true. Of course, we still need to be able to set these variables via touches on the screen. Very simply, this next code block sets the horizontal velocity to MAX_X_VELOCITY if `isPressingRight` is true or to -MAX_X_VELOCITY if `isPressingLeft` is true. If neither is true, it sets the horizontal velocity to zero, which is standing still.

```
public void update(long fps, float gravity) {
        if (isPressingRight) {
            this.setxVelocity(MAX_X_VELOCITY);
        } else if (isPressingLeft) {
            this.setxVelocity(-MAX_X_VELOCITY);
        } else {
            this.setxVelocity(0);
        }
```

Next, we check which way the player is moving and call `setFacing()` with either RIGHT or LEFT as the argument.

```
//which way is player facing?
if (this.getxVelocity() > 0) {
  //facing right
  setFacing(RIGHT);
} else if (this.getxVelocity() < 0) {
```

```
        //facing left
        setFacing(LEFT);
    }//if 0 then unchanged
```

Now, we can handle jumping. When the player presses the jump button, if successful, isJumping will be set to true and jumpTime will be set to whatever the current system time is. So we can then enter the if(isJumping) block on each frame, test how long Bob has been jumping for, and if he has not exceeded maxJumpTime take one of two possible actions.

Action one is; if we are less than half way through the jump, the *y* velocity is set to -gravity (going up). Action two is; if Bob is more than half way through the jump, his *y* velocity is set to gravity (going down).

When maxJumpTime is exceeded, isJumping is set back to false until the next time the player taps the jump button. The final else clause in the following code executes whenever isJumping is false and sets the player's y velocity to gravity. Note that the additional line of code that sets isFalling to true. As we will see, this variable is used to control what happens when the player initially tries to jump and also in parts of our collision detection code. It basically stops the player from being able to jump in mid air.

```java
// Jumping and gravity
if (isJumping) {
    long timeJumping = System.currentTimeMillis() - jumpTime;
    if (timeJumping < maxJumpTime) {
        if (timeJumping < maxJumpTime / 2) {
            this.setyVelocity(-gravity);//on the way up
            } else if (timeJumping > maxJumpTime / 2) {
                this.setyVelocity(gravity);//going down
            }
    } else {
        isJumping = false;
    }
} else {
        this.setyVelocity(gravity);
        // Read Me!
        // Remove this next line to make the game easier
        // it means the long jumps are less punishing
        // because the player can take off just after the platform
        // They will also be able to cheat by jumping in thin air
        isFalling = true;
}
```

Immediately after we handle jumping, we call move() to update the *x* and *y* coordinates, if they have changed.

```
// Let's go!
this.move(fps);
}// end update()
```

That was a bit of a mouthful, but apart from the actual controls, it is just about everything we need to allow the player to move. We just need to call the update() method from our PlatformView class's update method once each frame, and our player character will spring into action.

In the update method of the PlatformView class, add the following code as shown highlighted:

```
// Set visible flag to true
go.setVisible(true);

if (lm.isPlaying()) {
  // Run any un-clipped updates
  go.update(fps, lm.gravity);
}

} else {
  // Set visible flag to false
  //...
```

Next, we can see what is going on. Let's add some more text output to the if(debugging) block in the draw method of PlatformView. Add the new highlighted code as shown here:

```
canvas.drawText("playerY:" +
  lm.gameObjects.get(lm.playerIndex).getWorldLocation().y,
  10, 140, paint);

canvas.drawText("Gravity:" +
  lm.gravity, 10, 160, paint);

canvas.drawText("X velocity:" +
  lm.gameObjects.get(lm.playerIndex).getxVelocity(),
  10, 180, paint);

canvas.drawText("Y velocity:" +
  lm.gameObjects.get(lm.playerIndex).getyVelocity(),
  10, 200, paint);

//for reset the number of clipped objects each frame
```

Why not run the game now? You have probably noticed the next issue is that the player is gone.

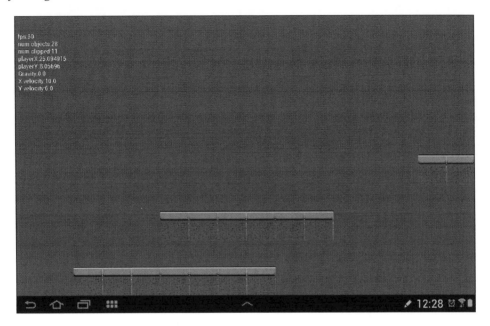

This is because we now have gravity, and also the thread that calls update() runs immediately as the application starts, even before our level and the player character is finished being set up.

We need to do two things. First, we only want update() to run when the LevelManager class has finished its work. Secondly, we need to update the focus of the Viewport class in every frame so that even if the player is falling to his death (as he will frequently) the screen will be centered on him, so we can watch his demise.

Let's start the game on paused mode so that the player isn't missing. First, we will add a method to our LevelManager class that will switch the playing status between playing and not playing. A good name may be switchPlayingStatus(). Add the new method to LevelManager as shown follows:

```
public void switchPlayingStatus() {
    playing = !playing;
    if (playing) {
        gravity = 6;
    } else {
        gravity = 0;
    }
}
```

Now, just delete or comment out the line of code in the LevelManager constructor that sets playing to true. Soon, this will be handled by screen touches and the method we just wrote:

```
// Load all the GameObjects and Bitmaps
loadMapData(context, pixelsPerMetre, px, py);

//playing = true;

//..
```

We will write a tiny bit of temporary code, just a tiny bit. We already know that we will eventually be delegating responsibility to monitor player input to our new InputController class. This little bit of code in the overridden onTouchEvent method is well worth the effort because we will be able to use a pause feature right now.

This code will toggle the playing status using the method we just wrote each time we touch the screen. Add the overridden method to the PlatformView class. We will eventually replace some of this code later in the chapter.

```
@Override
public boolean onTouchEvent(MotionEvent motionEvent) {
  switch (motionEvent.getAction() & MotionEvent.ACTION_MASK) {
    case MotionEvent.ACTION_DOWN:
        lm.switchPlayingStatus();
        break;
  }
return true;
}
```

You can set isPressingRight in the Player class to true, following which you can run the game and tap the screen. We will then see the player fall like a ghost off the bottom, while moving to the right of the screen:

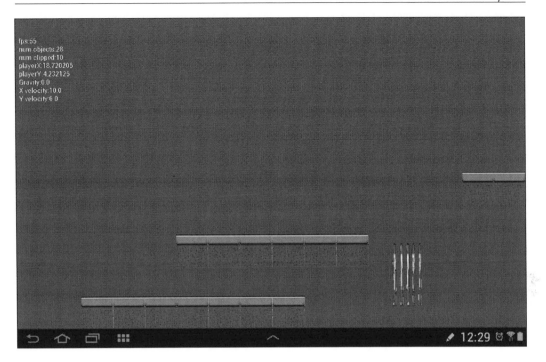

Now, let's update the viewport per frame to remain centered on the player. Add this highlighted code to the very end of the update method in the PlatformView class:

```
if (lm.isPlaying()) {
    //Reset the players location as the centre of the viewport
    vp.setWorldCentre(lm.gameObjects.get(lm.playerIndex)
        .getWorldLocation().x,
        lm.gameObjects.get(lm.playerIndex)
        .getWorldLocation().y);}
}// End of update()
```

If you run the game now, although the player still falls to his doom and to the right, at least the screen stays focused on him to watch it happen.

We will deal with the perpetual falling problem.

Multiphase collision detection

We have seen that our player character simply falls though the world and into oblivion. Of course we need the player to be able to stand on the platforms. Here is what we will do.

We will provide every object that matters with a hitbox as we can then provide methods in the `Player` class to test if a hitbox has made contact with the player. Once per frame, we will send all hitboxes that have not been clipped by the viewport to this new method where a collision can be tested for.

We do it like this for two main reasons. Firstly, by sending only unclipped hitboxes for collision testing, we drastically reduce the number of checks, as described in *Chapter 3, Tappy Defender – Taking Flight*, in the section *Things that go bump – collision detection*. Secondly, by handling the checks within the `Player` class, we can give the player multiple different hitboxes and respond slightly differently according to which one is hit.

Let's create our own class for a hitbox, so we can make it just how we want it. It needs to use float coordinates, it needs an `intersects` method and a bunch of getters and setters as well. Create a new class and call it `RectHitbox`.

Here, we see that `RectHitbox` simply has a bunch of self explanatory getters and setters. It also has the `intersects` method, which returns `true` if the `RectHitbox` passed into it intersects with itself. For an explanation of how the `intersects()` code works, see *Chapter 3, Tappy Defender – Taking Flight*. Enter the following code into the new class:

```
public class RectHitbox {
    float top;
    float left;
    float bottom;
    float right;
    float height;

    boolean intersects(RectHitbox rectHitbox){
        boolean hit = false;

        if(this.right > rectHitbox.left
                && this.left < rectHitbox.right ){
            // Intersecting on x axis

            if(this.top < rectHitbox.bottom
                    && this.bottom > rectHitbox.top ){
                // Intersecting on y as well
```

```
                    // Collision
                    hit = true;
                }
            }


        return hit;
    }

    public void setTop(float top) {
        this.top = top;
    }

    public float getLeft() {
        return left;
    }

    public void setLeft(float left) {
        this.left = left;
    }

    public void setBottom(float bottom) {
        this.bottom = bottom;
    }

    public float getRight() {
        return right;
    }

    public void setRight(float right) {
        this.right = right;
    }

    public float getHeight() {
        return height;
    }

    public void setHeight(float height) {
        this.height = height;
    }
}
```

Now, we can add a RectHitbox class as a member of GameObject. Add it right after the class declaration.

```
private RectHitbox rectHitbox = new RectHitbox();
```

Then, we add a method to initialize the hitbox and a method so that we can grab a copy of it when needed. Add these two methods to GameObject:

```
public void setRectHitbox() {
    rectHitbox.setTop(worldLocation.y);
    rectHitbox.setLeft(worldLocation.x);
    rectHitbox.setBottom(worldLocation.y + height);
    rectHitbox.setRight(worldLocation.x + width);
}

RectHitbox getHitbox(){
    return rectHitbox;
}
```

Now for our Grass object, we add a call to setRectHitbox() and then we can start bumping into it. Add this one line of highlighted code at the very end of the Grass class's constructor. It is important that the call to setRectHitbox() comes after the call to setWorldLocation() otherwise the hitbox won't be wrapped around the block of grass.

```
// Where does the tile start
// X and y locations from constructor parameters
setWorldLocation(worldStartX, worldStartY, 0);
setRectHitbox();
}// End of Grass constructor
```

Before we can begin to comprehend the code that will do the collision checking, we need the Player class to have its own set of hitboxes. We need to know the following things about the player character:

- When the head bumps something above it
- When the feet land on a platform below
- When the player walks into something either side of it

To achieve this, we will create four hitboxes; one for the head, one for the feet, and one for each of the left and right-hand sides. As they are unique to the player, we will create the hitboxes within the Player class.

Declare the four hitboxes as members just after the `Player` class declaration:

```
RectHitbox rectHitboxFeet;
RectHitbox rectHitboxHead;
RectHitbox rectHitboxLeft;
RectHitbox rectHitboxRight;
```

Now in the constructor, we call new `RectHitbox()` to prepare them. Note that we haven't bothered assigning any values to the hitboxes. We will see how we do that soon. Add the four calls to `new()` at the end of the `Player` constructor like this:

```
rectHitboxFeet = new RectHitbox();
rectHitboxHead = new RectHitbox();
rectHitboxLeft = new RectHitbox();
rectHitboxRight = new RectHitbox();
```

We will see were we will initialize them properly. The hitbox values in the code that follows, have been manually estimated based on the space taken up by the actual shape of the character within the rectangle that represents each frame of the character. If you use a different character graphic, you will likely need to adjust the precise values you use.

The diagram shows an approximate graphical representation of the locations that each hitbox will be positioned at. The apparent lack of closeness for the left and right hitboxes is because different frames of the animation are slightly wider than this one. This is a compromise.

The code must be placed after the call to `move()` within the `update` method in the `Player` class. This way, the hitboxes are updated each and every time the player position has changed. Add the highlighted code in exactly the position shown, and then we are one step closer to being able to start bumping in to stuff.

```
// Let's go!
this.move(fps);

// Update all the hitboxes to the new location
// Get the current world location of the player
// and save them as local variables we will use next
Vector2Point5D location = getWorldLocation();
float lx = location.x;
float ly = location.y;

//update the player feet hitbox
rectHitboxFeet.top = ly + getHeight() * .95f;
rectHitboxFeet.left = lx + getWidth() * .2f;
rectHitboxFeet.bottom = ly + getHeight() * .98f;
rectHitboxFeet.right = lx + getWidth() * .8f;

// Update player head hitbox
rectHitboxHead.top = ly;
rectHitboxHead.left = lx + getWidth() * .4f;
rectHitboxHead.bottom = ly + getHeight() * .2f;
rectHitboxHead.right = lx + getWidth() * .6f;

// Update player left hitbox
rectHitboxLeft.top = ly + getHeight() * .2f;
rectHitboxLeft.left = lx + getWidth() * .2f;
rectHitboxLeft.bottom = ly + getHeight() * .8f;
rectHitboxLeft.right = lx + getWidth() * .3f;

// Update player right hitbox
rectHitboxRight.top = ly + getHeight() * .2f;
rectHitboxRight.left = lx + getWidth() * .8f;
rectHitboxRight.bottom = ly + getHeight() * .8f;
rectHitboxRight.right = lx + getWidth() * .7f;

}// End update()
```

In the next stage, we can detect some collisions and react to them. Collisions which only concern the player, such as falling, bumping his head, or trying to walk through a wall are handled directly in this next method, within the `Player` class. Note that the method also returns an `int` value to represent if there was a collision and where on the player that collision occurred so that other collisions with things like pickups or pits of fire can be handled outside the class.

The new `checkCollisions` method receives a `RectHitbox` as a parameter. This will be the `RectHitbox` of whichever object we are currently checking against for collisions. Add the `checkCollisions` method to the `Player` class.

```
public int checkCollisions(RectHitbox rectHitbox) {
    int collided = 0;// No collision

    // The left
    if (this.rectHitboxLeft.intersects(rectHitbox)) {
        // Left has collided
        // Move player just to right of current hitbox
        this.setWorldLocationX(rectHitbox.right - getWidth() * .2f);
        collided = 1;
    }

    // The right
    if (this.rectHitboxRight.intersects(rectHitbox)) {
        // Right has collided
        // Move player just to left of current hitbox
        this.setWorldLocationX(rectHitbox.left - getWidth() * .8f);
        collided = 1;
    }

    // The feet
    if (this.rectHitboxFeet.intersects(rectHitbox)) {
        // Feet have collided
        // Move feet to just above current hitbox
        this.setWorldLocationY(rectHitbox.top - getHeight());
        collided = 2;
    }

    // Now the head
    if (this.rectHitboxHead.intersects(rectHitbox)) {
        // Head has collided. Ouch!
        // Move head to just below current hitbox bottom
        this.setWorldLocationY(rectHitbox.bottom);
        collided = 3;
```

```
    }

      return collided;
  }
```

As the previous code implies, we need to add some setter methods to the GameObject class so that the *x* and *y* world coordinates can be changed when a collision is detected. Add the following two methods to the GameObject class:

```
public void setWorldLocationY(float y) {
   this.worldLocation.y = y;
}

public void setWorldLocationX(float x) {
   this.worldLocation.x = x;
}
```

The final step is to select all relevant objects and test for collisions. We do this in the update method of the PlatformView class, following which we switch to take further actions based on which body part collides with what object type. Our switch block will only have a default case to begin with, since we have only one possible object type to collide with a grass platform. Note that when a collision with the feet is detected, we set our isFalling variable to false, enabling the player to jump. Enter the highlighted code where shown:

```
// Set visible flag to true
go.setVisible(true);

// check collisions with player
int hit = lm.player.checkCollisions(go.getHitbox());
if (hit > 0) {
  //collision! Now deal with different types
  switch (go.getType()) {

    default:// Probably a regular tile
         if (hit == 1) {// Left or right
            lm.player.setxVelocity(0);
            lm.player.setPressingRight(false);
          }

         if (hit == 2) {// Feet
            lm.player.isFalling = false;
         }

         break;
    }
}
```

We will make more use of the value that gets stored in `hit` for further collision-based decision making, as we progress with this project.

Let's take control of the player for real.

Player input

First, let's add some methods in the `Player` class that our input controller will be able to call, then manipulate the variables that the `Player` class's `update` method uses to move around.

We already played with the `isPressingRight` variable, and also have an `isPressingLeft` variable. Furthermore, we want to be able to jump. If you take a look at the `Player` class's `update` method, we already have the code to handle these situations. We just need the player to be able to initiate the movements via touches to the screen.

Our previous button layout design and the code we have written so far, suggests a method for going left, a method for going right, and a method for jumping.

You will also note that we pass a copy of `SoundManager` into the `startJump` method, which allows us to play a neat retro jumping sound, if the jump attempt is successful. Add these three new methods to the `Player` class:

```
public void setPressingRight(boolean isPressingRight) {
    this.isPressingRight = isPressingRight;
}

public void setPressingLeft(boolean isPressingLeft) {
    this.isPressingLeft = isPressingLeft;
}

public void startJump(SoundManager sm) {
    if (!isFalling) {//can't jump if falling
        if (!isJumping) {//not already jumping
            isJumping = true;
            jumpTime = System.currentTimeMillis();
            sm.playSound("jump");
        }
    }
}
```

Now, we can focus on the InputController class. Let's pass control from the onTouchEvent method to our InputController class. Change the code in the onTouchEvent method to the following in the PlatformView class:

```
@Override
    public boolean onTouchEvent(MotionEvent motionEvent) {
        if (lm != null) {
            ic.handleInput(motionEvent, lm, sm, vp);
        }
        //invalidate();
        return true;
    }
```

We have an error in our new method. This is simply because we have called the handleInput method but not implemented it yet. We will do that now.

 If you are wondering about the check for whether lm != null, that is because the onTouchEvent method is triggered from the Android UI thread and is not within our control. If we pass in lm and start trying to do things with it, when it is not initialized, the game will crash.

We can now get everything that we need done within the InputController class. Open that class now, and we will plan what we are going to do.

We need a button to go left, a button to go right, a button to jump, a button to toggle pause, and later we will also need a button to fire a machine gun. Therefore, we really need to highlight different areas of the screen to represent each of these tasks.

To do this, we will declare four Rect objects, one for each task. Then in the constructor, we will define the points of these four Rect objects by carrying out some simple calculations based on the players screen resolution.

We define some handy variables, buttonWidth, buttonHeight, and buttonPadding, based on the device's screen resolution to help us arrange our Rect coordinates neatly. Enter the following members and the InputController constructor as shown next:

```
import android.graphics.Rect;
import android.view.MotionEvent;
import java.util.ArrayList;

public class InputController {
```

```
Rect left;
Rect right;
Rect jump;
Rect shoot;
Rect pause;

InputController(int screenWidth, int screenHeight) {

    //Configure the player buttons
    int buttonWidth = screenWidth / 8;
    int buttonHeight = screenHeight / 7;
    int buttonPadding = screenWidth / 80;

    left = new Rect(buttonPadding,
        screenHeight - buttonHeight - buttonPadding,
        buttonWidth,
        screenHeight - buttonPadding);

    right = new Rect(buttonWidth + buttonPadding,
        screenHeight - buttonHeight - buttonPadding,
        buttonWidth + buttonPadding + buttonWidth,
        screenHeight - buttonPadding);

    jump = new Rect(screenWidth - buttonWidth - buttonPadding,
        screenHeight - buttonHeight - buttonPadding -
        buttonHeight - buttonPadding,
        screenWidth - buttonPadding,
        screenHeight - buttonPadding - buttonHeight -
        buttonPadding);

    shoot = new Rect(screenWidth - buttonWidth - buttonPadding,
        screenHeight - buttonHeight - buttonPadding,
        screenWidth - buttonPadding,
        screenHeight - buttonPadding);

    pause = new Rect(screenWidth - buttonPadding -
        buttonWidth,
        buttonPadding,
        screenWidth - buttonPadding,
        buttonPadding + buttonHeight);

}
```

We will use the four `Rect` objects to draw buttons on the screen. The `draw` method is going to need a copy of them. Enter the code for the `getButtons` method to achieve this:

```
public ArrayList getButtons(){
    //create an array of buttons for the draw method
    ArrayList<Rect> currentButtonList = new ArrayList<>();
    currentButtonList.add(left);
    currentButtonList.add(right);
    currentButtonList.add(jump);
    currentButtonList.add(shoot);
    currentButtonList.add(pause);
    return  currentButtonList;
}
```

We can now handle the actual player input. This project is different to the previous one because there are lots of different possible player actions that need to be monitored and responded to, sometimes simultaneously. As you expect, the Android API has the functionality to make this as easy as possible for us.

The `MotionEvent` class has a lot more data tucked away in it than we have seen so far. Previously, we simply checked for the `ACTION_DOWN` and `ACTION_UP` events. Now, we need to dig a little deeper to grab more of the event data.

In order to record and pass on the details of multiple fingers, touching, leaving, and moving on the screen, the `MotionEvent` class stores them all in an array. When the first finger of the player touches the screen, the details, coordinates, and so on, are stored at position zero. Subsequent actions are then stored later in the array.

The position in the array related to any such finger's activity is not consistent. In some situations, such as detecting specific gestures, this can be a problem and the programmer needs to capture, remember, and respond to the ID of a finger, also held in the `MotionEvent` class.

Fortunately in this situation, we have our clearly defined areas of the screen that represent our buttons, and the most we will ever need to know is if the finger has pressed or released the screen within one of these predefined areas.

We just need to find out how many fingers have caused events and are therefore stored in the array by calling `motionEvent.getPointerCount()`. We then loop through each of these events while providing a `switch` block to handle them, whatever area of the screen, where `ACTION_DOWN` or `ACTION_UP` has occurred. It won't matter which position in the array our event is stored at, as long as we detect it and respond to it.

The only other thing we need to know, before we can code our solution, is that the subsequent actions in the array are stored as ACTION_POINTER_DOWN and ACTION_POINTER_UP; therefore, with each pass through the loop, that we will shortly code, we need to check and handle both ACTION_DOWN and ACTION_POINTER_DOWN.

After all this talk, here is our handleInput method that gets called every time the screen is touched or released:

```java
public void handleInput(MotionEvent motionEvent,LevelManager l,
    SoundManager sound, Viewport vp){

    int pointerCount = motionEvent.getPointerCount();

    for (int i = 0; i < pointerCount; i++) {

        int x = (int) motionEvent.getX(i);
        int y = (int) motionEvent.getY(i);

        if(l.isPlaying()) {
            switch (motionEvent.getAction() &
            MotionEvent.ACTION_MASK) {

            case MotionEvent.ACTION_DOWN:
                    if (right.contains(x, y)) {
                    l.player.setPressingRight(true);
                    l.player.setPressingLeft(false);

                    } else if (left.contains(x, y)) {
                    l.player.setPressingLeft(true);
                    l.player.setPressingRight(false);

                    } else if (jump.contains(x, y)) {
                    l.player.startJump(sound);

                    } else if (shoot.contains(x, y)) {

                    } else if (pause.contains(x, y)) {
                    l.switchPlayingStatus();
                    }

            break;


            case MotionEvent.ACTION_UP:
```

```
        if (right.contains(x, y)) {
        l.player.setPressingRight(false);

        } else if (left.contains(x, y)) {
        l.player.setPressingLeft(false);
    }

break;


case MotionEvent.ACTION_POINTER_DOWN:
if (right.contains(x, y)) {
    l.player.setPressingRight(true);
    l.player.setPressingLeft(false);

    } else if (left.contains(x, y)) {
    l.player.setPressingLeft(true);
        l.player.setPressingRight(false);

    } else if (jump.contains(x, y)) {
    l.player.startJump(sound);

    } else if (shoot.contains(x, y)) {
    //Handle shooting here

    } else if (pause.contains(x, y)) {
    l.switchPlayingStatus();
}

    break;


case MotionEvent.ACTION_POINTER_UP:
    if (right.contains(x, y)) {
    l.player.setPressingRight(false);
    //Log.w("rightP:", "up" );

    } else if (left.contains(x, y)) {
    l.player.setPressingLeft(false);
    //Log.w("leftP:", "up" );

    } else if (shoot.contains(x, y)) {
    //Handle shooting here
    } else if (jump.contains(x, y)) {
```

```
                //Handle more jumping stuff here later
            }

            break;
}// End if(l.playing)

}else {// Not playing
    //Move the viewport around to explore the map
    switch (motionEvent.getAction() & MotionEvent.ACTION_MASK) {

    case MotionEvent.ACTION_DOWN:

        if (pause.contains(x, y)) {
            l.switchPlayingStatus();
            //Log.w("pause:", "DOWN" );
        }

        break;
            }
        }
    }
}
}
```

If you are wondering why we bothered to set up two sets of control code, one for playing and one for not playing, it is because in *Chapter 8, Putting It All Together*, we will add a cool new feature for the game while it is paused. Of course, the togglePlayingStatus method did not need to be done like this, and it would have worked fine without the test for the status of playing. It just saves us making minor intricate amendments to our code later on.

Now all we need to do is open up the PlatformView class, grab a copy of the array with all the control buttons in, and draw them to the screen. We use the drawRoundRect method to draw neat curved-corner rectangles to represent the areas of the screen that will respond to the player's touches. Enter this code in the draw method right before the call to unlockCanvasAndPost():

```
//draw buttons
paint.setColor(Color.argb(80, 255, 255, 255));
ArrayList<Rect> buttonsToDraw;
buttonsToDraw = ic.getButtons();

for (Rect rect : buttonsToDraw) {
    RectF rf = new RectF(rect.left, rect.top,
```

```
        rect.right, rect.bottom);

    canvas.drawRoundRect(rf, 15f, 15f, paint);
}
```

Also, right before we call `unlockCanvasAndPost()`, let's draw a simple pause screen so that we know when the game is paused or playing.

```
//draw paused text
if (!this.lm.isPlaying()) {
    paint.setTextAlign(Paint.Align.CENTER);
    paint.setColor(Color.argb(255, 255, 255, 255));

    paint.setTextSize(120);
    canvas.drawText("Paused", vp.getScreenWidth() / 2,
    vp.getScreenHeight() / 2, paint);
}
```

You can now jump and walk all over the place and a nice retro jumping sound plays as well. Why not add some more grass to the scene by editing `LevelCave` and replacing a few period characters (.) with a few more `1` characters. The next screenshot shows that the player has been jumping around a bit as well as the buttons used for controls:

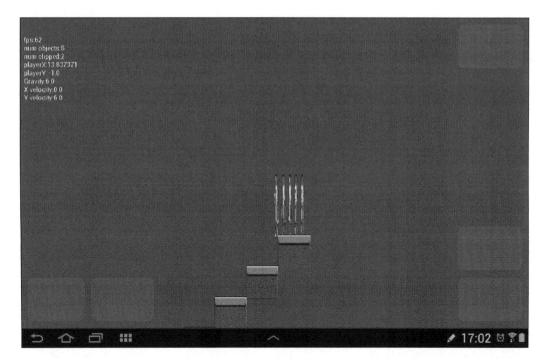

We will design some real-playable levels, as well as link them together in *Chapter 8, Putting It All Together*. For now, just do whatever seems like fun with `LevelCave`.

Now, we can get rid of that ugly squashed player graphic and make a neat little animation out of it.

Animating Bob

Sprite sheet animations work by quickly changing the image drawn to the screen. Exactly like a child may draw the phases of a stick-man moving on the corner of a book, and then quickly flicking through it to make it appear to move.

The frames of Bob's animation are already contained within the `player.png` file we have been using to represent him.

All we need to do is loop through them one at a time when the player is moving.

This is quite straightforward to implement. We will make a simple animation class that handles the function of keeping time and returning the appropriate part of the sprite sheet when requested. We can then initialize a new animation object for any `GameObject` that needs to be animated. In addition, when they are being drawn in the `draw` method of `PlatformView`, if the object is animated, we will handle it slightly differently.

In this section, we will also see how to use the facing variable that tracks which way the player is facing. It will enable us to reverse the sprite sheet depending on the way the player (or any future animated objects) is headed.

Let's start by making the animation class. Create a new Java class and call it `Animation`. The code that follows soon will declare variables that hold the bitmap to be manipulated, the name of the bitmap, and a `rect` parameter to define the area of the sprite sheet that is the coordinates of the currently relevant frame of animation.

In addition, we have `frameCount`, `currentFrame`, `frameTicker`, and `framePeriod` that hold and control the number of available frames, the current frame number, and the timing of the change of the frames. As you would expect, we also need to know the width and height of a frame of animation, these are held by `frameWidth` and `frameHeight`.

Furthermore, the `Animation` class will regularly refer to the number of pixels per meter; therefore, it makes sense to hold this value in a member variable.

Enter these member variables that we discussed in the `Animation` class:

```
import android.content.Context;
import android.graphics.Bitmap;
import android.graphics.Rect;

public class Animation {
    Bitmap bitmapSheet;
    String bitmapName;
    private Rect sourceRect;
    private int frameCount;
    private int currentFrame;
    private long frameTicker;
    private int framePeriod;
    private int frameWidth;
    private int frameHeight;
    int pixelsPerMetre;
```

Next, we have the constructor that prepares our animation object for use. We will see exactly how we prepare for the actual animation soon. Note that there are a fair few parameters in the signature indicating that the animation is quite configurable. Just note that FPS in this context is not referring to the frame rate of the game but the frame rate of the animation.

```
Animation(Context context,
    String bitmapName, float frameHeight,
    float frameWidth, int animFps,
    int frameCount, int pixelsPerMetre){

    this.currentFrame = 0;
    this.frameCount = frameCount;
    this.frameWidth = (int)frameWidth * pixelsPerMetre;
    this.frameHeight = (int)frameHeight * pixelsPerMetre;
    sourceRect = new Rect(0, 0, this.frameWidth,
    this.frameHeight);
```

```
        framePeriod = 1000 / animFps;
        frameTicker = 0l;
        this.bitmapName = "" + bitmapName;
        this.pixelsPerMetre = pixelsPerMetre;
    }
```

We can deal with the real functionality of the class. The `getCurrentFrame` method first checks to see if the object is moving or if it is capable of moving. At this stage, this may seem a little odd as this method will only ever be called by a `GameObject` class that is animated. The odd looking check, therefore, is determining if a new frame is required at the moment.

If an object moves, (such as Bob), but is standing still, then we don't need to change the frame of animation. However, if the animated object has no velocity ever, like a roaring fire, then we need to animate it all the time. It will never have any velocity so the `moves` variable will be `false`, but the method will proceed.

The method then uses `time`, `frameTicker` and `framePeriod`, to determine if it is time to show the next frame of animation and if it increments the frame number to display. Then, if the animation is on the last frame, it goes back to the first frame.

Finally, the precise left and right-hand positions that represent the portion of the sprite sheet that contains the needed frame, are calculated and returned to the calling code.

```
    public Rect getCurrentFrame(long time,
        float xVelocity, boolean moves){

        if(xVelocity!=0 || moves == false) {
        // Only animate if the object is moving
        // or it is an object which doesn't move
        // but is still animated (like fire)

            if (time > frameTicker + framePeriod) {
                frameTicker = time;
                currentFrame++;
                if (currentFrame >= frameCount) {
                    currentFrame = 0;
                }
            }
        }

        //update the left and right values of the source of
        //the next frame on the spritesheet
        this.sourceRect.left = currentFrame * frameWidth;
```

```
        this.sourceRect.right = this.sourceRect.left + frameWidth;

        return sourceRect;

    }


    }// End of Animation class
```

Next, we can add some members to the GameObject class.

```
// Most objects only have 1 frame
// And don't need to bother with these
private Animation anim = null;
private boolean animated;
private int animFps = 1;
```

Some methods to interact with our Animation class, which set and get variables, make the animation work and inform the draw method if the object is animated or not.

```
public void setAnimFps(int animFps) {
   this.animFps = animFps;
}

public void setAnimFrameCount(int animFrameCount) {
   this.animFrameCount = animFrameCount;
}

public boolean isAnimated() {
   return animated;
}
```

Lastly in GameObject, there is a method which the objects that require animating can use to set up their whole animation object. Note it is this setAnimated method that calls new() on a new animation object.

```
public void setAnimated(Context context, int pixelsPerMetre,
   boolean animated){

  this.animated = animated;
  this.anim = new Animation(context, bitmapName,
      height,
      width,
      animFps,
      animFrameCount,
      pixelsPerMetre );
}
```

The next method acts as a go between for the `draw` method of the `PlatformView` class and the `getRectToDraw` method of the `Animation` class.

```
public Rect getRectToDraw(long deltaTime){
  return anim.getCurrentFrame(
    deltaTime,
    xVelocity,
    isMoves());
}
```

Then, we need to update the `Player` class in order to initialize its animation object according to its own specific required number of frames and frames per second. The new code in the `Player` class is highlighted:

```
setBitmapName("player");

final int ANIMATION_FPS = 16;
final int ANIMATION_FRAME_COUNT = 5;

// Set this object up to be animated
setAnimFps(ANIMATION_FPS);
setAnimFrameCount(ANIMATION_FRAME_COUNT);
setAnimated(context, pixelsPerMetre, true);

// X and y locations from constructor parameters
setWorldLocation(worldStartX, worldStartY, 0);
```

We can use all this new code from the `draw` method to implement our animations. The next block of code checks if the current `GameObject` being drawn `isAnimated()`. If it is, it gets the appropriate rectangle from the sprite sheet using the `getNextRect()` method via the `GameObject` class's `getRectToDraw` method.

Note that, the next code listing from the `draw` method that made the original call to `drawBitmap()`, is now wrapped in an `else` clause at the end of the new code. Basically, the logic is this. If animated, execute the new code, otherwise just do it the usual way.

In addition to the animation code we know about, we also check `if(go.getFacing() == 1)` and use the `Matrix` class to flip the bitmap when required by scaling it by -1 on the *x* axis.

Here is all the new code, including the original `drawBitmap()` call wrapped in an `else` clause at the end:

```
toScreen2d.set(vp.worldToScreen
    go.getWorldLocation().x,
    go.getWorldLocation().y,
    go.getWidth(),
    go.getHeight()));

if (go.isAnimated()) {
    // Get the next frame of the bitmap
    // Rotate if necessary
    if (go.getFacing() == 1) {
        // Rotate
        Matrix flipper = new Matrix();
        flipper.preScale(-1, 1);
        Rect r = go.getRectToDraw(System.currentTimeMillis());
        Bitmap b = Bitmap.createBitmap(
        lm.bitmapsArray[lm.getBitmapIndex(go.getType())],
        r.left,
        r.top,
        r.width(),
        r.height(),
        flipper,
        true);
        canvas.drawBitmap(b, toScreen2d.left, toScreen2d.top, paint);
    } else {
        // draw it the regular way round
        canvas.drawBitmap(
        lm.bitmapsArray[lm.getBitmapIndex(go.getType())],
        go.getRectToDraw(System.currentTimeMillis()),
        toScreen2d, paint);
    }
} else { // Just draw the whole bitmap
        canvas.drawBitmap(
        lm.bitmapsArray[lm.getBitmapIndex(go.getType())],
        toScreen2d.left,
        toScreen2d.top, paint);
}
```

Now, you can run the game and see Bob in all his animated glory. The screenshot can't show his movements, but you can see he is now perfectly formed:

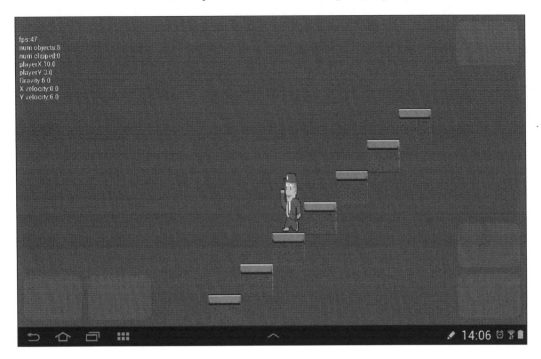

Summary

Our game is steadily coming together. At this stage, we can build a huge level design in LevelCave and go running and jumping all over the place. However, we will save to postpone trying to make the game playable until we have added a load more neat features.

These neat features will include a machine gun, which can be upgraded through collectible pickups and some enemies that Bob can shoot at. We will get going with that in the next chapter.

7
Platformer – Guns, Life, Money, and the Enemy

In this chapter, we will do many things. First, we will build a machine gun with a variable rate of fire and have it shoot bullets. Then, we will introduce pickups or collectibles. These give the player something to scavenge for while trying to escape into the next level.

Then, just as Bob was beginning to think that his life was a blissful one of grass and collectibles, we will build two adversaries for him to outsmart or kill. A homing drone and a patrolling guard. We will easily be able to add all these things into our level designs.

Ready aim fire

Now, we can give our hero a gun, and later, we can give him enemies to shoot at. We will create a `MachineGun` class to do all the work and a `Bullet` class to represent the projectiles that it fires. The `Player` class will control the `MachineGun` class, and the `MachineGun` class will control and keep track of all the `Bullet` objects that it fires.

Create a new Java class and call it `Bullet`. Bullets are not complicated. Ours will need a *x* and *y* location, a horizontal velocity, and a direction to help calculate the velocity.

This implies the following simple class, constructor, and a bunch of getters and setters:

```
public class Bullet  {

    private float x;
    private float y;
```

```java
    private float xVelocity;
    private int direction;

    Bullet(float x, float y, int speed, int direction){
        this.direction = direction;
        this.x = x;
        this.y = y;
        this.xVelocity = speed * direction;
    }

    public int getDirection(){
        return direction;
    }

    public void update(long fps, float gravity){
        x += xVelocity / fps;
    }

    public void hideBullet(){
        this.x = -100;
        this.xVelocity = 0;
    }

    public float getX(){
        return x;
    }

    public float getY(){
        return y;
    }



}
```

Now let's implement the MachineGun class.

Create a new Java class and call it MachineGun. First, we add some members. The maxBullets variable is not the amount of shots a player has, that is unlimited, it is the number of bullet objects the MachineGun class can have. Ten is sufficient for a very fast firing gun, as we will see. The members numBullets and nextBullet help the class to keep track of its 10 bullets. The rateOfFire variable controls how fast the player will be able to tap the fire button, and lastShotTime will help enforce the rateOfFire by keeping track of the system time that the last bullet was fired. It is the rate of fire that will be the upgradeable aspect of the weapon.

Enter the code that we discussed as follows.

```java
import java.util.concurrent.CopyOnWriteArrayList;

public class MachineGun extends GameObject{
    private int maxBullets = 10;
    private int numBullets;
    private int nextBullet;
    private int rateOfFire = 1;//bullets per second
    private long lastShotTime;

    private CopyOnWriteArrayList<Bullet> bullets;

    int speed = 25;
```

> For functional purposes, we can think of the
> CopyOnWriteArrayList bullets, which stores our bullets,
> as a plain old ArrayList object. We use this more complex
> and slightly slower class because it is thread safe and bullets
> can be accessed potentially simultaneously from the UI thread,
> when the player taps the fire button as well as from our own
> thread. This article explains CopyOnWriteArrayList, if you
> want to know more, visit:
>
> http://examples.javacodegeeks.com/
> java-basics/exceptions/java-util-
> concurrentmodificationexception-how-to-handle-
> concurrent-modification-exception/

We have the constructor that just initializes bullets, lastShotTime, and nextBullet:

```java
MachineGun(){
    bullets = new CopyOnWriteArrayList<Bullet>();
    lastShotTime = -1;
    nextBullet = -1;
}
```

Here, we update all the Bullet objects controlled by the gun by calling the bullet.update method for each bullet.

```java
public void update(long fps, float gravity){
        //update all the bullets
        for(Bullet bullet: bullets){
            bullet.update(fps, gravity);
        }
    }
```

Next, we have some getters that will let us find out things about our gun and its bullets, to do things like collision detection, and drawing bullets.

```
public int getRateOfFire(){
    return rateOfFire;
}

public void setFireRate(int rate){
    rateOfFire = rate;
}

public int getNumBullets(){
    //tell the view how many bullets there are
    return numBullets;
}

public float getBulletX(int bulletIndex){
    if(bullets != null && bulletIndex < numBullets) {
        return bullets.get(bulletIndex).getX();
      }

    return -1f;
}

public float getBulletY(int bulletIndex){
    if(bullets != null) {
        return bullets.get(bulletIndex).getY();
      }
        return -1f;
}
```

We also have a quick helper method for when we want to stop drawing a bullet. We hide it away until it is ready to be reassigned in our shoot method shortly.

```
public void hideBullet(int index){
    bullets.get(index).hideBullet();
}
```

A getter that returns the direction of travel:

```
public int getDirection(int index){
    return bullets.get(index).getDirection();
}
```

Now, we add a more comprehensive method that actually shoots a bullet. The method compares the time of the last fired shot against the current `rateOfFire`. It then proceeds to increment `nextBullet` and create a new `Bullet` object if permitted. The bullet is sent speeding off in the same direction as Bob is facing. Note that the method returns `true` if a bullet was successfully fired. This is so that the `InputController` class can play a sound effect to correspond with the player's button press.

```
public boolean shoot(float ownerX, float ownerY,
    int ownerFacing, float ownerHeight){

    boolean shotFired = false;
    if(System.currentTimeMillis() - lastShotTime  >
      1000/rateOfFire){

        //spawn another bullet;
        nextBullet ++;


        if(numBullets >= maxBullets){
            numBullets = maxBullets;
        }

        if(nextBullet == maxBullets){
            nextBullet = 0;
        }

        lastShotTime = System.currentTimeMillis();
        bullets.add(nextBullet,
                new Bullet(ownerX,
                (ownerY+ ownerHeight/3), speed, ownerFacing));

        shotFired = true;
        numBullets++;
    }
    return shotFired;
}
```

Finally, we have a method to call when the player finds a machine gun upgrade pickup. We will see more of them later in the chapter. Here, we simply increase `rateOfFire`, which enables the player to tap the fire button more furiously and still get results.

```
public void upgradeRateOfFire(){
    rateOfFire += 2;
}
}// End of MachineGun class
```

Now, we will modify the `Player` class to carry a `MachineGun`. Give `Player` a member variable that is a `MachineGun`.

```
public MachineGun bfg;
```

Next in the `Player` constructor, add a line of code to initialize our new `MachineGun` object:

```
bfg = new MachineGun();
```

In the `Player` class's `update` method, add a call to the `MachineGun` class's `update` method just before we call `move()` for the player. As highlighted next:

```
bfg.update(fps, gravity);

// Let's go!
this.move(fps);
```

Add a method to the `Player` class, so our `InputController` can access the virtual trigger. As we saw, the method returns `true` if a shot was successful so that the `InputController` class knows whether to play a shot sound or not.

```
public boolean pullTrigger() {
        //Try and fire a shot
        return bfg.shoot(this.getWorldLocation().x,
            this.getWorldLocation().y,
            getFacing(), getHeight());
}
```

Now, we can make some minor additions to our `InputController` class so that the player can fire a shot. The code to add is shown highlighted amongst the existing code:

```
} else if (jump.contains(x, y)) {
  l.player.startJump(sound);

} else if (shoot.contains(x, y)) {
  if (l.player.pullTrigger()) {
      sound.playSound("shoot");
    }

} else if (pause.contains(x, y)) {
  l.switchPlayingStatus();

}
```

Not forgetting the way that our new control system works, we also need to add the same piece of extra code further down the InputController class in the MotionEvent.ACTION_POINTER_DOWN case as well. As usual, here is the code highlighted and with plenty of context:

```
} else if (jump.contains(x, y)) {
  l.player.startJump(sound);

} else if (shoot.contains(x, y)) {
  if (l.player.pullTrigger()) {
     sound.playSound("shoot");
}

} else if (pause.contains(x, y)) {
  l.switchPlayingStatus();
}
```

Now we have a gun, it's loaded, and we know how to pull the trigger. We just need to draw the bullets.

Add the new code in the draw method, just before we draw the debugging text, as shown:

```
//draw the bullets
paint.setColor(Color.argb(255, 255, 255, 255));
for (int i = 0; i < lm.player.bfg.getNumBullets(); i++) {
    // Pass in the x and y coords as usual
    // then .25 and .05 for the bullet width and height
    toScreen2d.set(vp.worldToScreen
            (lm.player.bfg.getBulletX(i),
            lm.player.bfg.getBulletY(i),
            .25f,
            .05f));

        canvas.drawRect(toScreen2d, paint);
}

// Text for debugging
if (debugging) {
// etc
```

We will now fire some bullets. Note that the rate of fire is unsatisfying and slow. We will add some pickups, which the player can get to increase the rate of fire of his gun.

Pickups

Pickups are game objects that can be collected by the player. They include things like upgrades, extra lives, money, and so on. We will now implement one of each of those collectibles. As our game engine is setup the way it is, this will be surprisingly easy.

The first thing we will do is create a class to hold the state of the current player. We want to monitor the money collected, power of machine gun, and lives remaining. Let's call it `PlayerState`. Create a new Java class and name it `PlayerState`.

In addition to the variables, we have just talked about, we also want the `PlayerState` class to remember an *x* and *y* location to respawn at, when the player loses a life. Enter these member variables and the simple constructor:

```java
import android.graphics.PointF;

public class PlayerState {

    private int numCredits;
    private int mgFireRate;
    private int lives;
    private float restartX;
    private float restartY;

    PlayerState() {
        lives = 3;
        mgFireRate = 1;
        numCredits = 0;
    }
```

Now, we need a method that we can call to initialize the respawn location. We will use this later when we call this method. Also, we need a method to reload the location. These are our next two methods for the `PlayerState` class:

```java
public void saveLocation(PointF location) {
    // The location saves each time the player uses a teleport
    restartX = location.x;
    restartY = location.y;
}

public PointF loadLocation() {
    // Used every time the player loses a life
    return new PointF(restartX, restartY);
}
```

We just need a whole bunch of getters and setters to give us access to the members of this class:

```
public int getLives(){
  return lives;
}

public int getFireRate(){
  return mgFireRate;
}

public void increaseFireRate(){
  mgFireRate += 2;
}

public void gotCredit(){
  numCredits ++;
}

public int getCredits(){
  return numCredits;
}

public void loseLife(){
  lives--;
}

public void addLife(){
  lives++;
}

public void resetLives(){
  lives = 3;
}
public void resetCredits(){
  lives = 0;
}

}// End PlayerState class
```

Next, declare an object of the `PlayerState` type as a member of the `PlatformView` class:

```
// Our new engine classes
private LevelManager lm;
private Viewport vp;
InputController ic;
SoundManager sm;
private PlayerState ps;
```

Initialize it in the `PlatformView` constructor:

```
vp = new Viewport(screenWidth, screenHeight);
sm = new SoundManager();
sm.loadSound(context);
ps = new PlayerState();

loadLevel("LevelCave", 10, 2);
```

Now in the `loadLevel` method, create a `RectF` object, store the players starting location, and pass it in to the `PlayerState` object, `ps`, for safe keeping. Each time the player dies, he can be respawned using this location.

```
ic = new InputController(vp.getScreenWidth(),
vp.getScreenHeight());

PointF location = new PointF(px, py);
ps.saveLocation(location);

//set the players location as the world centre of the viewport
```

Now we will create three classes, one for each of our pickups. These classes are very simple. They extend `GameObject`, set a bitmap, have a hitbox, and a location in the world. Also note that they all receive a type in the constructor and use `setType()` to store this value. We will soon see how to use their type to handle what happens when the player "picks them up". Create three new Java classes: `Coin`, `ExtraLife`, and `MachineGunUpgrade`. Note that the pickups are a little smaller than a platform, perhaps as we may expect. Enter the code for each of them in turn.

The following is the code for `Coin`:

```
public class Coin extends GameObject{

    Coin(float worldStartX, float worldStartY, char type) {

        final float HEIGHT = .5f;
        final float WIDTH = .5f;

        setHeight(HEIGHT);
        setWidth(WIDTH);

        setType(type);

        // Choose a Bitmap
        setBitmapName("coin");
```

```
        // Where does the tile start
        // X and y locations from constructor parameters
        setWorldLocation(worldStartX, worldStartY, 0);
        setRectHitbox();
    }

    public void update(long fps, float gravity){}
}
```

Now, for ExtraLife:

```
public class ExtraLife extends GameObject{

    ExtraLife(float worldStartX, float worldStartY, char type) {

        final float HEIGHT = .8f;
        final float WIDTH = .65f;

        setHeight(HEIGHT);
        setWidth(WIDTH);

        setType(type);

        // Choose a Bitmap

        setBitmapName("life");

        // Where does the tile start
        // X and y locations from constructor parameters
        setWorldLocation(worldStartX, worldStartY, 0);
        setRectHitbox();
    }

    public void update(long fps, float gravity){}
}
```

Finally, the MachineGunUpgrade class:

```
public class MachineGunUpgrade extends GameObject{
    MachineGunUpgrade(float worldStartX,
        float worldStartY,
        char type) {

        final float HEIGHT = .5f;
        final float WIDTH = .5f;
```

```
            setHeight(HEIGHT);
            setWidth(WIDTH);

            setType(type);

            // Choose a Bitmap

            setBitmapName("clip");

            // Where does the tile start
            // X and y locations from constructor parameters
            setWorldLocation(worldStartX, worldStartY, 0);
            setRectHitbox();
        }

        public void update(long fps, float gravity){}
    }
```

Now, update the LevelManager class to expect these three new objects in our level designs and add them to ArrayList of GameObjects. To do this, we need to update the LevelManager class in three places: getBitmap(), getBitmapIndex(), and loadMapData(). Here are each of these minor updates, with the new code highlighted amongst the existing code.

Make the following additions to getBitmap():

```
case 'p':
   index = 2;
   break;

case 'c':
   index = 3;
   break;

case 'u':
   index = 4;
   break;

case 'e':
   index = 5;
   break;

default:
   index = 0;
   break;
```

Make identical additions, but this time to `getBitmapIndex()`:

```
case 'p':
  index = 2;
  break;

case 'c':
  index = 3;
  break;

case 'u':
  index = 4;
  break;

case 'e':
  index = 5;
  break;

default:
  index = 0;
  break;
```

Make the final changes within `LevelManager` with the following additions to `loadMapData()`:

```
case 'p':// a player
    // Add a player to the gameObjects
    gameObjects.add(new Player(context, px, py, pixelsPerMetre));
    // We want the index of the player
    playerIndex = currentIndex;
    // We want a reference to the player object
    player = (Player) gameObjects.get(playerIndex);
    break;

case 'c':
    // Add a coin to the gameObjects
    gameObjects.add(new Coin(j, i, c));
    break;

case 'u':
    // Add a machine gun upgrade to the gameObjects
    gameObjects.add(new MachineGunUpgrade(j, i, c));
    break;
```

```
case 'e':
    // Add an extra life to the gameObjects
    gameObjects.add(new ExtraLife(j, i, c));
    break;
}
```

Now, we can add the three appropriately named graphics to the drawable folder and start adding them to our LevelCave design. Go ahead and copy clip.png, coin.png, and life.png from the Chapter7/drawables folder in the download bundle to the drawable folder of your Android Studio project.

Add a handy list of comments that identify all the types of game object. We will add these over the course of this project and the alpha-numeric code that will represent them on our level designs. Add the following comments to the LevelData class:

```
// Tile types
// . = no tile
// 1 = Grass
// 2 = Snow
// 3 = Brick
// 4 = Coal
// 5 = Concrete
// 6 = Scorched
// 7 = Stone

//Active objects
// g = guard
// d = drone
// t = teleport
// c = coin
// u = upgrade
// f = fire
// e = extra life

//Inactive objects
// w = tree
// x = tree2 (snowy)
// l = lampost
// r = stalactite
// s = stalacmite
// m = mine cart
// z = boulders
```

Before we enhance our `LevelCave` class to use our new objects, we want to detect when the player collects them or collides with them and take appropriate action. We will first add a quick helper method to the `Player` class. The reason for this is because when the player collides with another object, the default action in the `Player` class's `checkCollisions` method is to stop the character moving. We don't want this to happen for pickups because it will be irritating for the player. Therefore, we will quickly add a `restorePreviousVelocity` method to the `Player` class that we can call whenever we don't want this default action to occur. Add this method to the `Player` class:

```
public void restorePreviousVelocity() {
    if (!isJumping && !isFalling) {
        if (getFacing() == LEFT) {
            isPressingLeft = true;
            setxVelocity(-MAX_X_VELOCITY);
        } else {
            isPressingRight = true;
                    setxVelocity(MAX_X_VELOCITY);
        }
    }
}
```

Now, we can handle the collisions for each of our pickups in turn. Add these cases to handle our three pickups within the switch block that handles our collisions in the `update` method of the `PlatformView` class:

```
switch (go.getType()) {
    case 'c':
        sm.playSound("coin_pickup");
        go.setActive(false);
        go.setVisible(false);
        ps.gotCredit();

        // Now restore state that was
        // removed by collision detection
        if (hit != 2) {// Any hit except feet
            lm.player.restorePreviousVelocity();
        }
        break;

    case 'u':
        sm.playSound("gun_upgrade");
        go.setActive(false);
        go.setVisible(false);
        lm.player.bfg.upgradeRateOfFire();
        ps.increaseFireRate();
```

```
        if (hit != 2) {// Any hit except feet
            lm.player.restorePreviousVelocity();
        }
        break;

    case 'e':
        //extralife
        go.setActive(false);
        go.setVisible(false);
        sm.playSound("extra_life");
        ps.addLife();

        if (hit != 2) {
            lm.player.restorePreviousVelocity();
        }
        break;

    default:// Probably a regular tile
        if (hit == 1) {// Left or right
            lm.player.setxVelocity(0);
            lm.player.setPressingRight(false);
        }

        if (hit == 2) {// Feet
            lm.player.isFalling = false;
        }
        break;
    }
```

Finally, add the new objects to our `LevelCave` class.

> The following code snippet, I suggest, is for a simple new layout that demonstrates our new objects, but your layout can be as big or elaborate as you like. We will do something more elaborate in the next chapter when we design and link some levels.

Enter the following code into `LevelCave` or elaborate with your own design:

```
public class LevelCave extends LevelData{
    LevelCave() {
        tiles = new ArrayList<String>();
        this.tiles.add("p..............................................");
        this.tiles.add("...............................................");
```

```
        this.tiles.add("................................................");
        this.tiles.add("................................................");
        this.tiles.add(".........................c......................");
        this.tiles.add(".............................1........u.........");
        this.tiles.add("....................c.........u1................");
        this.tiles.add("....................1.........u1................");
        this.tiles.add(".................c............u1................");
        this.tiles.add(".................1............u1................");
        this.tiles.add("........................e..1....e....e.........");
        this.tiles.add("....1111111111111111111111111111111111111....");
    }
```

This is what the simple layout will look like:

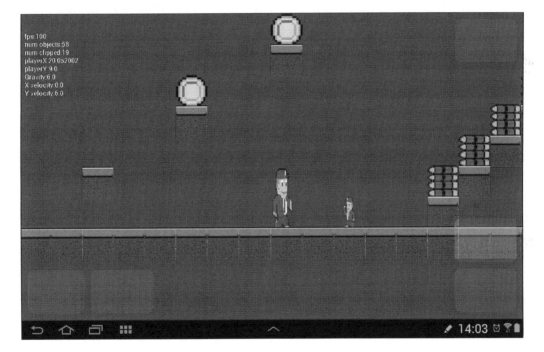

Try collecting the pickups, and you will hear the pleasing sound effects. In addition, each time we collect a pickup, the `PlayerState` class stores an update. This will be useful when we build a HUD in the next chapter. Most fun of all; if you collect the machine gun upgrades, then try shooting your gun, you will find it much more satisfying to wield.

We better make those bullets do something. However, before we do that, let's give the player a bit more cannon fodder in the form of a couple of enemies.

The drone

The drone is a simple but evil enemy. It will detect the player when it is within the viewport and fly straight at him. If the drone touches the player, death is immediate.

Let's build a `Drone` class. Create a new Java class and call it `Drone`. We need member variables to remember when we set the last waypoint. This will restrict the frequency with which the drone will get a navigation update of Bob's coordinates. This stops the drone from being too deadly accurate. It needs a waypoint/target coordinate and also needs to know the speed limit via `MAX_X_VELOCITY` and `MAX_Y_VELOCITY`.

```
import android.graphics.PointF;

public class Drone extends GameObject {

    long lastWaypointSetTime;
    PointF currentWaypoint;

    final float MAX_X_VELOCITY = 3;
    final float MAX_Y_VELOCITY = 3;
```

Now in the `Drone` constructor, initialize the usual `GameObject` members and specifically, the `Drone` class ones such as `currentWaypoint`. Not forgetting, that if we are going to shoot the drone, it will need a hitbox and we call `setRectHitBox()` after we have called `setWorldLocation()`.

```
Drone(float worldStartX, float worldStartY, char type) {
    final float HEIGHT = 1;
    final float WIDTH = 1;
    setHeight(HEIGHT); // 1 metre tall
    setWidth(WIDTH); // 1 metres wide

    setType(type);

    setBitmapName("drone");
    setMoves(true);
```

```
        setActive(true);
        setVisible(true);

        currentWaypoint = new PointF();

        // Where does the drone start
        // X and y locations from constructor parameters
        setWorldLocation(worldStartX, worldStartY, 0);
        setRectHitbox();
        setFacing(RIGHT);
    }
```

Here is the implementation of the update method, which compares the drone's coordinates with its currentWaypoint variable and changes its velocity accordingly. Then, we end update() by calling move() then setRectHitbox().

```
    public void update(long fps, float gravity) {
        if (currentWaypoint.x > getWorldLocation().x) {
            setxVelocity(MAX_X_VELOCITY);
        } else if (currentWaypoint.x < getWorldLocation().x) {
            setxVelocity(-MAX_X_VELOCITY);
        } else {
            setxVelocity(0);
        }

        if (currentWaypoint.y >= getWorldLocation().y) {
            setyVelocity(MAX_Y_VELOCITY);
        } else if (currentWaypoint.y < getWorldLocation().y) {
            setyVelocity(-MAX_Y_VELOCITY);
        } else {
            setyVelocity(0);
        }


    move(fps);

    // update the drone hitbox
    setRectHitbox();


}
```

In our last method for the `Drone` class, update the `currentWaypoint` variable by passing in Bob's coordinates as a parameter. Note that we check if enough time has elapsed for an update to make sure our drone is not too accurate.

```
public void setWaypoint(Vector2Point5D playerLocation) {
    if (System.currentTimeMillis() > lastWaypointSetTime + 2000)
    {//Has 2 seconds passed
        lastWaypointSetTime = System.currentTimeMillis();
        currentWaypoint.x = playerLocation.x;
        currentWaypoint.y = playerLocation.y;
    }
}
}// End Drone class
```

Add the drone graphic `drone.png` from `Chapter7/drawable` into the `drawable` folder of your project.

We then need to add drones to our `LevelManager` class in the usual three places, just as we did for each of our pickups. Now, add code to `getBitmap()`, `getBitmapIndex()`, and `loadMapData()`. These are the three minor code additions in order.

Add the highlighted code in the `getBitmap` method:

```
case 'e':
    index = 5;
    break;

case 'd':
    index = 6;
    break;

default:
    index = 0;
    break;
```

Add the highlighted code in the `getBitmapIndex` method:

```
case 'e':
    index = 5;
    break;

case 'd':
    index = 6;
    break;
```

```
default:
  index = 0;
  break;
```

Add the highlighted code in the `loadMapData` method:

```
case 'e':
   // Add an extra life to the gameObjects
   gameObjects.add(new ExtraLife(j, i, c));
   break;

case 'd':
   // Add a drone to the gameObjects
   gameObjects.add(new Drone(j, i, c));
   break;
```

The burning question is; how does the drone know where to go? In each frame, if there is a drone within the viewport, we can send the coordinates of the player. Do what is shown in this next code block within the `update` method of the `PlatformView` class.

As usual, the new code is shown highlighted and in the context of the existing code. If you remember the `setWaypoint()` code from the `Drone` class, it only accepts updates every 2 seconds. This stops the drone from being too accurate.

```
if (lm.isPlaying()) {
    // Run any un-clipped updates
    go.update(fps, lm.gravity);

    if (go.getType() == 'd') {
        // Let any near by drones know where the player is
        Drone d = (Drone) go;
        d.setWaypoint(lm.player.getWorldLocation());
    }
}
```

Now, these evil drones can be strategically placed around the level, and they will home in on the player. The last thing we need to do to make the drones fully operational is to detect when they actually collide with the player. This is nice and easy. Just add a case for drones in our collision detection `switch` block in the `update` method of the `PlatformView` class:

```
case 'e':
  //extralife
   go.setActive(false);
   go.setVisible(false);
```

```
            sm.playSound("extra_life");
            ps.addLife();
            if (hit != 2) {// Any hit except feet
                lm.player.restorePreviousVelocity();
            }
            break;

    case 'd':
            PointF location;
            //hit by drone
            sm.playSound("player_burn");
            ps.loseLife();
            location = new PointF(ps.loadLocation().x,
                ps.loadLocation().y);
            lm.player.setWorldLocationX(location.x);
            lm.player.setWorldLocationY(location.y);
            lm.player.setxVelocity(0);
            break;

    default:// Probably a regular tile
        if (hit == 1) {// Left or right
            lm.player.setxVelocity(0);
            lm.player.setPressingRight(false);
        }

        if (hit == 2) {// Feet
            lm.player.isFalling = false;
        }
```

Go ahead and add a whole bunch of drones to `LevelCave` and watch them fly at the player. Note that if a drone catches the player, he dies and respawns.

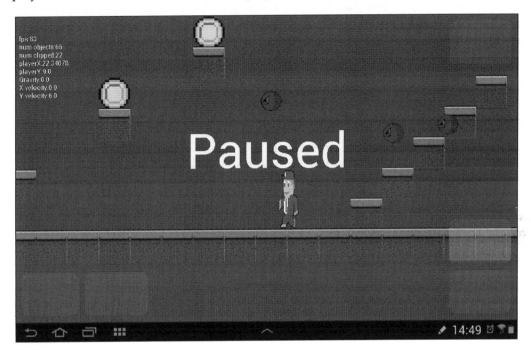

Now, as if the world wasn't a dangerous enough place with all those enemy drones, let's add another type of enemy.

The guard

The guard enemy will be an exercise in scripting. We will have our `LevelManager` class automatically generate a simple script, which generates a route for our guard to patrol.

The route will be the simplest one possible; it will be just two waypoints that the guard will walk between continuously. It will be much quicker and simpler to preprogram our guards with two predetermined waypoints. However, by taking the time to have it automatically generated, we can place guards wherever we like (within certain parameters) on any level we design, and the behavior will be taken care of for us.

Our guard will be animated, so we will be using a sprite sheet and configuring the animation details in the constructor; just as we did for the `Player` class.

Create a new class and call it `Guard`. First, handle the member variables. Our `Guard` class will not only need two waypoints, but also a variable to indicate which one the current waypoint is. Like other moving objects, it will need velocity. Here is the class declaration and member variables to start coding your class:

```
import android.content.Context;

public class Guard extends GameObject {

    // Guards just move on x axis between 2 waypoints

    private float waypointX1;// always on left
    private float waypointX2;// always on right
    private int currentWaypoint;
    final float MAX_X_VELOCITY = 3;
```

We need to set up our guards via the constructor. First, setup our animation variables, bitmap, and sizes. Then as usual, set the guard's position in the level, its hitbox, and the way that it is facing. However, in the last line of the constructor we set `currentWaypoint` to `1`; this is new. We will see how this informs our guard's behavior in this class's `update` method.

```
Guard(Context context, float worldStartX,
    float worldStartY, char type,
    int pixelsPerMetre) {

        final int ANIMATION_FPS = 8;
        final int ANIMATION_FRAME_COUNT = 5;
        final String BITMAP_NAME = "guard";
        final float HEIGHT = 2f;
        final float WIDTH = 1;

        setHeight(HEIGHT); // 2 metre tall
        setWidth(WIDTH); // 1 metres wide

        setType(type);

        setBitmapName("guard");
        // Now for the player's other attributes
        // Our game engine will use these
        setMoves(true);
        setActive(true);
        setVisible(true);

        // Set this object up to be animated
```

```
    setAnimFps(ANIMATION_FPS);
    setAnimFrameCount(ANIMATION_FRAME_COUNT);
    setBitmapName(BITMAP_NAME);
    setAnimated(context, pixelsPerMetre, true);

    // Where does the tile start
    // X and y locations from constructor parameters
    setWorldLocation(worldStartX, worldStartY, 0);
    setxVelocity(-MAX_X_VELOCITY);
    currentWaypoint = 1;
}
```

Next, add a method that our LevelManager class will use to let the Guard class know what its two waypoints are:

```
public void setWaypoints(float x1, float x2){
    waypointX1 = x1;
    waypointX2 = x2;
}
```

Now, we will code the "brains" of our Guard class, that is, its update method. You can basically break this method into two main parts. First, if(currentWaypoint == 1) and secondly, if(currentWaypoint == 2). Inside each of these if blocks, simply check if the guard has reached or passed the appropriate waypoint. If it has, switch waypoints, reverse the velocity, and make the guard face the other way.

Finally, call move() then setRectHitbox() to update the hitbox to the new location of the guard. Add the code for the update method and then we will see how to put it to work.

```
public void update(long fps, float gravity) {
    if(currentWaypoint == 1) {// Heading left
        if (getWorldLocation().x <= waypointX1) {
            // Arrived at waypoint 1
            currentWaypoint = 2;
            setxVelocity(MAX_X_VELOCITY);
            setFacing(RIGHT);
        }
    }

    if(currentWaypoint == 2){
        if (getWorldLocation().x >= waypointX2) {
            // Arrived at waypoint 2
            currentWaypoint = 1;
```

```
                setxVelocity(-MAX_X_VELOCITY);
                setFacing(LEFT);
            }
        }

    move(fps);
        // update the guards hitbox
        setRectHitbox();
    }
    }// End Guard class
```

Remember to add `guard.png` from the `Chapter7/drawables` folder of the download bundle to the `drawable` folder of the project.

Now, we can make the usual three additions to the `LevelManager` class to load any guards that may be found in our level designs.

In `getBitmap()`, add the highlighted code:

```
case 'd':
    index = 6;
    break;

case 'g':
    index = 7;
    break;

default:
    index = 0;
    break;
```

In `getBitmapIndex()`, add the highlighted code:

```
case 'd':
    index = 6;
    break;

case 'g':
    index = 7;
    break;

default:
    index = 0;
    break;
```

In `loadMapData()`, add the highlighted code:

```
case 'd':
    // Add a drone to the gameObjects
    gameObjects.add(new Drone(j, i, c));
    break;
case 'g':
    // Add a guard to the gameObjects
    gameObjects.add(new Guard(context, j, i, c, pixelsPerMetre));
    break;
```

We will soon add something totally new to `LevelManager`. That is a method that will create the script (set two waypoints to patrol). For this new method to work, it needs to know if the tile is suitable for walking on. We will add a new property, a getter, and a setter to `GameObject` so that this is easily discoverable.

Add this new member to the `GameObject` class right after the class declaration:

```
private boolean traversable = false;
```

Add these two methods to the `GameObject` class to get and set this variable:

```
public void setTraversable(){
    traversable = true;
}

public boolean isTraversable(){
    return traversable;
}
```

Now in the `Grass` class constructor, add a call to `setTraversable()`. We must remember to do this for all future `GameObject` derived classes that we design, if we want our guards to be able to patrol on them. In `Grass`, add this line at the top of the constructor:

```
setTraversable();
```

Next, we will look at the new `setWaypoints` method for our `LevelManager` class. It needs to examine the level design and calculate two waypoints for any `Guard` objects present in that level.

We will break this method into a few parts, so we can see what's happening at each stage.

First, we need to loop through all the gameObjects classes looking for the Guard objects.

```
public void setWaypoints() {
    // Loop through all game objects looking for Guards
    for (GameObject guard : this.gameObjects) {
        if (guard.getType() == 'g') {
```

If we reach this point in the code, it means we have found a guard who will need two waypoints to be set. First, we need to find the tile which the guard is "standing on". Then, we calculate the coordinate of the last traversable tile on either side, but with a maximum range of five tiles each way. These will be the two waypoints. Here, is the code to add to the setWaypoints method. It is heavily commented to make clear what is going on without interrupting the flow by stopping to talk about it.

```
// Set waypoints for this guard
// find the tile beneath the guard
// this relies on the designer putting
// the guard in sensible location

int startTileIndex = -1;
int startGuardIndex = 0;
float waypointX1 = -1;
float waypointX2 = -1;

for (GameObject tile : this.gameObjects) {
    startTileIndex++;
    if (tile.getWorldLocation().y ==
            guard.getWorldLocation().y + 2) {

        // Tile is two spaces below current guard
        // Now see if has same x coordinate
        if (tile.getWorldLocation().x ==
            guard.getWorldLocation().x) {

            // Found the tile the guard is "standing" on
            // Now go left as far as possible
            // before non travers-able tile is found
            // Either on guards row or tile row
            // upto a maximum of 5 tiles.
            //  5 is an arbitrary value you can
            // change it to suit

            for (int i = 0; i < 5; i++) {// left for loop
                if (!gameObjects.get(startTileIndex -
```

```
                    i).isTraversable()) {

                    //set the left waypoint
                    waypointX1 = gameObjects.get(startTileIndex -
                        (i + 1)).getWorldLocation().x;

                     break;// Leave left for loop
                     } else {
                    // Set to max 5 tiles as
                    // no non traversible tile found
                    waypointX1 = gameObjects.get(startTileIndex -
                        5).getWorldLocation().x;
                }
             }// end get left waypoint

             for (int i = 0; i < 5; i++) {// right for loop
                 if (!gameObjects.get(startTileIndex +
                     i).isTraversable()) {

                     //set the right waypoint
                     waypointX2 = gameObjects.get(startTileIndex +
                         (i - 1)).getWorldLocation().x;

                     break;// Leave right for loop
                     } else {
                     //set to max 5 tiles away
                     waypointX2 = gameObjects.get(startTileIndex +
                         5).getWorldLocation().x;
                 }

             }// end get right waypoint

         Guard g = (Guard) guard;
         g.setWaypoints(waypointX1, waypointX2);
     }
  }
  }
  }
  }
  }// End setWaypoints()
```

Now, we can call our new `setWaypoints` method as the last thing to do in the
`LevelManager` constructor. We need to call this method after the `GameObject`
class's `ArrayList` has been populated or there will be no guards in it. Add the
call to `setWaypoints()` as highlighted:

```
// Load all the GameObjects and Bitmaps
loadMapData(context, pixelsPerMetre, px, py);
// Set waypoints for our guards
setWaypoints();
```

Next, add this code to the collision detection switch block in the `update` method of
the `PlatformView` class, so we can bump into the guards.

```
case 'd':
    PointF location;
    //hit by drone
    sm.playSound("player_burn");
    ps.loseLife();
    location = new PointF(ps.loadLocation().x,
        ps.loadLocation().y);

    lm.player.setWorldLocationX(location.x);
    lm.player.setWorldLocationY(location.y);
    lm.player.setxVelocity(0);
    break;

case 'g':
    // Hit by guard
    sm.playSound("player_burn");
    ps.loseLife();
    location = new PointF(ps.loadLocation().x,
        ps.loadLocation().y);

    lm.player.setWorldLocationX(location.x);
    lm.player.setWorldLocationY(location.y);
    lm.player.setxVelocity(0);
    break;

default:// Probably a regular tile
    if (hit == 1) {// Left or right
        lm.player.setxVelocity(0);
        lm.player.setPressingRight(false);
    }
    if (hit == 2) {// Feet
        lm.player.isFalling = false;
    }
```

Finally, add some g letters to the `LevelCave` class. Make sure to place them with one space above the platform, because they are 2 meters high as in this pseudo code:

```
. . . . . . . . . . . . . . . g . . . . . . . . . . . . . . . . . . . . . . . . . . .
. . . . . . . . . . . . . . . . . . . . . . . . . d . . . . . . . . . . . . . . . .
1111111111111111111111111111111111111111111111111
```

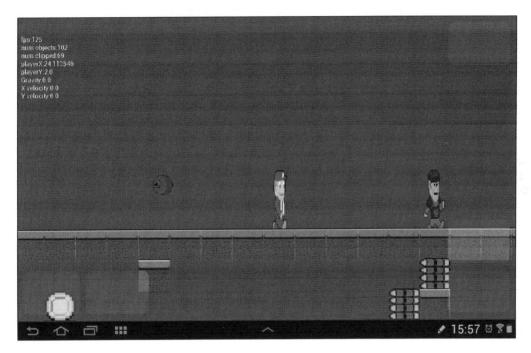

Summary

We implemented guns, pickups, drones, and guards. This means we now have plenty of dangers, but have a machine gun that can't do any damage. We will change that first thing in the next chapter, by implementing collision detection for our bullets. However, we will go slightly further than merely having them hit our enemies.

8
Platformer – Putting It All Together

Finally, we will make the bullets do some damage. The ricochet sound is very satisfying when the bullets energy is absorbed by a clump of grass. We will add an abundance of new platform types and inanimate scenery objects to make our levels more interesting. We will provide a real sense of motion and immersion by implementing multiple scrolling parallax backgrounds.

We will also add an animated fire tile for the player to avoid, and in addition, a special `Teleport` class to link levels together into one playable game. Then, we will use all of our game objects and backgrounds to create four, linked, and fully playable levels.

Then, we will add a HUD to keep track of pickups and lives. Finally, we will discuss some of the neat things that couldn't be fitted into this project in just four chapters.

Bullet collision detection

Detecting bullet collisions is fairly straightforward. We loop through all the existing `Bullet` objects held by our `MachineGun` object. Next, we convert the points of each bullet into a `RectHitBox` object and test it using `intersects()` against each object in our viewport.

If we get a hit, we check to see what type of object it has hit. We then switch to handle each type of object that we care about. If it is a `Guard` object, we knock it back a bit, if it is a `Drone` object, we destroy it, and if it is anything else, we just make the bullet disappear and play a kind of thudding/ricochet sound.

We simply place this logic we discussed after our `switch` block that handles collisions with the player, but before, we call `update()` on all our unclipped objects as shown next:

```
default:// Probably a regular tile
    if (hit == 1) {// Left or right
        lm.player.setxVelocity(0);
        lm.player.setPressingRight(false);
    }

    if (hit == 2) {// Feet
        lm.player.isFalling = false;
    }
    break;
}
}

//Check bullet collisions
for (int i = 0; i < lm.player.bfg.getNumBullets(); i++) {
    //Make a hitbox out of the the current bullet
    RectHitbox r = new RectHitbox();
    r.setLeft(lm.player.bfg.getBulletX(i));
    r.setTop(lm.player.bfg.getBulletY(i));
    r.setRight(lm.player.bfg.getBulletX(i) + .1f);
    r.setBottom(lm.player.bfg.getBulletY(i) + .1f);

    if (go.getHitbox().intersects(r)) {
        // Collision detected
        // make bullet disappear until it
        // is respawned as a new bullet
        lm.player.bfg.hideBullet(i);

        //Now respond depending upon the type of object hit
        if (go.getType() != 'g' && go.getType() != 'd') {
            sm.playSound("ricochet");

        } else if (go.getType() == 'g') {
            // Knock the guard back
            go.setWorldLocationX(go.getWorldLocation().x +
                2 * (lm.player.bfg.getDirection(i)));

            sm.playSound("hit_guard");
```

```
        } else if (go.getType() == 'd') {
            //destroy the droid
            sm.playSound("explode");
            //permanently clip this drone
            go.setWorldLocation(-100, -100, 0);
        }
    }
}

if (lm.isPlaying()) {
    // Run any un-clipped updates
    go.update(fps, lm.gravity);
        //...
```

Try it out, it is really satisfying, especially with a high rate of fire.

Adding some fire tiles

These new `GameObject` derived objects will mean instant death to Bob. They won't move, but they will be animated. We will see we can achieve this just by setting the already existing properties of `GameObject`.

Adding this feature into our game is simple because we have already implemented all the features we need. We already have a way to locate and add new tiles, a way to detect and respond to a collision, sprite sheet animation, and so on. Let's do it step-by-step, then we can add these dangerous and life-threatening elements into our world.

We can put the entire functionality of the class into its constructor. All we do is configure the object much like we did our `Grass` object, but in addition, we configure it with all the animation settings, like we did to the `Player` and `Guard` objects. The `fire.png` sprite sheet has three frames of animation that we want to play over the course of one second.

Create a new class, call it `Fire`, and add the following code to it:

```java
import android.content.Context;

public class Fire extends GameObject{

    Fire(Context context, float worldStartX,
    float worldStartY, char type, int pixelsPerMetre) {

        final int ANIMATION_FPS = 3;
        final int ANIMATION_FRAME_COUNT = 3;
        final String BITMAP_NAME = "fire";

        final float HEIGHT = 1;
        final float WIDTH = 1;

        setHeight(HEIGHT); // 1 metre tall
        setWidth(WIDTH); // 1 metre wide

        setType(type);
        // Now for the player's other attributes
        // Our game engine will use these
        setMoves(false);
        setActive(true);
        setVisible(true);

        // Choose a Bitmap
        setBitmapName(BITMAP_NAME);
        // Set this object up to be animated
        setAnimFps(ANIMATION_FPS);
        setAnimFrameCount(ANIMATION_FRAME_COUNT);
        setBitmapName(BITMAP_NAME);
        setAnimated(context, pixelsPerMetre, true);

        // Where does the tile start
        // X and y locations from constructor parameters
        setWorldLocation(worldStartX, worldStartY, 0);
        setRectHitbox();
    }

    public void update(long fps, float gravity) {
    }
}
```

Now, of course, we need to add the `fire.png` sprite sheet from `Chapter8/drawable` in the download bundle to the `drawable` folder of the project.

Then, we add to our `LevelManager` class, in the usual three ways that we have done for all our new `GameObject` derived classes.

In the `getBitmap` method, add the highlighted code:

```
case 'g':
    index = 7;
    break;

case 'f':
    index = 8;
    break;

default:
    index = 0;
    break;
```

In the `getBitmapIndex` method:

```
case 'g':
    index = 7;
    break;

case 'f':
    index = 8;
    break;

default:
    index = 0;
    break;
```

In the `loadMapData()` method:

```
case 'g':
    // Add a guard to the gameObjects
    gameObjects.add(new Guard(context, j, i, c, pixelsPerMetre));
    break;

    case 'f':
        // Add a fire tile the gameObjects
        gameObjects.add(new Fire
        (context, j, i, c, pixelsPerMetre));

        break;
```

Finally, we add to our collision detection `switch` block to handle the consequences of touching this terrible tile.

```
case 'g':
    //hit by guard
    sm.playSound("player_burn");
    ps.loseLife();
    location = new PointF(ps.loadLocation().x,
        ps.loadLocation().y);
    lm.player.setWorldLocationX(location.x);
    lm.player.setWorldLocationY(location.y);
    lm.player.setxVelocity(0);
    break;

case 'f':
    sm.playSound("player_burn");
    ps.loseLife();
    location = new PointF(ps.loadLocation().x,
        ps.loadLocation().y);
    lm.player.setWorldLocationX(location.x);
    lm.player.setWorldLocationY(location.y);
    lm.player.setxVelocity(0);
    break;

default:// Probably a regular tile
    if (hit == 1) {// Left or right
        lm.player.setxVelocity(0);
        lm.player.setPressingRight(false);
    }

    if (hit == 2) {// Feet
        lm.player.isFalling = false;
    }
    break;
```

Why not add a few f tiles to `LevelCave` and experiment with what the player is able to jump over. It will help us design some challenging levels later in the chapter.

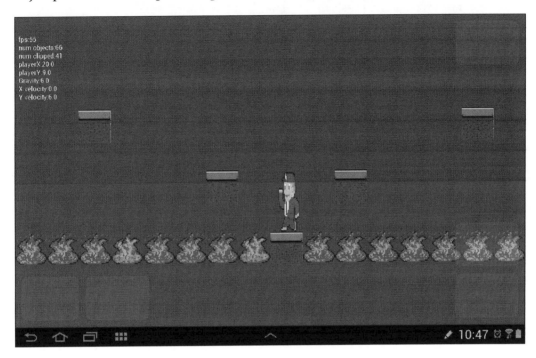

We don't want our player to be walking on the grass the whole time, so let's add some more variety.

Eye candy

The next three sections in this chapter will be purely aesthetic. We will add a whole bunch of different tile graphics with matching classes so that we can use a whole lot more artistic license to make our levels more interesting. The difference between the tiles will be purely visual, but it will be fairly simple to make them more functional than that.

For example, we can easily detect collision with a snow tile and have the player keep moving briefly after stopping to simulate skidding, or perhaps; the concrete tile can allow the player to move faster and therefore change the way we design big jumps and so on. The point is that you don't have to just copy paste the classes as they will be presented here.

We will also add some completely aesthetic props: mine carts, boulders, stalactites, and more. There will be no collision detection for these objects. They will allow the level designer to make the levels more visually interesting.

> It would be simple to make these aesthetics more functional. Just add a hitbox and a case in the collision detection switch block to handle the consequences.

Probably, the most visually significant improvement we add, will be scrolling backgrounds. We will add some classes to allow the level designer to add multiple different scrolling backgrounds to a level design.

> Why not add all the graphics from the Chapter8/drawable folder of the download bundle to the drawable folder of your project. Then, you will have all the graphics ready and in place, for this and the next two sections as well.

The new platform tiles

Now, add all these classes with the filenames as shown. I have removed all comments from the code because they are all functionally the same as the Grass class. Create each of the following classes with the name shown and enter the code:

Here is the code for the Brick class:

```
public class Brick extends GameObject {

    Brick(float worldStartX, float worldStartY, char type) {
        setTraversable();
        final float HEIGHT = 1;
        final float WIDTH = 1;
        setHeight(HEIGHT);
        setWidth(WIDTH);
        setType(type);
        setBitmapName("brick");
        setWorldLocation(worldStartX, worldStartY, 0);
        setRectHitbox();
    }

    public void update(long fps, float gravity) {
    }
}
```

This is the code for the Coal class:

```
public class Coal extends GameObject {

    Coal(float worldStartX, float worldStartY, char type) {
        setTraversable();
        final float HEIGHT = 1;
        final float WIDTH = 1;
        setHeight(HEIGHT);
        setWidth(WIDTH);
        setType(type);
        setBitmapName("coal");
        setWorldLocation(worldStartX, worldStartY, 0);
        setRectHitbox();
    }

    public void update(long fps, float gravity) {
    }
}
```

Here is the code for the Concrete class:

```
public class Concrete extends GameObject {

    Concrete(float worldStartX, float worldStartY, char type) {
        setTraversable();
        final float HEIGHT = 1;
        final float WIDTH = 1;
        setHeight(HEIGHT);
        setWidth(WIDTH);
        setType(type);
        setBitmapName("concrete");
        setWorldLocation(worldStartX, worldStartY, 0);
        setRectHitbox();
    }

    public void update(long fps, float gravity) {
    }
}
```

The following is the code for the `Scorched` class:

```
public class Scorched extends GameObject {

    Scorched(float worldStartX, float worldStartY, char type) {
        setTraversable();
        final float HEIGHT = 1;
        final float WIDTH = 1;
        setHeight(HEIGHT);
        setWidth(WIDTH);
        setType(type);
        setBitmapName("scorched");
        setWorldLocation(worldStartX, worldStartY, 0);
        setRectHitbox();
    }

    public void update(long fps, float gravity) {
    }
}
```

This is the code for the `Snow` class:

```
public class Snow extends GameObject {

    Snow(float worldStartX, float worldStartY, char type) {
        setTraversable();
        final float HEIGHT = 1;
        final float WIDTH = 1;
        setHeight(HEIGHT);
        setWidth(WIDTH);
        setType(type);
        setBitmapName("snow");
        setWorldLocation(worldStartX, worldStartY, 0);
        setRectHitbox();
    }

    public void update(long fps, float gravity) {
    }
}
```

Here is the code for the `Stone` class:

```
public class Stone extends GameObject {

    Stone(float worldStartX, float worldStartY, char type) {
        setTraversable();
```

```
            final float HEIGHT = 1;
            final float WIDTH = 1;
            setHeight(HEIGHT);
            setWidth(WIDTH);
            setType(type);
            setBitmapName("stone");
            setWorldLocation(worldStartX, worldStartY, 0);
            setRectHitbox();
        }

        public void update(long fps, float gravity) {
        }
    }
```

Now, as we are getting used to, we need to add them all into our LevelManager in the usual three places.

In getBitmap(), we simply add them in as normal. Note that although the values are arbitrary, we will use numbers for the type 2,3,4, and so on. This makes it easy to remember, while designing levels, that all our actual platforms are numbers. The actual index numbers are unimportant to us, as long as they are the same as in the getBitmapIndex method. Also, remember that we have a list of types in our LevelData class's comments, for easy reference when designing levels.

```
case 'f':
    index = 8;
    break;

case '2':
    index = 9;
    break;

case '3':
    index = 10;
    break;

case '4':
    index = 11;
    break;

case '5':
    index = 12;
    break;

case '6':
```

```
            index = 13;
            break;

    case '7':
        index = 14;
        break;

    default:
        index = 0;
        break;
```

In getBitmapIndex(), we do the same thing:

```
    case 'f':
        index = 8;
        break;

    case '2':
        index = 9;
        break;

    case '3':
        index = 10;
        break;

    case '4':
        index = 11;
        break;

    case '5':
        index = 12;
        break;

    case '6':
        index = 13;
        break;

    case '7':
        index = 14;
        break;

    default:
        index = 0;
        break;
```

In `loadMapData()`, we just call `new()` on our new `GameObjects` to add them to our `gameObjects` list.

```
case 'f':
    // Add a fire tile the gameObjects
    gameObjects.add(new Fire(context, j, i, c, pixelsPerMetre));
    break;

case '2':
    // Add a tile to the gameObjects
    gameObjects.add(new Snow(j, i, c));
    break;

case '3':
    // Add a tile to the gameObjects
    gameObjects.add(new Brick(j, i, c));
    break;

case '4':
    // Add a tile to the gameObjects
    gameObjects.add(new Coal(j, i, c));
    break;

case '5':
    // Add a tile to the gameObjects
    gameObjects.add(new Concrete(j, i, c));
    break;

case '6':
    // Add a tile to the gameObjects
    gameObjects.add(new Scorched(j, i, c));
    break;

case '7':
    // Add a tile to the gameObjects
    gameObjects.add(new Stone(j, i, c));
    break;
```

Now, go wild adding different terrains to the `LevelCave` class:

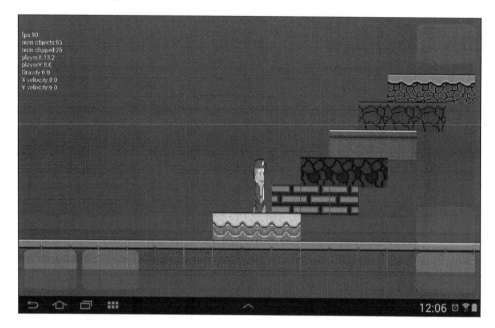

Now, to add some scenery objects.

The new scenery objects

Here, we will add some objects that don't do anything but look pretty. We will let the game engine know by simply not adding a hitbox and setting them randomly to either z layer -1, or 1. Then the player can appear either in front or behind them.

We will first add all the classes, and then update `LevelManager` in the usual three places. Create each of the new classes as follows:

Here is the `Boulders` class:

```
public class Boulders extends GameObject {

    Boulders(float worldStartX, float worldStartY, char type) {

        final float HEIGHT = 1;
        final float WIDTH = 3;

        setHeight(HEIGHT); // 1 metre tall
        setWidth(WIDTH); // 1 metre wide

        setType(type);
```

```
            // Choose a Bitmap
            setBitmapName("boulder");
            setActive(false);//don't check for collisions etc

            // Randomly set the tree either just in front or just
            //behind the player -1 or 1
            Random rand = new Random();
            if(rand.nextInt(2)==0) {
                setWorldLocation(worldStartX, worldStartY, -1);
            }else{
                setWorldLocation(worldStartX, worldStartY, 1);//
            }
            //No hitbox!!

        }

        public void update(long fps, float gravity) {
        }
    }
```

From now on, I removed all the comments to save digital ink. The class functionality is the same as it is in Boulders, just the attributes vary a bit.

Here is the Cart class:

```
    public class Cart extends GameObject {

        Cart(float worldStartX, float worldStartY, char type) {

            final float HEIGHT = 2;
            final float WIDTH = 3;
            setWidth(WIDTH);
            setHeight(HEIGHT);
            setType(type);
            setBitmapName("cart");
            setActive(false);
            Random rand = new Random();
            if(rand.nextInt(2)==0) {
              setWorldLocation(worldStartX, worldStartY, -1);
            }else{
              setWorldLocation(worldStartX, worldStartY, 1);
            }
        }

        public void update(long fps, float gravity) {
        }
    }
```

This is the code for the `Lampost` class:

```
public class Lampost extends GameObject {

    Lampost(float worldStartX, float worldStartY, char type) {

            final float HEIGHT = 3;
            final float WIDTH = 1;
            setHeight(HEIGHT);
            setWidth(WIDTH);
            setType(type);
            setBitmapName("lampost");
            setActive(false);
            Random rand = new Random();
            if(rand.nextInt(2)==0) {
              setWorldLocation(worldStartX, worldStartY, -1);
            }else{
              setWorldLocation(worldStartX, worldStartY, 1);
            }
    }

     public void update(long fps, float gravity) {
       }
    }
```

Here is the `Stalagmite` class:

```
import java.util.Random;

public class Stalagmite extends GameObject {

    Stalagmite(float worldStartX, float worldStartY, char type) {

            final float HEIGHT = 3;
            final float WIDTH = 2;
            setHeight(HEIGHT);
            setWidth(WIDTH);
            setType(type);
            setBitmapName("stalacmite");
            setActive(false);
            Random rand = new Random();
            if(rand.nextInt(2)==0) {
             setWorldLocation(worldStartX, worldStartY, -1);
            }else{
             setWorldLocation(worldStartX, worldStartY, 1);
```

```
                }
        }

        public void update(long fps, float gravity) {
        }
    }
```

This is the Stalactite **class:**

```
    import java.util.Random;

    public class Stalactite extends GameObject {

        Stalactite(float worldStartX, float worldStartY, char type) {

            final float HEIGHT = 3;
            final float WIDTH = 2;
            setHeight(HEIGHT);
            setWidth(WIDTH);
            setType(type);
            setBitmapName("stalactite");
            setActive(false);
            Random rand = new Random();
            if(rand.nextInt(2)==0) {
                setWorldLocation(worldStartX, worldStartY, -1);
            }else{
                setWorldLocation(worldStartX, worldStartY, 1);
            }
        }

        public void update(long fps, float gravity) {
        }
    }
```

Here is the Tree **class:**

```
    import java.util.Random;

    public class Tree extends GameObject {

        Tree(float worldStartX, float worldStartY, char type) {

            final float HEIGHT = 4;
            final float WIDTH = 2;
            setWidth(WIDTH);
```

```
            setHeight(HEIGHT);
            setType(type);
            setBitmapName("tree1");
            setActive(false);
            Random rand = new Random();
            if(rand.nextInt(2)==0) {
              setWorldLocation(worldStartX, worldStartY, -1);
            }else{
              setWorldLocation(worldStartX, worldStartY, 1);
            }
        }


        public void update(long fps, float gravity) {
        }
    }
```

And this is the Tree2 class:

```
    import java.util.Random;

    public class Tree2 extends GameObject {

      Tree2(float worldStartX, float worldStartY, char type) {

            final float HEIGHT = 4;
            final float WIDTH = 2;
            setWidth(WIDTH);
            setHeight(HEIGHT);
            setType(type);
            setBitmapName("tree2");
            setActive(false);
            Random rand = new Random();
            if(rand.nextInt(2)==0) {
              setWorldLocation(worldStartX, worldStartY, -1);
            }else{
              setWorldLocation(worldStartX, worldStartY, 1);
            }
        }


        public void update(long fps, float gravity) {
        }
    }
```

That's all the new classes for the scenery objects. Now, we can update the `getBitmap` method with the seven new types in the `LevelManager` class.

```
case '7':
    index = 14;
    break;

case 'w':
    index = 15;
    break;

case 'x':
    index = 16;
    break;

case 'l':
    index = 17;
    break;

case 'r':
    index = 18;
    break;

case 's':
    index = 19;
    break;

case 'm':
    index = 20;
    break;

case 'z':
    index = 21;
    break;

default:
    index = 0;
    break;
```

Update the `getBitmapIndex` method in the same way:

```
case '7':
    index = 14;
    break;
```

```
case 'w':
    index = 15;
    break;

case 'x':
    index = 16;
    break;

case 'l':
    index = 17;
    break;

case 'r':
    index = 18;
    break;

case 's':
    index = 19;
    break;

case 'm':
    index = 20;
    break;

case 'z':
    index = 21;
    break;

default:
    index = 0;
    break;
```

Finally, make sure our new scenery items are added to our gameObjects array list:

```
case '7':
    // Add a tile to the gameObjects
    gameObjects.add(new Stone(j, i, c));
    break;

case 'w':
    // Add a tree to the gameObjects
    gameObjects.add(new Tree(j, i, c));
    break;

case 'x':
    // Add a tree2 to the gameObjects
    gameObjects.add(new Tree2(j, i, c));
    break;
```

```
case 'l':
    // Add a tree to the gameObjects
    gameObjects.add(new Lampost(j, i, c));
    break;

case 'r':
    // Add a stalactite to the gameObjects
    gameObjects.add(new Stalactite(j, i, c));
    break;

case 's':
    // Add a stalagmite to the gameObjects
    gameObjects.add(new Stalagmite(j, i, c));
    break;

case 'm':
    // Add a cart to the gameObjects
    gameObjects.add(new Cart(j, i, c));
    break;

case 'z':
    // Add a boulders to the gameObjects
    gameObjects.add(new Boulders(j, i, c));
    break;
```

Now, we can design levels with scenery. Note the slight difference in appearance when an object is drawn on layer zero compared to layer one and how the player character passes either in front or behind:

Of course, if you want to bump into lamposts, get skewered by stalagmites, or jump on top of mine carts, then just give them a hitbox.

We have one more way to beautify our game world.

Scrolling parallax backgrounds

Parallax backgrounds are scrolling backgrounds, where we scroll them slower the farther away they are. So, if we have a grass verge at the player's feet, we will scroll it quickly. However, if we have a mountain range in the distance, we will scroll it slowly. This effect can give the sense of motion to the player.

To implement them, we will first add a data structure to represent the parameters of a background. We will call this class BackgroundData, we will then implement a Background class, which has the functionality necessary to control the scrolling and then we will see how to position and define backgrounds in our level design. Finally, we will write a drawBackground method that we will call from our regular draw method.

Make sure you added all the graphics from the Chapter8/drawable folder of the download bundle to the drawable folder of your project.

First, let's build a simple class to hold the data structure which will define our backgrounds. As we can see in the next block of code, we have quite a large number of parameters and member variables. We will need to know which bitmap will represent a background, which layer on the z axis to draw it (in front on 1 or behind on -1), where in the world on the y axis it starts and finishes, how fast the background will scroll, and how high the background will be.

The isParallax Boolean is intended to give the option to have a background which is static, but we will not be implementing this feature. When you see the code for the background class, you will see it is simple to add this functionality if you want to.

Create a new class and call it BackgroundData, then implement it with the following code:

```
public class BackgroundData {
  String bitmapName;
    boolean isParallax;
    //layer 0 is the map
    int layer;
    float startY;
    float endY;
```

```
        float speed;
        int height;
        int width;

        BackgroundData(String bitmap, boolean isParallax,
        int layer, float startY, float endY,
        float speed, int height){

          this.bitmapName = bitmap;
          this.isParallax = isParallax;
          this.layer = layer;
          this.startY = startY;
          this.endY = endY;
          this.speed = speed;
          this.height = height;
      }
   }
```

Now, we add an `ArrayList` of our new type to the `LevelData` class:

```
   ArrayList<String> tiles;
   ArrayList<BackgroundData> backgroundDataList;

   // This class will evolve along with the project
```

Next, let's create the `Background` class itself. Create a new class and name it `Background`. First, we set up a bunch of variables to hold a copy of the background image along with a reversed copy. We will make the backgrounds seem *endless* by putting the images back to back alternating between the regular image and a reversed image. We will see how to achieve this further on in the code.

We also have variables for the width and height of the image in pixels. The `reversedFirst` Boolean will determine which copy of the image is currently drawn on the left-hand side of the screen (first) and will change as the player moves and the image scrolls. The `xClip` variable will hold the precise pixel of the *x* axis (of the image), where we will cut the image and start to draw it from the left hand edge of the screen.

The `y`, `endY`, `z`, and `speed` member variables are to hold the related values passed in as parameters:

```
   import android.content.Context;
   import android.graphics.Bitmap;
   import android.graphics.BitmapFactory;
   import android.graphics.Matrix;
```

```
public class Background {

    Bitmap bitmap;
    Bitmap bitmapReversed;

    int width;
    int height;

    boolean reversedFirst;
    int xClip;// controls where we clip the bitmaps each frame
    float y;
    float endY;
    int z;

    float speed;
    boolean isParallax;//Not currently used
```

Now, in the constructor, we create an Android resource ID from the name of the graphic file passed in as a parameter. Then, create the actual bitmap by calling `BitmapFactory.decodeResource()`. We set `reversedFirst` to `false`, so we will start with the regular (non-reversed) copy of the image on the left-hand side of the screen. We initialize our member variables and then scale the bitmap we just created by calling `Bitmap.createScaledBitmap()` and passing in bitmap, the width of the screen and the height (in the game world) of our background multiplied by the `pixelsPerMetre`, making the bitmap exactly the right size for the current devices screen.

[Note that we must choose appropriate heights for our background designs or they will appear stretched.]

The last thing we do in the constructor is create a `Matrix` object and send it to the `createScaledBitmap` method along with the bitmap, so we now have a reversed copy of our background image stored in the `bitmapReversed` `Bitmap` object.

```
Background(Context context, int yPixelsPerMetre,
    int screenWidth, BackgroundData data){

    int resID =   context.getResources().getIdentifier
    (data.bitmapName, "drawable",
    context.getPackageName());

        bitmap = BitmapFactory.decodeResource
        (context.getResources(), resID);
```

```
// Which version of background (reversed or regular) is
// currently drawn first (on left)
reversedFirst = false;

//Initialize animation variables.
xClip = 0;   //always start at zero
y = data.startY;
endY = data.endY;
z = data.layer;
isParallax = data.isParallax;
speed = data.speed; //Scrolling background speed

//Scale background to fit the screen.
bitmap = Bitmap.createScaledBitmap(bitmap, screenWidth,
        data.height * yPixelsPerMetre
        , true);

width = bitmap.getWidth();
height = bitmap.getHeight();

// Create a mirror image of the background
Matrix matrix = new Matrix();
matrix.setScale(-1, 1); //Horizontal mirror effect.
bitmapReversed = Bitmap.createBitmap(
bitmap, 0, 0, width, height, matrix, true);


    }
}
```

Now, we add two backgrounds to our level design. We fill out the required parameters that we have already discussed. Note that the "grass" background on layer 1 scrolls much faster than the "skyline" background on layer -1. This will create the desired parallax effect. Add this code right at the end of the LevelCave constructor:

```
backgroundDataList = new ArrayList<BackgroundData>();
// note that speeds less than 2 cause problems
this.backgroundDataList.add(
  new BackgroundData("skyline", true, -1, 3, 18, 10, 15 ));

this.backgroundDataList.add(
  new BackgroundData("grass", true, 1, 20, 24, 24, 4 ));
```

It is certainly true that most caves do not have grass and a skyline. This is just a demonstration and to get the code working. We will redesign LevelCave and design some more appropriate levels a little later in this chapter.

Now, we load them with our LevelManager class by declaring a new Arraylist object as a member of our LevelManager class.

```
LevelData levelData;
ArrayList<GameObject> gameObjects;
ArrayList<Background> backgrounds;
```

Then, add a new method in LevelManager to load the background data:

```
private void loadBackgrounds(Context context,
    int pixelsPerMetre, int screenWidth) {

    backgrounds = new ArrayList<Background>();
        //load the background data into the Background objects and
        // place them in our GameObject arraylist
        for (BackgroundData bgData : levelData.backgroundDataList) {
            backgrounds.add(new Background(context,
            pixelsPerMetre, screenWidth, bgData));
        }
}
```

We call the new method in the LevelManager constructor:

```
// Load all the GameObjects and Bitmaps
loadMapData(context, pixelsPerMetre, px, py);
loadBackgrounds(context, pixelsPerMetre, screenWidth);
```

And, not for the last time, we will upgrade our Viewport class to enable our PlatformView methods to get the information they need, to draw the parallax backgrounds.

```
public int getPixelsPerMetreY(){
    return  pixelsPerMetreY;
}

public int getyCentre(){
    return screenCentreY;
}

public float getViewportWorldCentreY(){
    return currentViewportWorldCentre.y;
}
```

Then, we will add a method which actually does the drawing in the `PlatformView` class. We will call this method from `onDraw()`, in just the right places, next. Note that we are using the new methods that we just added to the `Viewport` class.

First, we define four `Rect` objects that we will use to hold the start and end points of `bitmap` and `reversedBitmap`.

Implement the first part of the `drawBackground` method as shown:

```
private void drawBackground(int start, int stop) {

    Rect fromRect1 = new Rect();
    Rect toRect1 = new Rect();
    Rect fromRect2 = new Rect();
    Rect toRect2 = new Rect();
```

Now, we simply loop through all our backgrounds using the `start` and `stop` parameters to decide which backgrounds have a *z* layer that we are currently interested in drawing.

```
    for (Background bg : lm.backgrounds) {
    if (bg.z < start && bg.z > stop) {
```

Next, we send the world coordinates of the background to the `Viewport` class for clipping. If it isn't clipped (and should be drawn), we get the starting pixel coordinates, and ending pixel coordinates on the *y* axis with the help of the new methods we added to our `Viewport` class previously. Note that we cast the results to `int` variables ready to be drawn to the screen.

```
        // Is this layer in the viewport?
        // Clip anything off-screen
        if (!vp.clipObjects(-1, bg.y, 1000, bg.height)) {
            float floatstartY = ((vp.getyCentre() -
                ((vp.getViewportWorldCentreY() - bg.y) *
                vp.getPixelsPerMetreY()))));

            int startY = (int) floatstartY;

            float floatendY = ((vp.getyCentre() -
                ((vp.getViewportWorldCentreY() - bg.endY) *
                vp.getPixelsPerMetreY()))));

            int endY = (int) floatendY;
```

This next block of code is where the real action takes place. We initialize the four `Rect` objects with the starting and ending coordinates of the first and second of our two `Bitmap` objects. Note that the point (or pixel) that is calculated, is determined by `xClip`, which is initially zero. So, to start with, we will simply see `background` (if it is not clipped) stretched across the width of the screen. Soon, we will see that we modify `xClip` based on Bob's velocity and cause different regions from each bitmap to be shown:

```
// Define what portion of bitmaps to capture
// and what coordinates to draw them at
fromRect1 = new Rect(0, 0, bg.width - bg.xClip,
    bg.height);

toRect1 = new Rect(bg.xClip, startY, bg.width, endY);
    fromRect2 = new Rect(bg.width - bg.xClip, 0,
        bg.width, bg.height);

toRect2 = new Rect(0, startY, bg.xClip, endY);
}// End if (!vp.clipObjects...
```

Now, we determine which background (regular or reversed) is currently being drawn first, and then draw that one first followed by the other.

```
//draw backgrounds
  if (!bg.reversedFirst) {

      canvas.drawBitmap(bg.bitmap,
          fromRect1, toRect1, paint);
      canvas.drawBitmap(bg.bitmapReversed,
          fromRect2, toRect2, paint);

  } else {
      canvas.drawBitmap(bg.bitmap,
          fromRect2, toRect2, paint);

      canvas.drawBitmap(bg.bitmapReversed,
          fromRect1, toRect1, paint);
  }
```

We can scroll along based on the speed and direction of Bob, `lv.player.getxVelocity()` and if `xClip` has reached the end of the current first background, `if (bg.xClip >= bg.width)`, simply set `xClip` to zero and change which bitmap we show first.

```
            // Calculate the next value for the background's
              // clipping position by modifying xClip
              // and switching which background is drawn first,
              // if necessary.
              bg.xClip -= lm.player.getxVelocity() / (20 / bg.speed);
              if (bg.xClip >= bg.width) {
                  bg.xClip = 0;
                  bg.reversedFirst = !bg.reversedFirst;
              }
              else if (bg.xClip <= 0) {
                  bg.xClip = bg.width;
                  bg.reversedFirst = !bg.reversedFirst;

              }
          }
      }
}
```

Then, we add a call to `drawBackground()` just before our game objects for backgrounds with a *z* layer less than zero.

```
// Rub out the last frame with arbitrary color
paint.setColor(Color.argb(255, 0, 0, 255));
canvas.drawColor(Color.argb(255, 0, 0, 255));

// Draw parallax backgrounds from -1 to -3
drawBackground(0, -3);

// Draw all the GameObjects
Rect toScreen2d = new Rect();
```

Just after the bullets are drawn, but before the debugging text for those backgrounds with a *z* order more than zero.

```
// Draw parallax backgrounds from layer 1 to 3
drawBackground(4, 0);

// Text for debugging
```

Now, we can really start to get creative with our level designs.

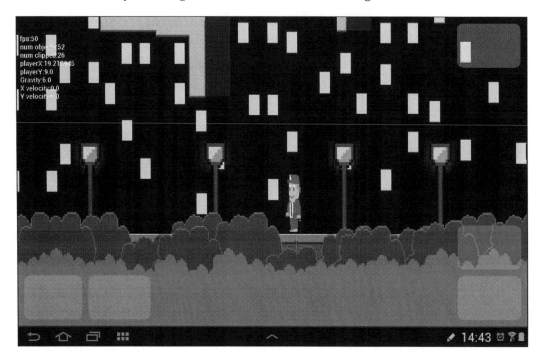

Very soon, we will make some real playable levels that use all the features we have implemented over the last four chapters. Before we do that, let's have a bit of fun with the Viewport class.

It will be really useful for the player to scan around a level and plan a route. Equally, it will be helpful when designing levels, to zoom around the level to see how a particular part of the level looks without having to get the player character to that part in order to see it on the screen. So, let's make the pause screen into a moveable viewport.

Pause menu with moveable viewport

This is nice and quick. We will just add a bunch of new methods to our Viewport class to change the center of focus. Then, we will call them from InputController.

If you remember when we implemented the InputController class back in *Chapter 6, Platformer – Bob, Beeps and Bumps*, we wrapped all the control logic in an if(playing) test. We also implemented the pause button already in the else clause. All we will do is use the left, right, jump, and shoot buttons as left, right, up, and down, respectively, for moving the viewport.

First, add these methods to the `Viewport` class:

```
public void moveViewportRight(int maxWidth){
   if(currentViewportWorldCentre.x < maxWidth -
     (metresToShowX/2)+3) {

     currentViewportWorldCentre.x += 1;
   }
}


public void moveViewportLeft(){
   if(currentViewportWorldCentre.x > (metresToShowX/2)-3){
     currentViewportWorldCentre.x -= 1;
     }
}

public void moveViewportUp(){
   if(currentViewportWorldCentre.y > (metresToShowY /2)-3) {
         currentViewportWorldCentre.y -= 1;
   }
}

public void moveViewportDown(int maxHeight){
   if(currentViewportWorldCentre.y <
     maxHeight - (metresToShowY / 2)+3) {

     currentViewportWorldCentre.y += 1;
   }
}
```

Now, add these calls to the methods from the `else` clause of the `if` condition in the `InputController` class that we were just discussing.

```
//Move the viewport around to explore the map
switch (motionEvent.getAction() & MotionEvent.ACTION_MASK) {
  case MotionEvent.ACTION_DOWN:
       if (right.contains(x, y)) {
          vp.moveViewportRight(l.mapWidth);
        } else if (left.contains(x, y)) {
          vp.moveViewportLeft();
        } else if (jump.contains(x, y)) {
          vp.moveViewportUp();
        } else if (shoot.contains(x, y)) {
          vp.moveViewportDown(l.mapHeight);
        } else if (pause.contains(x, y)) {
```

```
        l.switchPlayingStatus();
    }
    break;
}
```

On the pause screen, the player can look around and plan their route when they are on more complicated levels. They are probably going to need to.

Levels and game rules

We have implemented so many features, but we still don't have a way to put them altogether into a playable game. We need to be able to travel between levels, and have the player state persist when we do.

Traveling between levels

As we are going to design four levels, we want the player to be able to travel between them. First, let's add code to the `switch` statement at the start of the `LevelManager` constructor to include all four levels that we are about to build:

```
switch (level) {
  case "LevelCave":
      levelData = new LevelCave();
      break;

// We can add extra levels here
case "LevelCity":
    levelData = new LevelCity();
    break;

case "LevelForest":
    levelData = new LevelForest();
    break;

case "LevelMountain":
    levelData = new LevelMountain();
    break;
}
```

As we know, we start the game by calling `loadLevel()` from the `PlatformView` constructor. The arguments include the name of the level and the coordinates to spawn the player. If you are designing your own levels, then you need to decide which level and coordinates to start with. If you will be following along with the levels I have provided, set the call to `loadLevel()` in the constructor of `PlatformView` as follows:

```
loadLevel("LevelCave", 1, 16);
```

In the `if(lm.isPlaying())` block, in the `update` method, where we set the viewport to center on the player each frame; add the following code to detect (and brutally kill) the player if he falls out of the map as well as cause the game to restart with three lives, zero money, and no upgrades should he run out of lives:

```
if (lm.isPlaying()) {
    // Reset the players location as
    // the world centre of the viewport
    //if game is playing
    vp.setWorldCentre(lm.gameObjects.get(lm.playerIndex)
        .getWorldLocation().x,
        lm.gameObjects.get(lm.playerIndex)
        .getWorldLocation().y);

    //Has player fallen out of the map?
    if (lm.player.getWorldLocation().x < 0 ||
        lm.player.getWorldLocation().x > lm.mapWidth ||
        lm.player.getWorldLocation().y > lm.mapHeight) {

        sm.playSound("player_burn");
        ps.loseLife();
        PointF location = new PointF(ps.loadLocation().x,
         ps.loadLocation().y);

        lm.player.setWorldLocationX(location.x);
        lm.player.setWorldLocationY(location.y);
        lm.player.setxVelocity(0);
    }

    // Check if game is over
    if (ps.getLives() == 0) {
        ps = new PlayerState();
        loadLevel("LevelCave", 1, 16);
    }
}
```

Now, we can create a special `GameObject` class that when touched sends the player to a predetermined level and location. We can then strategically add these objects to our level designs, and they will act as the link between our levels. Create a new class and call it `Teleport`. If you haven't already done so, add the `door.png` file from `Chapter8/drawable` to the `drawable` folder of the project.

This is how our `Teleport` object will appear in the game:

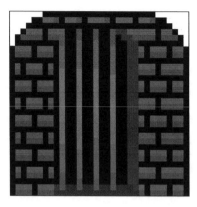

Let's make a simple class to hold the data that each `Teleport` object will need. Create a new class called `Location` like this:

```
public class Location {
    String level;
    float x;
    float y;

    Location(String level, float x, float y){
        this.level = level;
        this.x = x;
        this.y = y;
    }
}
```

The actual `Teleport` class looks just like any other `GameObject` class, but note that it also has a member `Location` variable. We will see how the level design will hold the destination of the `Teleport`, the `LevelManager` class will initialize it, and then when the player collides with it, we can load the new location, sending the player off to his destination.

```
public class Teleport extends GameObject {

    Location target;

    Teleport(float worldStartX, float worldStartY,
        char type, Location target) {
```

```
            final float HEIGHT = 2;
            final float WIDTH = 2;
            setHeight(HEIGHT); // 2 metres tall
            setWidth(WIDTH); // 1 metre wide
            setType(type);
            setBitmapName("door");

            this.target = new Location(target.level,
                target.x, target.y);

            // Where does the tile start
            // X and y locations from constructor parameters
            setWorldLocation(worldStartX, worldStartY, 0);

            setRectHitbox();
        }

        public Location getTarget(){
            return target;
        }

        public void update(long fps, float gravity){
        }
    }
```

To make our `Teleport` class work in a way that lets the level designer decide what it will do exactly, we need to add to our `LevelData` class like this:

```
ArrayList<String> tiles;
ArrayList<BackgroundData> backgroundDataList;
ArrayList<Location> locations;

// This class will evolve along with the project
```

Then, we need to add a `t` to the level design wherever we want our teleport/door, and an entry like the next line of code, within the constructor of the class of the level we are designing.

Note that you can have as many `Teleport` objects as you like in a map, as long as the order they are defined in code matches the order they appear in the design. We will see exactly how this works when we look at our actual level designs in a minute, but the code will look like this:

```
// Declare the values for the teleports in order of appearance
locations = new ArrayList<Location>();
this.locations.add(new Location("LevelCity", 118f, 18f));
```

As usual, we need to update the `LevelManager` class to load and locate our teleport(s). Here is the new code for `getBitmap()`:

```
case 'z':
   index = 21;
   break;

case 't':
   index = 22;
   break;

default:
   index = 0;
   break;
```

New code for `getBitmapIndex()`:

```
case 'z':
   index = 21;
      break;

case 't':
   index = 22;
   break;

default:
   index = 0;
   break;
```

We also need to keep track of our `Teleport` objects during the loading phase in case there is more than one. So, add a new local variable as shown in the `loadMapData` method:

```
//Keep track of where we load our game objects
int currentIndex = -1;
int teleportIndex = -1;
// how wide and high is the map? Viewport needs to know
```

Finally for the `LevelManager` class, we initialize all the teleport data from the level design, tuck it away in the object and add it to our `gameObject ArrayList`.

```
case 'z':
    // Add a boulders to the gameObjects
    gameObjects.add(new Boulders(j, i, c));
    break;

case 't':
    // Add a teleport to the gameObjects
    teleportIndex++;
    gameObjects.add(new Teleport(j, i, c,
    levelData.locations.get(teleportIndex)));

    break;
```

We are really close to being able to teleport all over the place. We need to detect a collision with a teleport, and then load a new level with the player at the desired location. This code will go in our collision detection switch block in the `PlatformView` class like this:

```
case 'f':
    sm.playSound("player_burn");
    ps.loseLife();
    location = new PointF(ps.loadLocation().x,
      ps.loadLocation().y);
    lm.player.setWorldLocationX(location.x);
    lm.player.setWorldLocationY(location.y);
    lm.player.setxVelocity(0);
    break;

case 't':
    Teleport teleport = (Teleport) go;
    Location t = teleport.getTarget();
    loadLevel(t.level, t.x, t.y);
    sm.playSound("teleport");
    break;

default:// Probably a regular tile
    if (hit == 1) {// Left or right
        lm.player.setxVelocity(0);
        lm.player.setPressingRight(false);
    }
```

```
    if (hit == 2) {// Feet
        lm.player.isFalling = false;
    }
    break;
```

When a new level is loaded, the `Player`, `MachineGun`, and `Bullet` objects are all created from scratch. Therefore, we need to add a line to our `loadLevel` method to reload the current machine gun fire rate from the `PlayerState` class into the `MachineGun` class. Add the highlighted code:

```
ps.saveLocation(location);

// Reload the players current fire rate from the player state
lm.player.bfg.setFireRate(ps.getFireRate());
```

Now, we can work on the level designs for real.

The level designs

You can just copy and paste four classes from the `Chapter8/java` folder into your project and start playing, or you can start from the beginning and design your own. The levels are quite large, intricate, and tough to beat. It is not physically possible to print the level designs in a book or e-book in any meaningful way, so you will need to open up the `LevelCave`, `LevelCity`, `LevelForest`, and `LevelMountain` design files in order to see the detail of the four levels.

However, a brief discussion of the levels, pictures, and some screenshots, but not actual code from the four designs follows.

 Note that the following screenshots feature the new HUD that is the last thing we will cover in this chapter.

The cave

The cave level is where the whole thing starts. It not only features modestly frustrating jumps, but also plenty of fire making a fall potentially deadly.

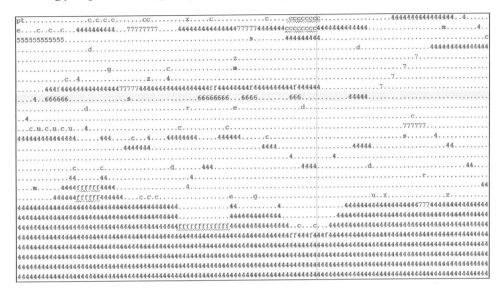

As the player starts with a puny machine gun, only a few drones are present in the level. But there are two awkward guards that will require vaulting.

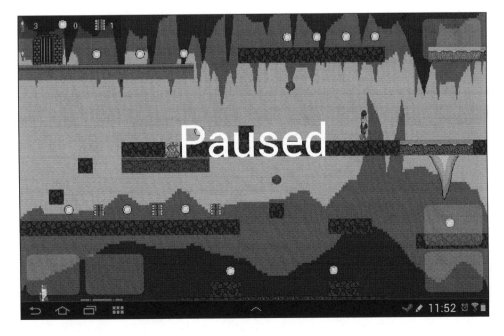

The city

The city holds vast rewards, especially in the bottom left-hand corner for coins and the top-left for machine gun upgrades.

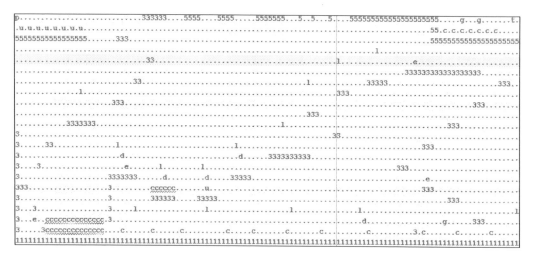

However, there is a very awkward-to-jump guard on the bottom level should the player want to get all those stray coins and not opt for leaving them behind. The near vertical ascent that must be traversed up the left-hand side is likely to frustrate and if the player opts not to go for the machine gun upgrades, he will probably struggle with the double-guard just outside the door to the next level.

The forest

The forest may be the overall toughest level of them all with a brutally long run of jumps, which are very easy to over or under jump.

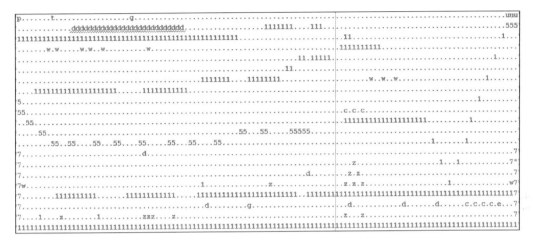

```
p......t.............g.                                                                           .uuu
..............dddddddddddddddddddddddddd                          1111111....111.               .555
1111111111111111111111111111111111111111111111111111111                    .11.                   .1...
......w.w.....w.w..w..........w.                                   1111111111
............................................11.11111                                        .1.....
.........................................11.
...............1111111....11111111.                               w..w..w.                 .1.
....1111111111111111111......11111111111.                                                 .1.......
5.                                                                                       .1.........
55.                                                               .c.c.c
..55.                                                             .11111111111111111111..........1..........
....55.                                           55...55.....55555.
.......55..55...55...55...55....55...55....55.                              .1......1.........
7........................d.                                                                      .7
7.                                                                .z.                .1...1..........7*
7.                                                                .z.z.                            .7
7.                                               .d.              .z.z.z.                .1.........w7
7w.................1...............z..............z.z.z...............1.............w7
7.......1111111111......111111111111.....1111111111111111111111.1111111111111111111111111111111111117
7.                               .d........g.              .d......d......d...c.c.c.e...7
7...1....z.......1.........zzz...z.                         .z..z.                                .7
1111111111111111111111111111111111111111111111111111111111111111111111111111111111111111111111111111
```

And with in excess of a dozen drones waiting to swoop on Bob, as his pixels hang precariously off a platform.

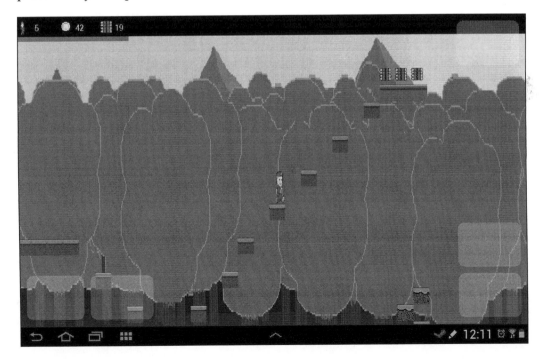

The mountains

The fresh mountain air means Bob has almost made it. Not a guard or a drone in sight.

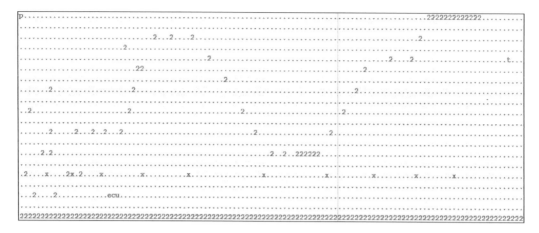

However, look at that winding path of jumps, most of which will see Bob thrown right back to the bottom if he puts a pixel out of place.

If you want to try out each of the levels without completing the grueling level(s) that precede it, you can of course, just start at the level and location of your choice. To do this, just change the call to `loadLevel()` in the `PlatformView` constructor to one of the following:

```
loadLevel("LevelMountain", 118, 17);
loadLevel("LevelForest", 1, 17);
loadLevel("LevelCity", 118, 18);
loadLevel("LevelCave", 1, 16);
```

The HUD

The finishing touch is to add a HUD. This code in the `draw` method of `PlatformView` uses the graphics from some of the existing game objects.

Add the code after the last call to `drawBackground()` and before the debugging text is drawn:

```
// Draw the HUD
// This code needs bitmaps: extra life, upgrade and coin
// Therefore there must be at least one of each in the level

int topSpace = vp.getPixelsPerMetreY() / 4;
int iconSize = vp.getPixelsPerMetreX();
int padding = vp.getPixelsPerMetreX() / 5;
int centring = vp.getPixelsPerMetreY() / 6;
paint.setTextSize(vp.getPixelsPerMetreY()/2);
paint.setTextAlign(Paint.Align.CENTER);

paint.setColor(Color.argb(100, 0, 0, 0));
canvas.drawRect(0,0,iconSize * 7.0f, topSpace*2 + iconSize,paint);
paint.setColor(Color.argb(255, 255, 255, 0));

canvas.drawBitmap(lm.getBitmap('e'), 0, topSpace, paint);
canvas.drawText("" + ps.getLives(), (iconSize * 1) + padding,
  (iconSize) - centring, paint);

canvas.drawBitmap(lm.getBitmap('c'), (iconSize * 2.5f) + padding,
  topSpace, paint);
```

```
canvas.drawText("" + ps.getCredits(), (iconSize * 3.5f) + padding
    * 2, (iconSize) - centring, paint);

canvas.drawBitmap(lm.getBitmap('u'), (iconSize * 5.0f) + padding,
    topSpace, paint);

canvas.drawText("" + ps.getFireRate(), (iconSize * 6.0f) + padding
    * 2, (iconSize) - centring, paint);
```

I think we are done!

Summary

We finished the platform game because that is all there is space for. Why not try to implement some or all of the following improvements and features?

Change the code in the `Player` class to make Bob gradually accelerate and decelerate instead of always running at full speed. Simply increment the velocity for each frame that the player is holding down left or right, and decrement it for each frame they are not.

Once you have achieved this, add the preceding code to the collision detection `switch` block in the `update` method to make the player skid on snow, speed up on concrete, and have a different walking/landing sound effect for each tile type.

Draw a gun on Bob, and adjust the height that the `Bullet` object is spawned at to appear as if it is coming from the barrel of his machine gun.

Make some objects pushable. Add an `isPushable` member to `GameObject` and make the collision detection simply knock the object back a little. Perhaps, Bob could push mine carts into fire to jump over extra wide fire pits. Note that pushing objects that fall down to another level will be more complicated than pushing objects that remain at the same *y* coordinate.

Destructible tiles sound like fun. Give them a strength variable that decrements when hit by a bullet and is removed from `gameObjects` when it reaches zero.

Moving platforms are a staple of great platformers. Simply add waypoints to a tile object and add the move code to the `update` method. The challenge will be assigning the waypoints. You can either have them all move a set number of spaces left and right or up and down, or do some kind of `setTileWaypoint` method similar to how we scripted the `Guard` object.

Make the game more persistent by saving the total number of coins collected ever, remembering which levels are unlocked, and offering access to replay any unlocked levels from the menu screen.

Make the game easier with teleports used as waypoints. Adjust the viewport zoom for different screen sizes. The current zoom can be a little too low for some small phones.

Add timed runs for high scores, leaderboards, and achievements, and add more levels.

In the next chapter, we will look at a much smaller project, but still an interesting one, as we will be using OpenGL ES for super-fast, smooth drawing.

9
Asteroids at 60 FPS with OpenGL ES 2

Welcome to the final project. Over the course of the next three chapters, we will build an Asteroids-like game using the OpenGL ES 2 graphics API. If you are wondering exactly what OpenGL ES 2 is, then we will discuss the details later in this chapter.

We will build a very simple but fun and challenging game, where we can draw and animate hundreds of objects at a time, even on quite old Android devices.

With OpenGL, we will take our drawing efficiency to a much higher level, and with some not-too-tricky math, our movement and collision detection will be greatly enhanced compared to our previous projects.

By the end of this chapter, we will have a basic working OpenGL ES 2 engine drawing our simple but temporarily static spaceship to the screen; at 60 FPS or higher.

> If you have never seen or played the '80s arcade hit (released in November 1979) Asteroids, why not go and check out a clone of it or a video now?
>
> Free web game at http://www.freeasteroids.org/.
>
> On YouTube at https://www.youtube.com/watch?v=WYSupJ5r2zo.

Let's discuss exactly what we intend to build.

Asteroids simulator

Our game will be set in a four directional scrolling world that the player will be able to traverse while hunting for asteroids. The world will be enclosed in a rectangular border to keep the asteroids from drifting off too far, and the border will also serve as another hazard for the player to avoid.

The game controls

We will reuse our `InputController` class with a few simple modifications and can even keep the same button layout. As we will see, however, we will draw the buttons on screen in a very different manner to our retro platformer. Also, instead of walking left and right, the player will rotate the ship left and right through 360 degrees. The jump button will become a thrust toggle switch to turn on and off forward motion, and the shoot button will remain just that. We will also have the pause button in the same place.

Rules for the game

When an asteroid hits the border, it will bounce back into the game world. If the player hits the border, a life will be lost and the ship will respawn in the center of the screen. If an asteroid hits the ship this will be fatal too.

The player will start with three lives and must clear the asteroids simulator of all asteroids. The HUD will show a tally of the remaining asteroids and lives. If the player clears all the asteroids, then the next wave will start with more than the last. They will also move a little faster. Each wave cleared will be rewarded with an extra life.

We will implement these rules as we proceed through the project.

Introducing OpenGL ES 2

OpenGL ES 2 is the second major version of the **Open Graphics Library** (**OpenGL**) for embedded systems. It is the mobile incarnation of OpenGL for desktop systems.

Why use it and how does it work?

OpenGL runs as a native process, not on the Dalvik virtual machine like the rest of our Java. This is one of the reasons it is super fast. The OpenGL ES API takes away all of the complexity of interacting with native code, and OpenGL itself also provides very efficient and fast algorithms within its native code base.

The first version of OpenGL was completed in 1992. The point is that even back then OpenGL used arguably the most efficient code and algorithms to draw graphics. Now, more than 20 years on, it has been continually refined and improved as well as adapted to work with the latest graphics hardware, both mobile and desktop. All the mobile GPU manufacturers specifically design their hardware to be compatible with the latest version of OpenGL ES.

Trying to improve on OpenGL ES is, therefore, probably a fool's errand.

 There is another viable Graphics API option when developing exclusively for Windows devices called DirectX.

What is neat about Version 2?

The first version of OpenGL ES certainly impressed at the time. I remember almost falling off my chair when I first played a 3D shooter on a phone! Now this is of course commonplace. However, compared to the desktop version of OpenGL, OpenGL ES 1 had a major drawback.

OpenGL ES 1 had, what is known as, a fixed function pipeline. The geometry to draw went into the GPU and it was drawn, but any further manipulation of individual pixels needed to take place before OpenGL ES took over the drawing of a frame of the game.

Now, with OpenGL ES 2, we have access to what is called a programmable pipeline. That is, we can send our graphics off to be drawn, but we can also write code that runs on the GPU that is capable of manipulating each and every pixel independently. This is a very powerful feature, although we will not get to explore it in much depth.

This extra code that runs on the GPU is called a **shader** program. We can write code to manipulate the geometry (position) of our graphics in what is called a **vertex shader**. We can also write code that manipulates the appearance of each and every pixel individually called a **fragment shader**.

 Actually, we can do better than even pixel manipulation. A fragment is not necessarily a pixel. It depends on the hardware and the specific nature of the graphics being processed. It can be more than one pixel or a sub-pixel: one light of several that makes up a pixel in the screen hardware.

The disadvantage of OpenGL ES 2 for simple games like this is that you must provide at least one vertex and one fragment shader, even if you are not going to do a whole lot with them. As we will see, however, this is not very difficult. Although we will not be exploring shaders in any depth, we will write some shader code using **GL Shader Language** (**GLSL**) and get a glimpse at the possibilities they offer.

If the power of programmable graphics pipelines and shaders is just too exciting to leave for another day, then I can highly recommend *GLSL Essentials* by Jacobo Rodríguez.

`https://www.packtpub.com/hardware-and-creative/glsl-essentials`

The book explores OpenGL shaders on the desktop and is highly accessible to any reader with basic programming knowledge and a willingness to learn a different language (GLSL), yet one with some syntax similarities to Java.

How will we be using OpenGL ES 2?

How we will use OpenGL ES 2?

In OpenGL, everything is a point, a line, or a triangle. In addition, we can attach colors and textures to this basic geometry and also combine these elements to make the complex graphics that we see in today's modern mobile games.

We will use some of each type of element (points, lines, and triangles) that are collectively referred to as primitives.

We will not be using textures on this project. Fortunately, the appearance of untextured primitives is appropriate for building our Asteroids-like game.

In addition to primitives, Open GL uses matrices. **Matrices** are a method and structure for performing arithmetic. This arithmetic can range from extremely simple high-school level calculations to move (translate) a coordinate or it can be quite complex to perform more advanced mathematics to convert our game world coordinates into OpenGL screen coordinates that the GPU can use.

The point is that both the matrices and methods to use them are entirely provided by the OpenGL API. This means that we just have to learn what methods do which graphical manipulation and do not have to concern ourselves with the potentially complex math that goes on behind the scenes (on the GPU).

The best way to learn about shaders, primitives, and matrices in OpenGL is to go ahead and start using them.

Preparing OpenGL ES 2

First we start off with our `Activity` class, which as before is the entry point into our game. Create a new project and in the **Application Name** field enter `C9 Asteroids`. Choose **Phones and tablets**, then **Blank Activity** when prompted. In the **Activity Name** field type `AsteroidsActivity`.

> Obviously you don't have to follow my exact naming choices but just remember to make the minor alterations in code to reflect your own naming choices.

You can delete `activity_asteroids.xml` from the `layout` folder. You can also delete all the code within the `AsteroidsActivity.java` file. Just leave the package declaration.

Locking the layout to landscape

Just as we did for the previous two projects, we will make sure the game runs in landscape mode only. We will make our `AndroidManifest.xml` file, force our `AsteroidsActivity` class to run with a full screen, and lock it to a landscape orientation. Let's make these changes:

1. Open the `manifests` folder now and double-click the `AndroidManifest.xml` file to open it in the code editor.

2. In the `AndroidManifest.xml` file, find the following line of code:

   `android:name=".AsteroidsActivity"`

3. Immediately, type or copy and paste these two lines to make `PlatformActivity` run in full screen and lock it in the landscape orientation:

   `android:theme="@android:style/Theme.NoTitleBar.Fullscreen"`
   `android:screenOrientation="landscape"`

Now we can move on to implementing our Asteroids simulator game with OpenGL.

Activity

First of all, we have our familiar `Activity` class. The only thing that is new here is the type of our view class. We declare a member called `asteroidsView` of type `GLSurfaceView`. This is the class that will provide us with easy access to OpenGL. We will see exactly how very soon. Note that all we do is initialize `GLSurfaceView` by passing in the `Activity` context and the screen resolution that we obtain in the usual manner. Implement the `AsteroidsActivity` class as shown:

```
package com.gamecodeschool.c9asteroids;

import android.app.Activity;
import android.graphics.Point;
import android.opengl.GLSurfaceView;
import android.os.Bundle;
import android.view.Display;

public class AsteroidsActivity extends Activity {

    private GLSurfaceView asteroidsView;

    @Override
    public void onCreate(Bundle savedInstanceState) {
        super.onCreate(savedInstanceState);

        // Get a Display object to access screen details
        Display display = getWindowManager().getDefaultDisplay();

        // Load the resolution into a Point object
        Point resolution = new Point();
        display.getSize(resolution);

        asteroidsView = new AsteroidsView
          (this, resolution.x, resolution.y);

        setContentView(asteroidsView);
    }

    @Override
    protected void onPause() {
        super.onPause();

        asteroidsView.onPause();

    }

    @Override
    protected void onResume() {
        super.onResume();

        asteroidsView.onResume();
```

```
        }
    }
```

Next, we will get to see some OpenGL code.

The view

Here, we will implement the `GLSurfaceView` class. Actually, this isn't where the real action will take place but it does allow us to attach an OpenGL renderer. This is a class that implements the `Renderer` interface. As well as in this critical `Renderer`, the `GLSurfaceView` class enables us to override the `onTouchListener` method that will allow us to detect player input in the same way that `SurfaceView` did in the previous projects.

 Android Studio does not auto-import or even suggest all of the OpenGL imports required. Therefore, I included all of the imports for some classes in the code listings. In addition, you will note that sometimes we use static imports. This will make the code more readable too.

In the code that follows, we declare and initialize a new object of type `GameManager` that we will implement soon. We set the OpenGL version to two by calling `setEGLContextClientVersion(2)`, and we set our vital renderer object by calling `setRenderer()` and passing in our `GameManager` object. Create a new class called `AsteroidsView` and implement it as follows:

```
import android.content.Context;
import android.opengl.GLSurfaceView;

public class AsteroidsView extends GLSurfaceView{

    GameManager gm;

    public AsteroidsView(Context context, int screenX, int
       screenY) {
        super(context);

        gm = new GameManager(screenX, screenY);

        // Which version of OpenGl we are using
        setEGLContextClientVersion(2);

        // Attach our renderer to the GLSurfaceView
        setRenderer(new AsteroidsRenderer(gm));
```

```
        }

    }
```

Now, we can take a look at what is involved in our `GameManager` class.

A class to manage our game

This class will control things like the level the player is on, the number of lives, as well as things like the overall size of the game world. It will evolve a little as the project progresses, but it will remain quite simple in comparison to the combined depth of the LevelManager and PlayerState classes from the previous project, although it effectively replaces both.

In the code that follows, we declare `int` members to hold the width and height of the game world; we can make this much bigger or smaller as we see fit. We keep track of the games status with the Boolean `playing`.

The `GameManager` class also needs to know the height and width of the screen in pixels, and this information is passed in to the constructor when the object is initialized back in the `AsteroidsView` class.

Note also the `metresToShowX` and `metresToShowY` member variables. These probably sound familiar from our `Viewport` class from the last project. These variables will be used for exactly the same thing: defining the current viewable area of the game world. This time, however, OpenGL will take care of what objects to clip before drawing (using a matrix). We will soon see where this happens.

 Note that although OpenGL takes care of clipping and scaling the area of the game world that we want to show, it doesn't have any effect on which objects are updated each frame. As we will see, however, this is just what we want for this game because we want all our objects to update themselves each frame, even when they are offscreen. Therefore, no `Viewport` class is necessary for this game.

Lastly, we want a convenient way to pause and unpause the game, and we provide this functionality with the `switchPlayingStatus` method. Create a new class called `GameManager` and implement it as shown:

```
public class GameManager {

    int mapWidth = 600;
    int mapHeight = 600;
    private boolean playing = false;
```

```
// Our first game object
SpaceShip ship;

int screenWidth;
int screenHeight;

// How many metres of our virtual world
// we will show on screen at any time.
int metresToShowX = 390;
int metresToShowY = 220;

public GameManager(int x, int y){

    screenWidth = x;
    screenHeight = y;

}

public void switchPlayingStatus() {
    playing = !playing;

}

public boolean isPlaying(){
    return playing;
}
}
```

We can now take our first look at these all powerful shaders and how we will manage them.

Managing simple shaders

An application can have many shaders. We can then attach different shaders to different game objects to create the desired effects.

We will only have one vertex and one fragment shader in this game. However, when you see how to attach a shader to primitives, it will be plain that it is simple to have more shaders.

1. First of all, we need the code for the shader that will be executed in the GPU.
2. Then we need to compile that code.
3. Finally, we need to link together the two compiled shaders into a GL program.

As we implement this next simple class, we will see how we can bundle up this functionality into a single method call, which can be made by an object from our game and have the ready-to-run GL program returned to the game object. When we build our `GameObject` class later in the chapter, we will see how we use this GL program.

Let's go ahead and implement the necessary three steps in a new class. Create a new class and call it `GLManager`. Add the static imports as shown here:

```
import static android.opengl.GLES20.GL_FRAGMENT_SHADER;
import static android.opengl.GLES20.GL_VERTEX_SHADER;
import static android.opengl.GLES20.glAttachShader;
import static android.opengl.GLES20.glCompileShader;
import static android.opengl.GLES20.glCreateProgram;
import static android.opengl.GLES20.glCreateShader;
import static android.opengl.GLES20.glLinkProgram;
import static android.opengl.GLES20.glShaderSource;
```

Next, we will add some public static final member variables that we can use in our `GameObject` class later in the chapter. Although we will see exactly how they work when we get around to using them, here is a quick preliminary explanation.

`COPONENTS_PER_VERTEX` is the number of values that will be used to represent a single vertex (point) in our primitives that will make up our game objects. As you can see, we initialize this to three coordinates: x, y, and z.

We also have `FLOAT_SIZE`, which is initialized to 4. This is the number of bytes in a Java float. As we will see soon, OpenGL likes all its primitives passed into it in the form of a `ByteBuffer`. We need to make sure we are precise about where in the `ByteBuffer` each piece of information is.

Next, we declare `STRIDE` and initialize it to `COMPONENTS_PER_VERTEX * FLOAT_SIZE`. As OpenGL uses the float type to hold virtually all of the data it works with, `STRIDE` now equals the size in bytes of the data that represents a single vertex of an object. Go ahead and add these members at the top of the class:

```
public class GLManager {

    // Some constants to help count the number of bytes between
    // elements of our vertex data arrays
    public static final int COMPONENTS_PER_VERTEX = 3;
    public  static final int FLOAT_SIZE = 4;
    public static final int STRIDE =
      (COMPONENTS_PER_VERTEX)
        * FLOAT_SIZE;

    public static final int ELEMENTS_PER_VERTEX = 3;// x,y,z
```

GLSL is a language in its own right and it also has its own types, and variables of those types can be utilized. Here, we declare and initialize some strings that we can use to refer to these variables more cleanly in our code.

Discussion of these types is beyond the scope of this book, but simply explained they will represent a matrix (u_matrix), a location (a_position), and a color (u_Color). We will see examples of the actual GLSL types these variables are in our shader code very soon.

After the strings, we declare three int types. These three public static (but not final) members will be used to store the location of there namesake types within our shaders. This allows us to manipulate the values within the shader program before we give OpenGL the final instruction to draw our primitives.

```
// Some constants to represent GLSL types in our shaders
public static final String U_MATRIX = "u_Matrix";
public static final String A_POSITION = "a_Position";
public static final String U_COLOR = "u_Color";


// Each of the above constants also has a matching int
// which will represent its location in the open GL glProgram
public static int uMatrixLocation;
public static int aPositionLocation;
public static int uColorLocation;
```

At last, we come to our GLSL code that is a vertex shader packed up in a string. Note that we declare a variable called u_Matrix of type uniform mat4 and a_Position of type attribute vec4. We will see in our GameObject class later how to get the locations of these variables to enable us to pass in values for them from our Java code.

The line in the code that starts with void main() is were the actual shader code executes from. Note that gl_position is assigned the value of the product of the two variables we just declared. Also gl_PointSize is assigned the value of 3.0. This will be the size we draw all our point primitives. Enter the code for the vertex shader right after the previous block of code:

```
// A very simple vertexShader glProgram
// that we can define with a String

private static String vertexShader =
    "uniform mat4 u_Matrix;" +
    "attribute vec4 a_Position;" +

    "void main()" +
    "{" +
```

```
        "gl_Position = u_Matrix * a_Position;" +
        "gl_PointSize = 3.0;"+
    "}";
```

Next, we will implement the fragment shader. A few things are happening here. First, the line precision `mediump` float tells OpenGL to draw with medium precision and therefore medium speed. Then we can see our variable `u_Color` being declared to type uniform `vec4`. We will see how we can pass a `color` value to this variable in the `GameObject` class soon.

When execution begins at `void main()`, we simply assign `u_Color` to `gl_FragColor`. So, whatever color is assigned to `u_Colour`, all the fragments will be that color. Just after the fragment shader, we declare an `int` called `program` that will act as a handle to our GL program.

Enter the code for the fragment shader right after the previous block of code:

```
// A very simple vertexShader glProgram
// that we can define with a String

private static String vertexShader =
    "uniform mat4 u_Matrix;" +
    "attribute vec4 a_Position;" +

    "void main()" +
    "{" +
        "gl_Position = u_Matrix * a_Position;" +
        "gl_PointSize = 3.0;"+
    "}";
```

This is a getter method that returns a handle to the GL program:

```
public static int getGLProgram(){
    return program;
}
```

This next method may look complex, but all it does is return a compiled and linked program to the caller. It does so by calling the OpenGL's `linkProgram` method with `compileVertexShader()` and `compileFragmentShader()` as arguments. Next, we see these two new methods and that all they need to do is call our method `compileShader()` with the OpenGL constant representing the type of shader and the appropriate string that holds the matching shader GLSL code.

Enter the three methods that we have just discussed into the GLManager class:

```
public static int buildProgram(){
    // Compile and link our shaders into a GL glProgram object
    return linkProgram(compileVertexShader(),compileFragmentShader());

}

private static int compileVertexShader() {
    return compileShader(GL_VERTEX_SHADER, vertexShader);
}

private static int compileFragmentShader() {
    return compileShader(GL_FRAGMENT_SHADER, fragmentShader);
}
```

Now we see what happens when our methods called compileShader(). First, we create a handle to a shader based on the type parameter. Then, we pass in that handle and the code to glShaderSource(). Finally, we compile the shader with glCompileShader() and return a handle to the calling method:

```
private static int compileShader(int type, String shaderCode) {

    // Create a shader object and store its ID
    final int shader = glCreateShader(type);

    // Pass in the code then compile the shader
    glShaderSource(shader, shaderCode);
    glCompileShader(shader);

    return shader;
}
```

Now we can see the final step in the process. We create an empty program with glCreateProgram(). Then we attach each of the compiled shaders in turn with glAttachShader(), and finally link them into a program we can actually use with glLinkProgram():

```
private static int linkProgram(int vertexShader, int fragmentShader) {

    // A handle to the GL glProgram -
    // the compiled and linked shaders
        program = glCreateProgram();
```

```
        // Attach the vertex shader to the glProgram.
        glAttachShader(program, vertexShader);

        // Attach the fragment shader to the glProgram.
        glAttachShader(program, fragmentShader);

        // Link the two shaders together into a glProgram.
        glLinkProgram(program);

        return program;
    }
}// End GLManager
```

Note that we created a program and we have access to it via its handle and the getProgram method. We also have access to all those public static members we created, so we will be able to tinker with the variables in the shader programs from our Java code.

The game's main loop – the renderer

Now we will see where the real meat of our code will go. Create a new class and call it AsteroidsRenderer. This is the class that we attached as our renderer to the GLSurfaceView. Add the import statements as follows, noting that some of them are static:

```
import android.graphics.PointF;
import android.opengl.GLSurfaceView.Renderer;
import android.util.Log;
import javax.microedition.khronos.egl.EGLConfig;
import javax.microedition.khronos.opengles.GL10;
import static android.opengl.GLES20.GL_COLOR_BUFFER_BIT;
import static android.opengl.GLES20.glClear;
import static android.opengl.GLES20.glClearColor;
import static android.opengl.GLES20.glViewport;
import static android.opengl.Matrix.orthoM;
```

Now we will build the class. The first thing to note that we have mentioned before is that the class implements Renderer, so we need to override three methods. They are onSurfaceCreated(), onSurfaceChanged(), and onDrawFrame(). Also, into this class, we will initially add a constructor to get everything set up, a createObjects method where we will eventually initialize all our game objects, an update method were we will update all our objects each frame, and a draw method were we will draw all our objects each frame.

We will explore and explain each method as we implement it, and we will also see how our methods fit in to the OpenGL renderer system, which dictates the flow of this class.

To get started, we have some member variables that are worth looking at quite closely.

The Boolean debugging will be used to toggle output to the console on and off. The `frameCounter`, `averageFPS`, and `fps` variables will not only be used for checking what frame rates we are reaching but also for passing to our game objects that will update themselves based on the elapsed time each frame.

Our first really interesting variable is the float array `viewportMatrix`. As the name suggests, it will hold a matrix that OpenGL can use to calculate the viewport into our game world.

We have a `GameManager` to hold a reference to the `GameManager` object, that `AsteroidsView` passed into this class's constructor. Finally, we have two `PointF` objects.

We will initialize the `PointF` objects in the constructor and use them for a few different things to avoid dereferencing any objects in the main game loop. When the garbage collector starts cleaning up discarded objects, even OpenGL will slow down. Avoiding summoning the garbage collector will be a goal for the entire game.

Enter the member variables at the top of the `AsteroidsRenderer` class:

```
public class AsteroidsRenderer implements Renderer {

// Are we debugging at the moment

boolean debugging = true;

// For monitoring and controlling the frames per second

long frameCounter = 0;
long averageFPS = 0;
private long fps;

// For converting each game world coordinate
// into a GL space coordinate (-1,-1 to 1,1)
// for drawing on the screen

private final float[] viewportMatrix = new float[16];

// A class to help manage our game objects
// current state.
```

```
    private GameManager gm;

    // For capturing various PointF details without
    // creating new objects in the speed critical areas

    PointF handyPointF;
    PointF handyPointF2;
```

Here is our constructor, where we initialize our GameManager reference from the parameter and create our two handy PointF objects ready for use:

```
    public AsteroidsRenderer(GameManager gameManager) {

        gm = gameManager;

        handyPointF = new PointF();
        handyPointF2 = new PointF();

    }
```

This is the first overridden method. It is called every time a GLSurfaceView class with attached renderer is created. We call glClearColor() to set which color OpenGL will use each time it clears the screen. We then build our shader program using our GLManager.buildProgram() method and call our createObjects method that we will code soon.

```
    @Override
    public void onSurfaceCreated(GL10 glUnused, EGLConfig config) {

        // The color that will be used to clear the
        // screen each frame in onDrawFrame()
        glClearColor(0.0f, 0.0f, 0.0f, 0.0f);

        // Get GLManager to compile and link the shaders into an object
        GLManager.buildProgram();

        createObjects();

    }
```

This next overridden method is called once after onSurfaceCreated() and any time the screen orientation changes. Here, we call the glViewport() method to tell OpenGL the pixel coordinates to map the OpenGL coordinate system onto.

The OpenGL coordinate system is very different from the pixel coordinates we are used to deal with in the previous two projects. The center of the screen is 0,0, the left and bottom are -1, and the top and right are 1.

The preceding situation is further complicated by the fact that most screens are not square, yet the range -1 to 1 must represent both x and y axes. Fortunately, our glViewport() has dealt with this for us.

The last thing we see in this method is calling the orthoM method with our viewportMatrix as the first parameter. OpenGL will now prepare viewportMatrix for use within OpenGL itself. The method orthoM() creates a matrix to convert coordinates into an orthographic view. If our coordinates are three-dimensional, it will have the effect of making all the objects appear the same distance away. As we are making a two-dimensional game, this is also suitable for us.

Enter the code for the onSurfaceChanged method:

```
@Override
    public void onSurfaceChanged(GL10 glUnused, int width, int height)
{

        // Make full screen
        glViewport(0, 0, width, height);

        /*
            Initialize our viewport matrix by passing in the starting
            range of the game world that will be mapped, by OpenGL to
            the screen. We will dynamically amend this as the player
            moves around.
```

```
        The arguments to setup the viewport matrix:
        our array,
        starting index in array,
        min x, max x,
        min y, max y,
        min z, max z)
    */

        orthoM(viewportMatrix, 0, 0,
    gm.metresToShowX, 0,
    gm.metresToShowY, 0f, 1f);
}
```

Here is our `createObjects` method and, as you can see, we create an object of type `SpaceShip` and pass in the map height and width to the constructor. We will build the `SpaceShip` class and its parent class `GameObject` later in this chapter. Enter the `createObjects` method:

```
    private void createObjects() {
        // Create our game objects

        // First the ship in the center of the map
        gm.ship = new SpaceShip(gm.mapWidth / 2, gm.mapHeight /
        2);
    }
```

This is the overridden `onDrawFrame` method. It is called continuously by the system. We can control when this is called by setting a render mode when we attach the `AsteroidsRenderer` to the view but the default OpenGL controlled continuous calling is exactly what we need.

We set `startFrameTime` to whatever the current system time is. Then, if `isPlaying()` returns `true`, we call our soon-to-be-implemented `update` method. Then, we call `draw()`, which will tell all of our objects to draw themselves.

We then update `timeThisFrame` and `fps` optionally outputting the average frames per second, every 100 frames, if we are debugging.

Now we know that OpenGL will call `onDrawFrame()` up to hundreds of times per second. We will conditionally call our `update` method each time as well as call our `draw` method. We have effectively implemented our game loop apart from the actual draw and update methods themselves.

Add the `onDrawFrame` method to the class:

```java
@Override
public void onDrawFrame(GL10 glUnused) {

    long startFrameTime = System.currentTimeMillis();

    if (gm.isPlaying()) {
        update(fps);
    }

    draw();

    // Calculate the fps this frame
    // We can then use the result to
    // time animations and more.
    long timeThisFrame = System.currentTimeMillis() -
    startFrameTime;
    if (timeThisFrame >= 1) {
        fps = 1000 / timeThisFrame;
    }

    // Output the average frames per second to the console
    if (debugging) {
        frameCounter++;
        averageFPS = averageFPS + fps;
        if (frameCounter > 100) {
            averageFPS = averageFPS / frameCounter;
            frameCounter = 0;
            Log.e("averageFPS:", "" + averageFPS);
        }
    }
}
```

Here is our `update` method, leave an empty body for now:

```java
private void update(long fps) {

}
```

Now, we come to our `draw` method, which is called once per frame from the `onDrawFrame` method. Here, we load up the ships current location into one of our handy `PointF` objects. Clearly, as we haven't implemented our `SpaceShip` class yet, this method call will produce an error.

The next thing we do in `draw()` is quite interesting. We modify our `viewportMatrix` based on the current location in the game world and the values assigned to `metresToShowX` and `metresToShowY`. Simply, we are centering on wherever the ship is and extending out by half the distance we wish to show in all four directions. Remember that, this happens in every frame, so our viewport will constantly follow the player ship.

Next, we call `glClear()` to clear the screen with the color we set in `onSurfaceCreated()`. The last thing we do in `draw()` is call a `draw` method on our `SpaceShip` object. This implies quite a fundamental design change from both of our previous games.

We mentioned this already, but here we can see it in action: each object will draw itself. Also, notice that we pass in our newly configured `viewportMatrix`.

Enter the code for the `draw` method:

```
private void draw() {

    // Where is the ship?
    handyPointF = gm.ship.getWorldLocation();

    // Modify the viewport matrix orthographic projection
    // based on the ship location
    orthoM(viewportMatrix, 0,
        handyPointF.x - gm.metresToShowX / 2,
        handyPointF.x + gm.metresToShowX / 2,
        handyPointF.y - gm.metresToShowY / 2,
        handyPointF.y + gm.metresToShowY / 2,
        0f, 1f);

    // Clear the screen
    glClear(GL_COLOR_BUFFER_BIT);

    // Start drawing!

    // Draw the ship
    gm.ship.draw(viewportMatrix);
    }
}
```

Now, we can build our `GameObject` super class, closely followed by its first child, `SpaceShip`. We will see how these objects will manage to use OpenGL to draw themselves.

Building an OpenGL-friendly, GameObject super class

Let's dive straight into the code. As we will see, this `GameObject` will have a lot in common with the `GameObject` class from the previous project. The most significant difference will be that this latest `GameObject` will of course draw itself using a handle to the GL program, primitive (vertex) data from a child class, and the viewport matrix contained in `viewportMatrix`.

Create a new class, call it `GameObject`, and enter these import statements, noting again that that some of them are static:

```
import android.graphics.PointF;
import java.nio.ByteBuffer;
import java.nio.ByteOrder;
import java.nio.FloatBuffer;
import static android.opengl.GLES20.GL_FLOAT;
import static android.opengl.GLES20.GL_LINES;
import static android.opengl.GLES20.GL_POINTS;
import static android.opengl.GLES20.GL_TRIANGLES;
import static android.opengl.GLES20.glDrawArrays;
import static android.opengl.GLES20.glEnableVertexAttribArray;
import static android.opengl.GLES20.glGetAttribLocation;
import static android.opengl.GLES20.glGetUniformLocation;
import static android.opengl.GLES20.glUniform4f;
import static android.opengl.GLES20.glUniformMatrix4fv;
import static android.opengl.GLES20.glUseProgram;
import static android.opengl.Matrix.multiplyMM;
import static android.opengl.Matrix.setIdentityM;
import static android.opengl.Matrix.setRotateM;
import static android.opengl.Matrix.translateM;
import static android.opengl.GLES20.glVertexAttribPointer;
import static com.gamecodeschool.c9asteroids.GLManager.*;
```

There are lots of member variables, many are self-explanatory and commented just to refresh our memories, but there are some totally new ones as well.

For example, we have an `enum` to represent each type of `GameObject` we will create. The reason for this is we will draw some objects as points, some as lines, and one as a triangle. The way that we use OpenGL is consistent between different types of primitive; hence, it is why we have bundled the code into this parent class. However, the final call to draw the primitive varies dependent on the type of primitive. We can use the `type` variable in a `switch` statement to execute the correct type of a `draw` method.

We also have an `int numElements` and `numVertices` that holds the number of points that make up any given `GameObject`. These will be set from the child class as we will see soon.

We have another float array called `modelVertices`, which will hold all the vertices that make up a model.

Enter the first batch of member variables in the `GameObject` class and take a look at the comments to refresh your memory or make clear what the various members will eventually be used for:

```
public class GameObject {

    boolean isActive;

    public enum Type {SHIP, ASTEROID, BORDER, BULLET, STAR}

    private Type type;

    private static int glProgram =-1;

    // How many vertices does it take to make
    // this particular game object?
    private int numElements;
    private int numVertices;

    // To hold the coordinates of the vertices that
    // define our GameObject model
    private float[] modelVertices;


    // Which way is the object moving and how fast?
    private float xVelocity = 0f;
    private float yVelocity = 0f;
    private float speed = 0;
    private float maxSpeed = 200;

    // Where is the object centre in the game world?
    private PointF worldLocation = new PointF();
```

Next, we will add another batch of member variables. First, and most notably, we have a `FloatBuffer` called `vertices`. As we know, OpenGL executes in native code and `FloatBuffers` are how it likes to consume its data. We will see how we pack all our vertices into this `FloatBuffer`.

We will also use all the public static members from our `GLManager` class to help us get it right.

Probably the second most interesting new member where OpenGL is concerned is we have another three float arrays called `modelMatrix`, `viewportModelMatrix`, and `rotateViewportModelMatrix`. These will be instrumental in helping OpenGL to draw the `GameObject` class exactly as required. We will examine exactly how they are initialized and used when we get to the `draw` method of this class.

We also have a bunch of members that hold different angles and rotation rates. How we use and update these in order to inform OpenGL of the orientation of our objects, we will see soon:

```
// This will hold our vertex data that is
// passed into the openGL glProgram
// OPenGL likes FloatBuffer
private FloatBuffer vertices;

// For translating each point from the model (ship, asteroid etc)
// to its game world coordinates
private final float[] modelMatrix = new float[16];

// Some more matrices for Open GL transformations
float[] viewportModelMatrix = new float[16];
float[] rotateViewportModelMatrix = new float[16];

// Where is the GameObject facing?
private float facingAngle = 90f;

// How fast is it rotating?
private float rotationRate = 0f;

// Which direction is it heading?
private float travellingAngle = 0f;

// How long and wide is the GameObject?
private float length;
private float width;
```

We now implement the constructor. First, we check if we have previously compiled the shaders, because we only need to do it once. If we haven't, this is what happens inside the `if(glProgarm == -1)` block.

We call `setGLProgram()` followed by `glUseProgram()` with `glProgram` as the argument. That is all we have to do, `GLManager` does the rest and our OpenGL program is ready to use.

Before we go on, however, we save the locations of our key shader variables by calling the respective methods (`glGetUniformLocation()` and `glGetAttrtibuteLocation`) to get their locations within our GL program. We will see in the `draw` method of this class how we use those locations to manipulate values within the shaders.

Finally, we set `isActive` to `true`. Enter this method into the `GameObject` class:

```
public GameObject(){
    // Only compile shaders once
    if (glProgram == -1){
        setGLProgram();

        // tell OpenGl to use the glProgram
        glUseProgram(glProgram);

        // Now we have a glProgram we need the locations
        // of our three GLSL variables.
        // We will use these when we call draw on the object.
        uMatrixLocation = glGetUniformLocation(glProgram, U_MATRIX);
        aPositionLocation = glGetAttribLocation(glProgram, A_
            POSITION);
        uColorLocation = glGetUniformLocation(glProgram, U_COLOR);
    }

    // Set the object as active
    isActive = true;

}
```

Now we have a few getters and setters including `getWorldLocation()`, which we called from the `draw` method in `AsteroidsRenderer` and `setGLProgram()`. This uses the `GLManager` class's static method `getGLProgram()` to get the handle to our GL program.

Enter all these methods into the `GameObject` class:

```
public boolean isActive() {
    return isActive;
}

public void setActive(boolean isActive) {
    this.isActive = isActive;
```

```
    }

    public void setGLProgram(){
        glProgram = GLManager.getGLProgram();
    }

    public Type getType() {
        return type;
    }

    public void setType(Type t) {
        this.type = t;
    }

    public void setSize(float w, float l){
        width = w;
        length = l;

    }

    public PointF getWorldLocation() {
        return worldLocation;
    }

    public void setWorldLocation(float x, float y) {
        this.worldLocation.x = x;
        this.worldLocation.y = y;
    }
```

The next method, setVertices() is a vital step in preparing an object to be drawn by OpenGL. In each of our child classes, we will build an array of float types to represent the vertices that make up the shape of the game object. Each game object will obviously be different in shape, but the setVertices method does not need to appreciate the difference, it just needs the data.

As we can see in the next block of code, the method receives a float array as a parameter. It then stores the number of elements that is equal to the length of the array in numElements. Note that the number of elements is different from the number of vertices the elements represent. It takes three elements (*x*, *y*, and *z*) to make one vertex. Therefore, we can store into numVertices the correct value by dividing numElements by ELEMENTS_PER_VERTEX.

Now we can actually initialize up our `ByteBuffer` by calling `allocateDirect()` and passing in our newly initialized variables along with `FLOAT_SIZE`. The `ByteOrder.nativeOrder` method simply detects if the particular system's endianness, and `asFloatBuffer()` tells `ByteBuffer` the type of data that will stored. We can now store our array of vertices into our vertices `ByteBuffer` by calling `vertices.put(modelVertices)`. This data is now ready to be passed to OpenGL.

 If you want to learn more about endianness, take a look at this Wikipedia article:

http://en.wikipedia.org/wiki/Endianness

Enter the `setVertices` method into the `GameObject` class:

```
public void setVertices(float[] objectVertices){

    modelVertices = new float[objectVertices.length];
    modelVertices = objectVertices;

    // Store how many vertices and elements there is for future use
    numElements = modelVertices.length;

    numVertices = numElements/ELEMENTS_PER_VERTEX;

    // Initialize the vertices ByteBuffer object based on the
    // number of vertices in the ship design and the number of
    // bytes there are in the float type
    vertices = ByteBuffer.allocateDirect(
            numElements
            * FLOAT_SIZE)
            .order(ByteOrder.nativeOrder()).asFloatBuffer();

    // Add the ship into the ByteBuffer object
    vertices.put(modelVertices);

}
```

Now we get to see how we actually draw the contents of our `ByteBuffer`. At a glance, the following code may look complex, but when we discuss the nature of the data in our `ByteBuffer` and the steps that OpenGL goes through to draw this data, we will see that it is actually quite straightforward.

As we have not written the code for our first `GameObject` child class, there is one key thing to point out. The vertices that represent the shape of a game object are zero based on its own center.

The OpenGL coordinate system has **0,0** as its center but, to make it clear, this is not related. This is called model space. The next image is a representation of our spaceship, in model space, that we will soon create:

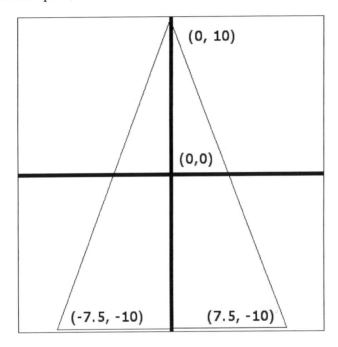

It is this data that is contained within our `ByteBuffer`. This data takes no account of orientation (is the ship or asteroid rotated), it takes no account of its position in the game world and, as a reminder, it is totally unrelated to the OpenGL coordinate system.

Therefore, before we draw our `ByteBuffer`, we need to convert this data, or, more accurately, we need to prepare an appropriate matrix, which we will pass into OpenGL with the data so that OpenGL will know how to use or convert the data.

I have split the `draw` method up into six chunks to talk about how we do this. Note that our `viewPort` matrix is prepared in our `AsteroidsRenderer` class's `draw` method, which is centered upon the location of the ship and based around the proportion of game world we want to show and is passed in as a parameter.

First, we call `glUseProgram()` and pass in the handle to our program. Then we set the internal pointer of our `ByteBuffer` to the start with `vertices.position(0)`.

The `glVertexAttributePointer` method uses our `aPositionLocation` variable along with our `GLManager` static constants and of course the `vertices` `ByteBuffer` to associate our vertices with the `aPosition` variable in the vertex shader. Finally, for this chunk of code, we tell OpenGL to enable the attribute array:

```
public void draw(float[] viewportMatrix){

    // tell OpenGl to use the glProgram
    glUseProgram(glProgram);

    // Set vertices to the first byte
    vertices.position(0);

    glVertexAttribPointer(
        aPositionLocation,
        COMPONENTS_PER_VERTEX,
        GL_FLOAT,
        false,
        STRIDE,
        vertices);

    glEnableVertexAttribArray(aPositionLocation);
```

Now, we put our matrices to work. We create an identity matrix out of our `modelMatrix` array by calling `setIndentityM()`.

As we will see, we are going to be using and combining quite a lot of matrices. An identity matrix acts as a starting point or container on which we can build a matrix, which combines all the transformations that we need to occur. A very simple but not entirely accurate way of thinking about an identity matrix is that it is like the number 1. When you multiply by an identity matrix, it doesn't cause any alteration to the other part of the sum. However, the answer is correct for moving on to the next part of the equation. If this is annoying you and you want to know more, take a look at these really quick tutorials on matrices and the identity matrix.

Matrices:

```
https://www.khanacademy.org/math/precalculus/precalc
-matrices/Basic_matrix_operations/v/introduction-to
-the-matrix
```

Identity matrix:

```
https://www.khanacademy.org/math/precalculus/
precalc-matrices/zero-identity-matrix-tutorial/v/
identity-matrix
```

We then pass our new `modelMatrix` into the `translateM` method. Translate is math speak for move. Look closely at the arguments passed into `translateM()`. We are passing in the *x* any *y* world locations of the object. This is how OpenGL knows where the object is:

```
// Translate model coordinates into world coordinates
// Make an identity matrix to base our future calculations on
// Or we will get very strange results
setIdentityM(modelMatrix, 0);
// Make a translation matrix

/*
    Parameters:
    m     matrix
    mOffset index into m where the matrix starts
    x     translation factor x
    y     translation factor y
    z     translation factor z
*/
translateM(modelMatrix, 0, worldLocation.x, worldLocation.y, 0);
```

We know that OpenGL has a matrix to translate our object to its world location. It also has a `ByteBuffer` class with the model space coordinates, but how does it convert translated model space coordinates to our viewport drawn using OpenGL coordinate system?

It uses the viewport matrix, which is modified by each frame and passed into this method. All we need to do is multiply `viewportMatrix` and the recently translated `modelMatrix` together using `multiplyMM()`. This method creates the combined or multiplied matrix and stores the result in `viewportModelMatrix`:

```
// Combine the model with the viewport
// into a new matrix
multiplyMM(viewportModelMatrix, 0,
    viewportMatrix, 0, modelMatrix, 0);
```

We are almost done creating our matrix. The only other possible distortion that OpenGL will need to make to the vertices in the `ByteBuffer` is to rotate them to the `facingAngle` parameter.

Next, we create a rotation matrix appropriate to the current object's facing angle and storing the result back in `modelMatrix`.

Then, we combine or multiply the newly rotated `modelMatrix` with our `viewportModelMatrix` and store the result in `rotateViewportModelMatrix`. This is our final matrix that we will pass into the OpenGL system:

```
/*
     Now rotate the model - just the ship model

     Parameters
     rm   returns the result
     rmOffset     index into rm where the result matrix starts
     a    angle to rotate in degrees
     x    X axis component
     y    Y axis component
     z    Z axis component
*/
setRotateM(modelMatrix, 0, facingAngle, 0, 0, 1.0f);

// And multiply the rotation matrix into the model-viewport
// matrix
multiplyMM(rotateViewportModelMatrix, 0,
  viewportModelMatrix, 0, modelMatrix, 0);
```

Now we pass in the matrix using the `glUniformMatrix4fv()` method and use the `uMatrixLocation` variable (which is the location of the matrix-related variable in the vertex shader) and our final matrix in the arguments.

We also choose the color by calling `glUniform4f()` with the `uColorLocation` and an RGBT (Red, Green, Blue, Transparency) value. All values are set to 1.0, so the fragment shader will draw white.

```
// Give the matrix to OpenGL

glUniformMatrix4fv(uMatrixLocation, 1, false,
rotateViewportModelMatrix, 0);

// Assign a color to the fragment shader
glUniform4f(uColorLocation, 1.0f, 1.0f, 1.0f, 1.0f);
```

Finally, we switch based on the object type and draw either points, lines, or triangle primitives:

```
// Draw the point, lines or triangle
switch (type){
    case SHIP:
    glDrawArrays(GL_TRIANGLES, 0, numVertices);
```

```
            break;

        case ASTEROID:
        glDrawArrays(GL_LINES, 0, numVertices);
        break;

        case BORDER:
        glDrawArrays(GL_LINES, 0, numVertices);
        break;

    case STAR:
        glDrawArrays(GL_POINTS, 0, numVertices);
        break;

        case BULLET:
        glDrawArrays(GL_POINTS, 0, numVertices);
        break;
    }

} // End draw()

}// End class
```

Now that we have the fundamentals of our `GameObject` class, we can make a class to represent our spaceship and draw it to the screen.

The spaceship

This class is nice and simple, although it will evolve with the project. The constructor receives the starting location within the game world. We set the ship's type and world location using the methods from the `GameObject` class, and we set a width and height.

We declare and initialize some variables to simplify the initialization of the model space coordinates, and then we go ahead and initialize a float array with three vertices that represent the triangle that is our ship. Note that the values are based around a center of $x = 0$ and $y = 0$.

All we do next is, call `setVertices()`, and `GameObject` will prepare the `ByteBuffer` ready for OpenGL:

```
public class SpaceShip extends GameObject{

    public SpaceShip(float worldLocationX, float worldLocationY){
        super();
```

```
// Make sure we know this object is a ship
// So the draw() method knows what type
// of primitive to construct from the vertices

setType(Type.SHIP);

setWorldLocation(worldLocationX,worldLocationY);

float width = 15;
float length = 20;

setSize(width, length);

// It will be useful to have a copy of the
// length and width/2 so we don't have to keep dividing by
2
float halfW = width / 2;
float halfL = length / 2;

// Define the space ship shape
// as a triangle from point to point
// in anti clockwise order
float [] shipVertices = new float[]{

        - halfW, - halfL, 0,
        halfW, - halfL, 0,
        0, 0 + halfL, 0

};


    setVertices(shipVertices);

    }

}
```

At last, we can see the fruits of our labor.

Drawing at 60 + FPS

In three simple steps, we will be able to glimpse our spaceship:

- Add a `SpaceShip` object to the `GameManager` member variables:

  ```
  private boolean playing = false;

      // Our first game object
      SpaceShip ship;

      int screenWidth;
  ```

- Add a call to the new `SpaceShip()` to the `createObjects` method:

  ```
  private void createObjects() {

      // Create our game objects
      // First the ship in the center of the map
      gm.ship = new SpaceShip(gm.mapWidth / 2, gm.mapHeight / 2);
  }
  ```

- Add the call to draw the spaceship in each frame in the `draw` method of `AsteroidsRenderer`:

  ```
  // Start drawing!
  // Draw the ship
  gm.ship.draw(viewportMatrix);
  ```

Run the game and see the output:

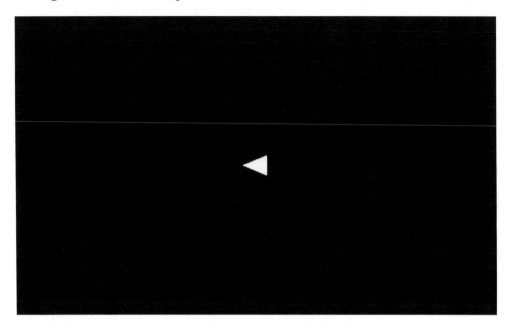

Not exactly impressive visuals, but it is running between 67 and 212 frames per second in debug mode while outputting to the console on an ageing Samsung Galaxy S2 phone.

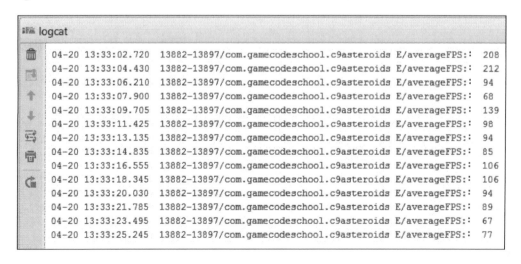

It will be our aim throughout the project to add hundreds of objects and keep the frames per second over 60.

One of the book's reviewers reported frame rates in excess of 1000 per second on a Nexus 5! It will therefore be worth considering a maximum frame rate locking strategy to save battery life if you were planning to release this to the Google Play store.

Summary

Setting up a drawing system was a little bit long-winded. However, now that it is done, we can churn out new objects much more easily. All we have to do is define the type and the vertices, then we can draw them with ease.

It is because of this ground work that the next chapter will be much more visually rewarding. Next, we will create blinking stars, a game world border, spinning and moving asteroids, whizzing bullets, and a HUD, as well as add full controls and motion to the spaceship.

10
Move and Draw with OpenGL ES 2

In this chapter, we will implement all the graphics, game play, and movement. In just over 30 pages, we will complete everything except collision detection. We can achieve this much because of the groundwork we laid in the last chapter.

First, we will draw a static border around our game world, then some blinking stars, followed by adding movement to our spaceship as well as some bullets. After that, we will quickly add controls for the player and we will be whizzing around the screen.

We will also make some noise by implementing our SoundManager class with some new sound FX.

Once this is done, we will add randomly shaped asteroids that move across the world while spinning around at the same time.

Then, we can add a HUD to highlight the touchable areas of the screen and provide a tally of the remaining player lives and asteroids that need destroying before the next level.

Drawing a static game border

In this simple class, we define four sets of points that will represent four lines. Unsurprisingly, the GameObject class will draw the border using these points as the end points of lines.

In the constructor, which is the entirety of the class, we set the type by calling setType(), the world location as the center of the map, and height and width as the height and width of the entire map.

Then, we define the four lines in a float array and call `setVertices()` to prepare a `FloatBuffer`.

Create a new class called `Border` and add the following code:

```
public class Border extends GameObject{

    public Border(float mapWidth, float mapHeight){

            setType(Type.BORDER);
            //border center is the exact center of map
            setWorldLocation(mapWidth/2,mapHeight/2);

            float w = mapWidth;
            float h = mapHeight;
            setSize(w, h);

            // The vertices of the border represent four lines
            // that create a border of a size passed into the constructor
            float[] borderVertices = new float[]{
                // A line from point 1 to point 2
                - w/2, -h/2, 0,
                w/2, -h/2, 0,
                // Point 2 to point 3
                w/2, -h/2, 0,
                w/2, h/2, 0,
                // Point 3 to point 4
                w/2, h/2, 0,
                -w/2, h/2, 0,
                // Point 4 to point 1
                -w/2, h/2, 0,
                - w/2, -h/2, 0,
        };

            setVertices(borderVertices);

    }

}
```

We can then declare a `Border` object as a member of `GameManager` like this:

```
// Our game objects
SpaceShip ship;
Border border;
```

Initialize it in the `createObjects` method of `AsteroidsRenderer` like this:

```
// Create our game objects

// First the ship in the center of the map
gm.ship = new SpaceShip(gm.mapWidth / 2, gm.mapHeight / 2);

// The deadly border
gm.border = new Border(gm.mapWidth, gm.mapHeight);
```

Now, we can draw our border by adding a line of code into the `draw` method of the `AsteroidsRendrer` class:

```
gm.ship.draw(viewportMatrix);
gm.border.draw(viewportMatrix);
```

You can now run the game. If you want to actually see the border, you can change the location to which we initialize the ship to somewhere near the border. Remember that in the `draw` method, we center the viewport around the ship. To see the border, change this one line in the `SpaceShip` class to this:

```
setWorldLocation(10,10);
```

Run the game to take a look.

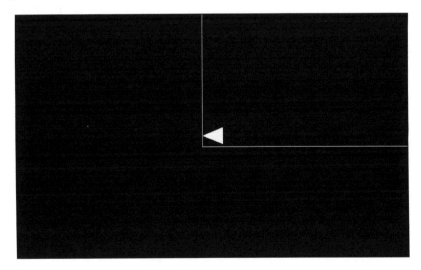

Change it back to this:

```
setWorldLocation(worldLocationX,worldLocationY);
```

Now, we will fill up the area within the border with stars.

Twinkling stars

We will get a bit more mobile than a static border. Here, we will add an `update` method to a simple `Star` class, which can be used to randomly switch the star on and off.

We set the type as `normal` and create a random location for the star within the confines of the border and call `setWorldLocation()` as always.

Stars will be drawn as points, so our vertex array will simply contain one vertex at model space 0,0,0. Then, we call `setVertices()` as usual.

Create a new class, call it `Star`, and enter the discussed code:

```
public class Star extends GameObject{

    // Declare a random object here because
    // we will use it in the update() method
    // and we don't want GC to have to keep clearing it up
    Random r;

    public Star(int mapWidth, int mapHeight){
    setType(Type.STAR);
    r = new Random();
    setWorldLocation(r.nextInt(mapWidth),r.nextInt(mapHeight));

    // Define the star
    // as a single point
    // in exactly the coordinates as its world location
    float[] starVertices = new float[]{

                0,
                0,
                0

    };

    setVertices(starVertices);


    }
```

Here is our `Star` class's `update` method. As we can see, there is a one in a 1000 chance in each frame that the star will switch its status. For more blinking, use a lower seed, and for less blinking, use a higher seed.

```
public void update(){

    // Randomly twinkle the stars
        int n = r.nextInt(1000);
        if(n == 0){
            // Switch on or off
            if(isActive()){
                setActive(false);
            }else{
                setActive(true);
            }
        }

    }

}
```

We then declare a `Star` array, as a member of `GameManager`, and an extra `int` variable to control how many stars we want to draw, as follows:

```
// Our game objects
SpaceShip ship;
Border border;
Star[] stars;
int numStars = 200;
```

Initialize the array of `Star` objects in the `createObjects` method of `AsteroidsRenderer` as follows:

```
// The deadly border
gm.border = new Border(gm.mapWidth, gm.mapHeight);

// Some stars
gm.stars = new Star[gm.numStars];
for (int i = 0; i < gm.numStars; i++) {

    // Pass in the map size so the stars no where to spawn
    gm.stars[i] = new Star(gm.mapWidth, gm.mapHeight);
}
```

Now, we can draw our stars by adding these lines of code into the draw method of the AsteroidsRenderer class. Note that we draw the stars first as they are in the background.

```
// Start drawing!

// Some stars
for (int i = 0; i < gm.numStars; i++) {

    // Draw the star if it is active
    if(gm.stars[i].isActive()) {
        gm.stars[i].draw(viewportMatrix);
    }
}

gm.ship.draw(viewportMatrix);
gm.border.draw(viewportMatrix);
```

Of course, to make them blink, we call their update method from the AsteroidsRenderer class's update method like this:

```
private void update(long fps) {

        // Update (twinkle) the stars
        for (int i = 0; i < gm.numStars; i++) {
        gm.stars[i].update();
        }


    }
```

You can now run the game:

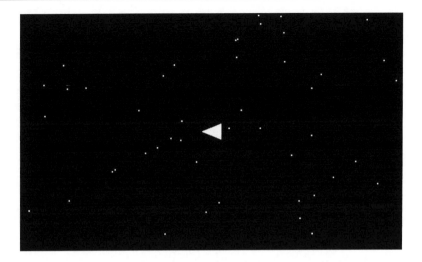

Bringing the spaceship to life

First, we need to add a bit more functionality to our GameObject class. We do so in GameObject because bullets and asteroids share a surprising amount of similarities with a spaceship.

We need a bunch of getters and setters to get and set the rotation rate, traveling angle, and facing angle. Add the following methods to the GameObject class:

```
public void setRotationRate(float rotationRate) {
   this.rotationRate = rotationRate;
}

public float getTravellingAngle() {
   return travellingAngle;
}

public void setTravellingAngle(float travellingAngle) {
   this.travellingAngle = travellingAngle;
}

public float getFacingAngle() {
   return facingAngle;
}

public void setFacingAngle(float facingAngle) {
   this.facingAngle = facingAngle;
}
```

Now, we add a move method, which adjusts the *x* and *y* coordinates as well as the facingAngle of the object based on the current frames per second. Add the move method:

```
void move(float fps){
    if(xVelocity != 0) {
        worldLocation.x += xVelocity / fps;
    }

    if(yVelocity != 0) {
        worldLocation.y += yVelocity / fps;
    }

    // Rotate
    if(rotationRate != 0) {
        facingAngle = facingAngle + rotationRate / fps;
    }

}
```

To complete our additions to the GameObject class, add these getters and setters for velocity, speed, and maximum speed:

```
public float getxVelocity() {
    return xVelocity;
}

public void setxVelocity(float xVelocity) {
    this.xVelocity = xVelocity;
}

public float getyVelocity() {
    return yVelocity;
}

public void setyVelocity(float yVelocity) {
    this.yVelocity = yVelocity;
}

public float getSpeed() {
    return speed;
}

public void setSpeed(float speed) {
```

```
    this.speed = speed;
}

public float getMaxSpeed() {
    return maxSpeed;
}

public void setMaxSpeed(float maxSpeed) {
    this.maxSpeed = maxSpeed;
}
```

We can make some additions to the SpaceShip class. Add these three members to the SpaceShip class to control if the player's ship is turning or moving forward:

```
boolean isThrusting;
private boolean isPressingRight = false;
private boolean isPressingLeft = false;
```

Now, inside the SpaceShip constructor, let's set the maximum speed of the ship. I have highlighted the new line of code among the existing code:

```
setSize(width, length);

setMaxSpeed(150);

// It will be useful to have a copy of the
```

Next, in the SpaceShip class, we add an update method that, first of all, increases and decreases the speed based on whether isThrusting is true or false.

```
public void update(long fps){

float speed = getSpeed();
if(isThrusting) {
   if (speed < getMaxSpeed()){
       setSpeed(speed + 5);
     }

     }else{
       if(speed > 0) {
         setSpeed(speed - 3);
       }else {
         setSpeed(0);
       }
}
```

Then, we set the *x* and *y* velocity based on the angle, which way the ship is facing, and the speed.

> We use speed multiplied by the cosine of the angle the ship is facing to set the velocity on the *x* axis. This works because the cosine function is a perfect variant that will return a value of -1 or 1, when the ship is facing exactly left or right, respectively; the variant returns a precise value of 0 when the ship is pointing exactly up or down. It also returns fine values in between as well. The sine of the angle works in exactly the same way on the *y* axis. The slightly convoluted looking code is because we need to convert our angle to radians and we must add 90 degrees to our facingAngle because 0 degrees is pointing to three o'clock. This fact is not conducive to using it on an *x*, *y* plane the way we have it, so we modify it by 90 degrees and the ship moves as expected. For more information about how this works check out this tutorial:
> http://gamecodeschool.com/essentials/calculating-heading-in-2d-games-using-trigonometric-functions-part-1/

```
setxVelocity((float)
   (speed* Math.cos(Math.toRadians(getFacingAngle() + 90))));

setyVelocity((float)
   (speed* Math.sin(Math.toRadians(getFacingAngle() + 90))));
```

Now, we set the rotation rate based on whether the player is turning left or right. Finally, we call move() to put all the updates into effect.

```
if(isPressingLeft){
   setRotationRate(360);
}

else if(isPressingRight){
   setRotationRate(-360);
      }else{
         setRotationRate(0);
      }

      move(fps);
}
```

Now, we need to add a `pullTrigger` method, which for now, we just return `true`. We also provide three methods for our future `InputController` to call and trigger the `update` method to make its various changes.

```
public boolean pullTrigger() {
  //Try and fire a shot
  // We could control rate of fire from here
  // But lets just return true for unrestricted rapid fire
  // You could remove this method and any code which calls it

   return true;
}



public void setPressingRight(boolean pressingRight) {
  isPressingRight = pressingRight;
}

public void setPressingLeft(boolean pressingLeft) {
  isPressingLeft = pressingLeft;
}

public void toggleThrust() {
  isThrusting = ! isThrusting;
}
```

We are already drawing the ship in each frame, but we need to add one line of code in the `AsteroidsRenderer` class's `update` method. Add this line of code to call the `SpaceShip` class's `update` method:

```
// Update (twinkle) the stars
for (int i = 0; i < gm.numStars; i++) {
  gm.stars[i].update();
}

// Run the ship,s update() method
gm.ship.update(fps);
```

Obviously, we can't actually move until we add the player controls. Let's quickly add some bullets to the game. Then, we will add sound and controls so that we can see and hear the cool new features we added.

Rapid fire bullets

I've been addicted to games since Pong in the '70s, and remember my delight when a friend actually had a Space Invaders machine in his home for about a week. Although what really made asteroids so much better than Space Invaders, was how quickly you could shoot. In that tradition, we will make a satisfying, rapid fire stream of bullets.

Create a new class called `Bullet`, which has one vertex and will be drawn with a point. Note that we also declare and initialize an `inFlight` Boolean.

```
public class Bullet extends GameObject {

    private boolean inFlight = false;

    public Bullet(float shipX, float shipY) {
        super();

        setType(Type.BULLET);

        setWorldLocation(shipX, shipY);

        // Define the bullet
        // as a single point
        // in exactly the coordinates as its world location
        float[] bulletVertices = new float[]{

                0,
                0,
                0

        };

        setVertices(bulletVertices);


    }
```

Next, we have the `shoot` method that sets the `facingAngle` of the bullet to that of the ship. This will cause the bullet to move in the direction the ship was facing at the time the fire button was pressed. We also set `inFlight` to true and see how this is used in the `update` method. Finally, we set the speed to `300`.

We also add a `resetBullet` method, which sets the bullet inside the ship and cancels its velocity and speed. This gives us a clue as to how we will implement our bullets. The bullets will sit invisibly inside the ship until they are fired.

```java
public void shoot(float shipFacingAngle){

    setFacingAngle(shipFacingAngle);
    inFlight = true;
    setSpeed (300);
}

public void resetBullet(PointF shipLocation){

    // Stop moving if bullet out of bounds
    inFlight = false;
    setxVelocity(0);
    setyVelocity(0);
    setSpeed(0);
    setWorldLocation(shipLocation.x, shipLocation.y);

}

public boolean isInFlight(){
    return  inFlight;
}
```

Now, we move the bullet based on its `facingAngle` and speed, only if `inFlight` is true. Otherwise, we keep the bullet inside the ship. Then, we call `move()`.

```java
public void update(long fps, PointF shipLocation){
        // Set the velocity if bullet in flight
        if(inFlight){
            setxVelocity((float)(getSpeed()*
                Math.cos(Math.toRadians(getFacingAngle() + 90))));
            setyVelocity((float)(getSpeed()*
                Math.sin(Math.toRadians(getFacingAngle() + 90))));
        }else{
            // Have it sit inside the ship
            setWorldLocation(shipLocation.x, shipLocation.y);
        }

        move(fps);
    }
}
```

Now, we have a `Bullet` class, we can declare an array, to hold a bunch of objects of this type in our `GameManager` class.

```
int numStars = 200;
Bullet [] bullets;
int numBullets = 20;
```

Initialize them in `createObjects()` right after our stars from the last section in `AsteroidsRenderer`. Note how we initialize their location in the game world as the center of the ship.

```
// Some bullets
gm.bullets = new Bullet[gm.numBullets];
for (int i = 0; i < gm.numBullets; i++) {
  gm.bullets[i] = new Bullet(
      gm.ship.getWorldLocation().x,
      gm.ship.getWorldLocation().y);
}
```

Update them in the `update` method, again right after our blinking stars.

```
// Update all the bullets
for (int i = 0; i < gm.numBullets; i++) {

    // If not in flight they will need the ships location
     gm.bullets[i].update(fps, gm.ship.getWorldLocation());

}
```

Draw them in the `draw` method, once more, after the stars.

```
for (int i = 0; i < gm.numBullets; i++) {
  gm.bullets[i].draw(viewportMatrix);
}
```

The bullets are now ready to be fired!

We will add a `SoundManager` and `InputController` class, then we can see our ship and its rapid fire gun in action.

Reusing existing classes

Let's quickly add our SoundManager and InputController classes to this project because they only need a little tweak to accommodate our needs here too.

Add a member for a SoundManager and an InputController object in both the AsteroidsView and AsteroidsRenderer classes.

```
private InputController ic;
private SoundManager sm;
```

Initialize the new objects in the onCreate method of the AsteroidsView class and call the loadSound method like this:

```
public AsteroidsView(Context context, int screenX, int screenY) {
    super(context);

        sm = new SoundManager();
        sm.loadSound(context);
        ic = new InputController(screenX, screenY);
        gm = new GameManager(screenX, screenY);
```

Also in AsteroidsView, add an extra two arguments to the call to the AsteroidsRenderer constructor to pass in references to the SoundManager and InputController objects.

```
setEGLContextClientVersion(2);
setRenderer(new AsteroidsRenderer(gm,sm,ic));
```

Now in the AsteroidsRenderer constructor add the two extra parameters and initialize the two new members like this:

```
public AsteroidsRenderer(GameManager gameManager,
    SoundManager soundManager, InputController inputController) {

        gm = gameManager;
        sm = soundManager;
        ic = inputController;

        handyPointF = new PointF();
        handyPointF2 = new PointF();

    }
```

You will have errors in your IDE until we add the two classes. We will do that now.

Adding the SoundManager class

The SoundManager class works exactly the same way as it did with the previous project, so there is nothing new to explain here.

Add all the sound files from the download bundle Chapter10/assets folder to the assets folder of your project. As in the last two projects, you may need to create the assets folder in the .../app/src/main folder of your project.

 As usual, you can use the sound effects provided or create your own.

Now, add a new class to the project called SoundManager. Note that the functionality of the class is identical to the last project, but the code is different simply because of the names of the sound files and their related variables. Add this code to the SoundManager class:

```
public class SoundManager {
    private SoundPool soundPool;
    private int shoot = -1;
    private int thrust = -1;
    private int explode = -1;
    private int shipexplode = -1;
    private int ricochet = -1;
    private int blip = -1;
    private int nextlevel = -1;
    private int gameover = -1;

    public void loadSound(Context context){
        soundPool = new SoundPool(10,
        AudioManager.STREAM_MUSIC,0);
        try{
            //Create objects of the 2 required classes
            AssetManager assetManager = context.getAssets();
            AssetFileDescriptor descriptor;

            //create our fx
            descriptor = assetManager.openFd("shoot.ogg");
            shoot = soundPool.load(descriptor, 0);

            descriptor = assetManager.openFd("thrust.ogg");
```

```
        thrust = soundPool.load(descriptor, 0);

        descriptor = assetManager.openFd("explode.ogg");
        explode = soundPool.load(descriptor, 0);

        descriptor = assetManager.openFd("shipexplode.ogg");
        shipexplode = soundPool.load(descriptor, 0);

        descriptor = assetManager.openFd("ricochet.ogg");
        ricochet = soundPool.load(descriptor, 0);

        descriptor = assetManager.openFd("blip.ogg");
        blip = soundPool.load(descriptor, 0);

        descriptor = assetManager.openFd("nextlevel.ogg");
        nextlevel = soundPool.load(descriptor, 0);

        descriptor = assetManager.openFd("gameover.ogg");
        gameover = soundPool.load(descriptor, 0);

    }catch(IOException e){
        //Print an error message to the console
        Log.e("error", "failed to load sound files");
    }
}

public void playSound(String sound){
    switch (sound){
        case "shoot":
            soundPool.play(shoot, 1, 1, 0, 0, 1);
            break;

        case "thrust":
            soundPool.play(thrust, 1, 1, 0, 0, 1);
            break;

        case "explode":
            soundPool.play(explode, 1, 1, 0, 0, 1);
            break;

        case "shipexplode":
            soundPool.play(shipexplode, 1, 1, 0, 0, 1);
```

```
                break;

            case "ricochet":
                soundPool.play(ricochet, 1, 1, 0, 0, 1);
                break;

            case "blip":
                soundPool.play(blip, 1, 1, 0, 0, 1);
                break;

            case "nextlevel":
                soundPool.play(nextlevel, 1, 1, 0, 0, 1);
                break;

            case "gameover":
                soundPool.play(gameover, 1, 1, 0, 0, 1);
                break;


        }

    }
}
```

We are now ready to call playSound() from anywhere we have a reference to our new class.

Adding the InputController class

This works the same way as it did in the last project, except that we call the appropriate PlayerShip methods instead of Bob's. Furthermore, we will not be moving the viewport while paused, so it is not necessary to handle the screen touches differently when the game is paused; making this InputController a little simpler and shorter.

Add the onTouchEvent method to the AsteroidsView class to pass responsibility for handling touches to InputController:

```
@Override
    public boolean onTouchEvent(MotionEvent motionEvent) {
        ic.handleInput(motionEvent, gm, sm);
        return true;
    }
```

Add a new class called InputController, and add the following code which is straightforward, except for the way that we handle the player firing a shot.

We declare a member int currentBullet that keeps track of which bullet from our soon-to-be-declared array we are going to shoot next. Then, we can count the bullets out when the fire button is pressed and go back to the first bullet, right after the last one in the array is fired.

Create a new class called InputController and enter the following code:

```
public class InputController {

    private int currentBullet;

    Rect left;
    Rect right;
    Rect thrust;
    Rect shoot;
    Rect pause;

    InputController(int screenWidth, int screenHeight) {

        //Configure the player buttons
        int buttonWidth = screenWidth / 8;
        int buttonHeight = screenHeight / 7;
        int buttonPadding = screenWidth / 80;

        left = new Rect(buttonPadding,
            screenHeight - buttonHeight - buttonPadding,
            buttonWidth,
            screenHeight - buttonPadding);

        right = new Rect(buttonWidth + buttonPadding,
            screenHeight - buttonHeight - buttonPadding,
            buttonWidth + buttonPadding + buttonWidth,
            screenHeight - buttonPadding);

        thrust = new Rect(screenWidth - buttonWidth -
            buttonPadding,
            screenHeight - buttonHeight - buttonPadding -
            buttonHeight - buttonPadding,
            screenWidth - buttonPadding,
            screenHeight - buttonPadding - buttonHeight -
            buttonPadding);
```

```
        shoot = new Rect(screenWidth - buttonWidth -
            buttonPadding,
            screenHeight - buttonHeight - buttonPadding,
            screenWidth - buttonPadding,
            screenHeight - buttonPadding);

        pause = new Rect(screenWidth - buttonPadding -
            buttonWidth,
            buttonPadding,
            screenWidth - buttonPadding,
            buttonPadding + buttonHeight);
```

Let's bundle all our buttons together in a list and make them available with a public method.

```
    }
    public ArrayList getButtons(){

        //create an array of buttons for the draw method
        ArrayList<Rect> currentButtonList = new ArrayList<>();
        currentButtonList.add(left);
        currentButtonList.add(right);
        currentButtonList.add(thrust);
        currentButtonList.add(shoot);
        currentButtonList.add(pause);
        return   currentButtonList;
    }
```

Next, we handle the input as we have before, except we call our Ship class's methods.

```
    public void handleInput(MotionEvent motionEvent,GameManager l,
        SoundManager sound){

        int pointerCount = motionEvent.getPointerCount();

        for (int i = 0; i < pointerCount; i++) {
        int x = (int) motionEvent.getX(i);
        int y = (int) motionEvent.getY(i);

            switch (motionEvent.getAction() &
                MotionEvent.ACTION_MASK) {

            case MotionEvent.ACTION_DOWN:
                    if (right.contains(x, y)) {
```

```
                l.ship.setPressingRight(true);
                l.ship.setPressingLeft(false);
            } else if (left.contains(x, y)) {
                l.ship.setPressingLeft(true);
                l.ship.setPressingRight(false);
            } else if (thrust.contains(x, y)) {
                l.ship.toggleThrust();
            } else if (shoot.contains(x, y)) {
                if (l.ship.pullTrigger()) {
                    l.bullets[currentBullet].shoot
                            (l.ship.getFacingAngle());

                    currentBullet++;
                // If we are on the last bullet restart
                // from the first one again
                if(currentBullet == l.numBullets){
                    currentBullet = 0;
                }

                    sound.playSound("shoot");
            }

            } else if (pause.contains(x, y)) {
            l.switchPlayingStatus();
            }
            break;

    case MotionEvent.ACTION_UP:
    if (right.contains(x, y)) {
            l.ship.setPressingRight(false);
        } else if (left.contains(x, y)) {
            l.ship.setPressingLeft(false);
        }

        break;


    case MotionEvent.ACTION_POINTER_DOWN:
    if (right.contains(x, y)) {
            l.ship.setPressingRight(true);
            l.ship.setPressingLeft(false);
        } else if (left.contains(x, y)) {
            l.ship.setPressingLeft(true);
        l.ship.setPressingRight(false);
```

```
      } else if (thrust.contains(x, y)) {
          l.ship.toggleThrust();
      } else if (shoot.contains(x, y)) {
          if (l.ship.pullTrigger()) {
          l.bullets[currentBullet].shoot
                  (l.ship.getFacingAngle());

              currentBullet++;
          // If we are on the last bullet restart
          // from the first one again
          if(currentBullet == l.numBullets){
              currentBullet = 0;
          }
          sound.playSound("shoot");
          }
      } else if (pause.contains(x, y)) {
          l.switchPlayingStatus();
      }
      break;


  case MotionEvent.ACTION_POINTER_UP:
  if (right.contains(x, y)) {
          l.ship.setPressingRight(false);
      } else if (left.contains(x, y)) {
          l.ship.setPressingLeft(false);
      }

      break;
      }
  }

  }
}
```

Now, we can fly around and loose off a few space rounds! Of course, you will have to estimate the screen positions until we get our HUD drawn later in this chapter. Don't forget that the player needs to tap the pause button (top-right) first.

Note that at the moment, we don't use the `resetBullet` method, and that once you have shot your twenty bullets, you will not be able to shoot any more. We can do a quick check to see if the bullet was at a location outside the border and then call `resetBullet`, but we will handle this fully, in conjunction with all the collision detection, in the next chapter.

Of course, we can't have an asteroids game without any asteroids.

Drawing and moving the asteroids

At last, we will add our cool, spinning asteroids. First, we will look at the constructor that is fairly similar to the other game object constructors, except that we set the world location randomly. However, take a little extra care not to spawn them in the center of the map, where the spaceship starts the game.

Create a new class called `Asteroid` and add this constructor. Note that we have not defined any vertices. We delegate this to the `generatePoints` method that we will see soon.

```
public class Asteroid extends GameObject{

    PointF[] points;

    public Asteroid(int levelNumber, int mapWidth, int mapHeight){
        super();

        // set a random rotation rate in degrees per second
        Random r = new Random();
        setRotationRate(r.nextInt(50 * levelNumber) + 10);

        // travel at any random angle
        setTravellingAngle(r.nextInt(360));

        // Spawn asteroids between 50 and 550 on x and y
        // And avoid the extreme edges of map
        int x = r.nextInt(mapWidth - 100)+50;
        int y = r.nextInt(mapHeight - 100)+50;

        // Avoid the center where the player spawns
        if(x > 250 && x < 350){ x = x + 100;}
        if(y > 250 && y < 350){ y = y + 100;}

        // Set the location
```

```
setWorldLocation(x,y);

// Make them a random speed with the maximum
// being appropriate to the level number
setSpeed(r.nextInt(25 * levelNumber)+1);

setMaxSpeed(140);

// Cap the speed
if (getSpeed() > getMaxSpeed()){
    setSpeed(getMaxSpeed());
}

// Make sure we know this object is a ship
setType(Type.ASTEROID);

// Define a random asteroid shape
// Then call the parent setVertices()
generatePoints();


}
```

Our update method simply calculates the velocity based on speed and traveling angle as we did for the SpaceShip class. It then calls move() in the usual way.

```
public void update(float fps){

    setxVelocity ((float) (getSpeed() * Math.cos(Math.toRadians
    (getTravellingAngle() + 90))));

    setyVelocity ((float) (getSpeed() *
    Math.sin(Math.toRadians(getTravellingAngle() + 90))));

        move(fps);

}
```

Here we see the generatePoints method, which will create a randomly shaped asteroid. Simply explained, each asteroid will have six vertices. Each vertex has a randomly generated position but within fairly strict limits, so we don't get any overlapping lines.

```
// Create a random asteroid shape
public void generatePoints(){
```

```
points = new PointF[7];

Random r = new Random();
int i;

    // First a point roughly centre below 0
    points[0] = new PointF();
    i = (r.nextInt(10))+1;
    if(i % 2 == 0){i = -i;}
    points[0].x = i;
    i = -(r.nextInt(20)+5);
    points[0].y = i;

    // Now a point still below centre but to the right and up a
    bit
    points[1] = new PointF();
    i = r.nextInt(14)+11;
    points[1].x = i;
    i = -(r.nextInt(12)+1);
    points[1].y = i;

    // Above 0 to the right
    points[2] = new PointF();
    i = r.nextInt(14)+11;
    points[1].x = i;
    i = r.nextInt(12)+1;
    points[2].y = i;

    // A point roughly centre above 0
    points[3] = new PointF();
    i = (r.nextInt(10))+1;
    if(i % 2 == 0){i = -i;}
    points[3].x = i;
    i = r.nextInt(20)+5;
    points[3].y = i;

    // left above 0
    points[4] = new PointF();
    i = -(r.nextInt(14)+11);
    points[4].x = i;
    i = r.nextInt(12)+1;
    points[4].y = i ;

    // left below 0
```

```
points[5] = new PointF();
i = -(r.nextInt(14)+11);
points[5].x = i;
i = -(r.nextInt(12)+1);

points[5].y = i;
```

Now, we have our six points that we use to build our array of floats that represent the vertices. Finally, we call `setVertices()` to create our `ByteBuffer`. Note that the asteroids will be drawn as a series of lines, which is why the last vertex in the array is the same as the first.

```
// Now use these points to draw our asteroid
float[] asteroidVertices = new float[]{
    // First point to second point
    points[0].x, points[0].y, 0,
    points[1].x, points[1].y, 0,

    // 2nd to 3rd
    points[1].x, points[1].y, 0,
    points[2].x, points[2].y, 0,

    // 3 to 4
    points[2].x, points[2].y, 0,
    points[3].x, points[3].y, 0,

    // 4 to 5
    points[3].x, points[3].y, 0,
    points[4].x, points[4].y, 0,

    // 5 to 6
    points[4].x, points[4].y, 0,
    points[5].x, points[5].y, 0,

    // 6 back to 1
    points[5].x, points[5].y, 0,
    points[0].x, points[0].y, 0,
};

setVertices(asteroidVertices);

}// End method

}// End class
```

Now as you have probably come to expect, we add an array to GameManager to hold all our asteroids. At the same time, we will declare some variables which will hold the level the player is currently on, as well as the starting (base) number of asteroids. Then soon, when we initialize all our asteroids, we will see how we will determine the number of asteroids that will need to be destroyed to clear a level.

```
Asteroid [] asteroids;
int numAsteroids;
int numAsteroidsRemaining;
int baseNumAsteroids = 10;
int levelNumber = 1;
```

Initialize the array in the GameManager constructor:

```
// For all our asteroids
asteroids = new Asteroid[500];
```

Initialize the objects themselves in the createObjects method using our previously declared variables to determine the number of asteroids based on the current level.

```
// Determine the number of asteroids
gm.numAsteroids = gm.baseNumAsteroids * gm.levelNumber;
// Set how many asteroids need to be destroyed by player
gm.numAsteroidsRemaining = gm.numAsteroids;
// Spawn the asteroids

for (int i = 0; i < gm.numAsteroids * gm.levelNumber; i++) {
    // Create a new asteroid
    // Pass in level number so they can be made
    // appropriately dangerous.
    gm.asteroids[i] = new Asteroid
      (gm.levelNumber, gm.mapWidth, gm.mapHeight);

}
```

Update them in the update method.

```
// Update all the asteroids
for (int i = 0; i < gm.numAsteroids; i++) {
  if (gm.asteroids[i].isActive()) {
    gm.asteroids[i].update(fps);
  }
}
```

Finally, we can draw all our asteroids in the draw method.

```
// The bullets
for (int i = 0; i < gm.numBullets; i++) {
  gm.bullets[i].draw(viewportMatrix);
}

for (int i = 0; i < gm.numAsteroids; i++) {
  if (gm.asteroids[i].isActive()) {
      gm.asteroids[i].draw(viewportMatrix);
  }

}
```

Now, run the game and check out those smooth, 60+ FPS, spinning asteroids.

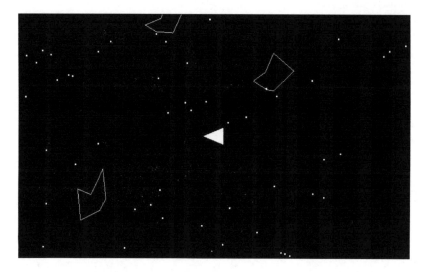

Now, we need to make it easy to control the ship by adding button graphics, as well as some other overlay information, with a HUD.

Scores and the HUD

The HUD objects will never be rotated. In addition, they are defined in the InputController class based on screen coordinates, not the game world or even Open GL coordinates. Therefore, our GameObject class is not a suitable parent class.

For the sake of simplicity, each of the three HUD classes will have their own draw method. We will see how we draw them at a consistent size and screen position using a new viewport matrix.

Once we have created all three of our HUD classes, we will add all of the object declarations, initializations, and drawing code.

Adding control buttons

The first HUD object we will make a class for, is a simple button.

I am showing all the imports explicitly, as they do not get imported automatically. Note that the next two classes will need these as well. The code is all in the download bundle as usual, if you wish to just copy and paste it.

Create a new class and call it `GameButton`, then add the following import statements. Be sure to state the correct package name based on which chapter's code you are using or the name you gave your project.

```
import android.graphics.PointF;
import java.nio.ByteBuffer;
import java.nio.ByteOrder;
import java.nio.FloatBuffer;
import static android.opengl.GLES20.GL_FLOAT;
import static android.opengl.GLES20.GL_LINES;
import static android.opengl.GLES20.glDrawArrays;
import static android.opengl.GLES20.glEnableVertexAttribArray;
import static android.opengl.GLES20.glGetAttribLocation;
import static android.opengl.GLES20.glGetUniformLocation;
import static android.opengl.GLES20.glUniform4f;
import static android.opengl.GLES20.glUniformMatrix4fv;
import static android.opengl.GLES20.glUseProgram;
import static android.opengl.Matrix.orthoM;
import static android.opengl.GLES20.glVertexAttribPointer;
import static
com.gamecodeschool.c10asteroids.GLManager.A_POSITION;
import static
com.gamecodeschool.c10asteroids.GLManager.COMPONENTS_PER_VERTEX;
import static
com.gamecodeschool.c10asteroids.GLManager.FLOAT_SIZE;
import static com.gamecodeschool.c10asteroids.GLManager.STRIDE;
import static com.gamecodeschool.c10asteroids.GLManager.U_COLOR;
import static com.gamecodeschool.c10asteroids.GLManager.U_MATRIX;
```

First, we declare some members; `viewportMatrix` into which we will put our new matrix for the viewport transformation from the `InputController` class's screen based coordinates — An int `glprogram` value, an int `numVertices` value, and a `FloatBuffer` class.

```
public class GameButton {

    // For button coordinate
    // into a GL space coordinate (-1,-1 to 1,1)
    // for drawing on the screen
    private final float[] viewportMatrix = new float[16];

    // A handle to the GL glProgram -
    // the compiled and linked shaders
    private static int glProgram;

    // How many vertices does it take to make
    // our button
    private int numVertices;

    // This will hold our vertex data that is
    // passed into openGL glProgram
    private FloatBuffer vertices;
```

The first thing we do in the constructor is make our viewport matrix by calling `orthoM()` with the screen height and width as `0,0`. This makes OpenGL map a coordinate range that is identical to the device resolution over the top of the OpenGL coordinate range.

We then get the coordinates of the passed in button and shrink it down to make it smaller. Then, we initialize a vertex array as four lines to represent a button. Clearly, we will need to create a new button object to represent each and every button from our `InputController` class.

```
public GameButton(int top, int left,
    int bottom, int right, GameManager gm){

    //The HUD needs its own viewport
    // notice we set the screen height in pixels as the
    // starting y coordinates because
    // OpenGL is upside down world :-)
    orthoM(viewportMatrix, 0, 0,
        gm.screenWidth, gm.screenHeight, 0, 0, 1f);

        // Shrink the button visuals to make
```

```
// them less obtrusive while leaving
// the screen area they represent the same.
int width = (right - left) / 2;
int height = (top - bottom) / 2;
left = left + width / 2;
right = right - width / 2;
top = top - height / 2;
bottom = bottom + height / 2;

PointF p1 = new PointF();
p1.x = left;
p1.y = top;

PointF p2 = new PointF();
p2.x = right;
p2.y = top;

PointF p3 = new PointF();
p3.x = right;
p3.y = bottom;

PointF p4 = new PointF();
p4.x = left;
p4.y = bottom;

// Add the four points to an array of vertices
// This time, because we don't need to animate the border
// we can just declare the world space coordinates, the
// same as above.
float[] modelVertices = new float[]{
        // A line from point 1 to point 2
        p1.x, p1.y, 0,
        p2.x, p2.y, 0,
        // Point 2 to point 3
        p2.x, p2.y, 0,
        p3.x, p3.y, 0,
        // Point 3 to point 4
        p3.x, p3.y, 0,
        p4.x, p4.y, 0,
        // Point 4 to point 1
        p4.x, p4.y, 0,
        p1.x, p1.y, 0
};
```

Now, we duplicate a little of the code from `GameObject` to prepare `ByteBuffer`, but still we use our static `GLManager.getGLProgram()` to get a handle to a GL program.

```
// Store how many vertices and
// elements there is for future use
final int ELEMENTS_PER_VERTEX = 3;// x,y,z
int numElements = modelVertices.length;
numVertices = numElements/ELEMENTS_PER_VERTEX;

// Initialize the vertices ByteBuffer object based on the
// number of vertices in the button and the number of
// bytes there are in the float type
vertices = ByteBuffer.allocateDirect(
        numElements
      * FLOAT_SIZE)
      .order(ByteOrder.nativeOrder()).asFloatBuffer();

// Add the button into the ByteBuffer object
vertices.put(modelVertices);

glProgram = GLManager.getGLProgram();


}
```

Finally, we implement the `draw` method, which is a simplified version of the `draw` method from `GameObject`. Note that we don't need to mess around with model, translation, and rotation matrices, and also that we pass a different color to the fragment shader.

```
public void draw(){

    // And tell OpenGl to use the glProgram
    glUseProgram(glProgram);

    // Now we have a glProgram we need the locations
    // of our three GLSL variables
    int uMatrixLocation = glGetUniformLocation(glProgram, U_MATRIX);

    int aPositionLocation =
        glGetAttribLocation(glProgram, A_POSITION);

    int uColorLocation = glGetUniformLocation(glProgram, U_COLOR);
```

```
    vertices.position(0);

    glVertexAttribPointer(
        aPositionLocation,
        COMPONENTS_PER_VERTEX,
        GL_FLOAT,
        false,
        STRIDE,
        vertices);

    glEnableVertexAttribArray(aPositionLocation);

    // give the new matrix to OpenGL
    glUniformMatrix4fv(uMatrixLocation, 1, false, viewportMatrix, 0);

    // Assign a different color to the fragment shader
    glUniform4f(uColorLocation, 0.0f, 0.0f, 1.0f, 1.0f);

    // Draw the lines
    // start at the first element of the
    // vertices array and read in all vertices
    glDrawArrays(GL_LINES, 0, numVertices);

}
}// End class
```

Tally icons

This class is the same as `GameButton`, except that a tally icon will be a single straight vertical line; therefore, we only need two vertices.

However, note that we have a parameter in the constructor called `nthIcon`. It will be the responsibility of the calling code to let `TallyIcon` know the total quantity of already created `TallyIcon` objects, plus one. Then, the current `TallyIcon` object can use the padding variable to position itself appropriately.

Create a new class called `TallyIcon` and enter the following code. As we have, previously, include the static imports as required. Here is the code for all the declarations and the constructor:

```
public class TallyIcon {

    // For button coordinate
    // into a GL space coordinate (-1,-1 to 1,1)
    // for drawing on the screen
    private final float[] viewportMatrix = new float[16];

    // A handle to the GL glProgram -
    // the compiled and linked shaders
    private static int glProgram;

    // How many vertices does it take to make
    // our button
    private int numVertices;

    // This will hold our vertex data that is
    // passed into openGL glProgram
    //private final FloatBuffer vertices;
    private FloatBuffer vertices;

    public TallyIcon(GameManager gm, int nthIcon){

        // The HUD needs its own viewport
        // notice we set the screen height in pixels as the
        // starting y coordinates because
        // OpenGL is upside down world :-)
        orthoM(viewportMatrix, 0, 0,
          gm.screenWidth, gm.screenHeight, 0, 0f, 1f);

        float padding = gm.screenWidth / 160;
        float iconHeight = gm.screenHeight / 15;
        float iconWidth = 1; // square icons
        float startX = 10 + (padding + iconWidth)* nthIcon;
        float startY = iconHeight * 2 + padding;

        PointF p1 = new PointF();
        p1.x = startX;
        p1.y = startY;

        PointF p2 = new PointF();
```

```
        p2.x = startX;
        p2.y = startY - iconHeight;

        // Add the four points to an array of vertices
        // This time, because we don't need to animate the border
        // we can just declare the world space coordinates, the
        // same as above.
        float[] modelVertices = new float[]{
                // A line from point 1 to point 2
                p1.x, p1.y, 0,
                p2.x, p2.y, 0,


        };


        // Store how many vertices and
        //elements there is for future use
        final int ELEMENTS_PER_VERTEX = 3;// x,y,z
        int numElements = modelVertices.length;
        numVertices = numElements/ELEMENTS_PER_VERTEX;

        // Initialize the vertices ByteBuffer object based on the
        // number of vertices in the button and the number of
        // bytes there are in the float type
        vertices = ByteBuffer.allocateDirect(
                numElements
                * FLOAT_SIZE)
                .order(ByteOrder.nativeOrder()).asFloatBuffer();

        // Add the button into the ByteBuffer object
        vertices.put(modelVertices);

        glProgram = GLManager.getGLProgram();
    }
```

This is the draw method which is probably looking quite familiar by now.

```
    public void draw(){

        // And tell OpenGl to use the glProgram
        glUseProgram(glProgram);

        // Now we have a glProgram we need the locations
```

```
            // of our three GLSL variables
            int uMatrixLocation =
            glGetUniformLocation(glProgram, U_MATRIX);

            int aPositionLocation =
            glGetAttribLocation(glProgram, A_POSITION);

            int uColorLocation =
            glGetUniformLocation(glProgram, U_COLOR);

            vertices.position(0);

            glVertexAttribPointer(
                    aPositionLocation,
                    COMPONENTS_PER_VERTEX,
                    GL_FLOAT,
                    false,
                    STRIDE,
                    vertices);

            glEnableVertexAttribArray(aPositionLocation);

            // Just give the passed in matrix to OpenGL
            glUniformMatrix4fv(uMatrixLocation, 1,
              false, viewportMatrix, 0);

            // Assign a color to the fragment shader
            glUniform4f(uColorLocation, 1.0f, 1.0f, 0.0f, 1.0f);

            // Draw the lines
            // start at the first element of the vertices array and read
            in all vertices
            glDrawArrays(GL_LINES, 0, numVertices);
    }
```

Now for the final HUD element.

Life icons

Our last icon will be a kind of mini-ship to indicate how many lives the player
has remaining.

We will construct a triangle shape out of lines to create a nice hollow effect. Note that
the `LifeIcon` constructor also uses an `nthIcon` element to control the padding and
on screen position.

Create a new class called `LifeIcon` and enter the following code, remembering all
the imports that will not auto-import. Here are the declarations and the constructor:

```
public class LifeIcon {

    // Remember the static import for GLManager

    // For button coordinate
    // into a GL space coordinate (-1,-1 to 1,1)
    // for drawing on the screen
    private final float[] viewportMatrix = new float[16];

    // A handle to the GL glProgram -
    // the compiled and linked shaders
    private static int glProgram;

    // Each of the above constants also has a matching int
    // which will represent its location in the open GL glProgram
    // In GameButton they are declared as local variables

    // How many vertices does it take to make
    // our button
    private int numVertices;

    // This will hold our vertex data that is
    // passed into openGL glProgram
    //private final FloatBuffer vertices;
    private FloatBuffer vertices;

    public LifeIcon(GameManager gm, int nthIcon){

        // The HUD needs its own viewport
        // notice we set the screen height in pixels as the
        // starting y coordinates because
```

```
// OpenGL is upside down world :-)
orthoM(viewportMatrix, 0, 0,
  gm.screenWidth, gm.screenHeight, 0, 0f, 1f);

float padding = gm.screenWidth / 160;
float iconHeight = gm.screenHeight / 15;
float iconWidth = gm.screenWidth / 30;
float startX = 10 + (padding + iconWidth)* nthIcon;
float startY = iconHeight;

PointF p1 = new PointF();
p1.x = startX;
p1.y = startY;

PointF p2 = new PointF();
p2.x = startX + iconWidth;
p2.y = startY;

PointF p3 = new PointF();
p3.x = startX + iconWidth/2;
p3.y = startY - iconHeight;


// Add the four points to an array of vertices
// This time, because we don't need to animate the border
// we can just declare the world space coordinates, the
// same as above.
float[] modelVertices = new float[]{
        // A line from point 1 to point 2
        p1.x, p1.y, 0,
        p2.x, p2.y, 0,
        // Point 2 to point 3
        p2.x, p2.y, 0,
        p3.x, p3.y, 0,
        // Point 3 to point 1
        p3.x, p3.y, 0,
        p1.x, p1.y, 0,

};

// Store how many vertices and elements there is for future
// use
final int ELEMENTS_PER_VERTEX = 3;// x,y,z
```

```
    int numElements = modelVertices.length;
    numVertices = numElements/ELEMENTS_PER_VERTEX;

    // Initialize the vertices ByteBuffer object based on the
    // number of vertices in the button and the number of
    // bytes there are in the float type
    vertices = ByteBuffer.allocateDirect(
            numElements
          * FLOAT_SIZE)
          .order(ByteOrder.nativeOrder()).asFloatBuffer();

    // Add the button into the ByteBuffer object
    vertices.put(modelVertices);

      glProgram = GLManager.getGLProgram();
    }
```

Here is the draw method of the LifeIcon class:

```
    public void draw(){

            // And tell OpenGl to use the glProgram
            glUseProgram(glProgram);

            // Now we have a glProgram we need the locations
            // of our three GLSL variables
            int uMatrixLocation = glGetUniformLocation
              (glProgram, U_MATRIX);
            int aPositionLocation = glGetAttribLocation
              (glProgram, A_POSITION);
            int uColorLocation = glGetUniformLocation
              (glProgram, U_COLOR);

            vertices.position(0);

            glVertexAttribPointer(
                  aPositionLocation,
                  COMPONENTS_PER_VERTEX,
                  GL_FLOAT,
                  false,
                  STRIDE,
                  vertices);

            glEnableVertexAttribArray(aPositionLocation);
```

```
            // Just give the passed in matrix to OpenGL
            glUniformMatrix4fv(uMatrixLocation, 1,
              false, viewportMatrix, 0);
            // Assign a color to the fragment shader
            glUniform4f(uColorLocation, 1.0f,
              1.0f, 0.0f, 1.0f);
            // Draw the lines
            // start at the first element of
            // the vertices array and read in all vertices
            glDrawArrays(GL_LINES, 0, numVertices);
        }


    }
```

We have our three HUD classes, and we can draw them to the screen.

Declaring, initializing, and drawing the HUD objects

We will declare, initialize, and draw our HUD objects just like all the GameObject classes. However, note that, as expected, we don't pass a viewport matrix to the draw method because the HUD classes provide their own.

Add these members to GameManager:

```
TallyIcon[] tallyIcons;
int numLives = 3;
LifeIcon[] lifeIcons;
```

As we did with the asteroids array, initialize tallyIcons and lifeIcons in the GameManager constructor:

```
lifeIcons = new LifeIcon[50];
tallyIcons = new TallyIcon[500];
```

Add a new member array to the AsteroidsRenderer class:

```
// This will hold our game buttons
private final GameButton[] gameButtons = new GameButton[5];
```

Add this code to create objects of all our new HUD classes. Add it to the
`createObjects` method just before the closing curly brace:

```
// Now for the HUD objects
// First the life icons
for(int i = 0; i < gm.numLives; i++) {
    // Notice we send in which icon this represents
    // from left to right so padding and positioning is correct.
    gm.lifeIcons[i] = new LifeIcon(gm, i);
}

// Now the tally icons (1 at the start)
for(int i = 0; i < gm.numAsteroidsRemaining; i++) {
    // Notice we send in which icon this represents
    // from left to right so padding and positioning is correct.
    gm.tallyIcons[i] = new TallyIcon(gm, i);
}

// Now the buttons
ArrayList<Rect> buttonsToDraw = ic.getButtons();
int i = 0;
for (Rect rect : buttonsToDraw) {
    gameButtons[i] = new GameButton(rect.top, rect.left,
        rect.bottom, rect.right, gm);

    i++;

}
```

Now we can draw our HUD based on the number of lives remaining and the number
of asteroids left before the next level. Add this code to the end of the `draw` method:

```
// the buttons
for (int i = 0; i < gameButtons.length; i++) {
  gameButtons[i].draw();
}

// Draw the life icons
for(int i = 0; i < gm.numLives; i++) {
    // Notice we send in which icon this represents
    // from left to right so padding and positioning is correct.
    gm.lifeIcons[i].draw();
}
```

```
// Draw the level icons
for(int i = 0; i < gm.numAsteroidsRemaining; i++) {
   // Notice we send in which icon this represents
   // from left to right so padding and positioning is correct.
   gm.tallyIcons[i].draw();
}
```

You can now fly around and admire your new HUD.

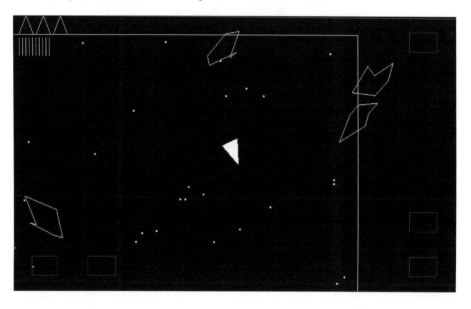

Obviously, if we are going to make any use of our lives and asteroid tally indicators, then we first need to be able to shoot asteroids as well as detect them when the ship gets hit.

Summary

We achieved lots in this chapter, and indeed it would be simple to quickly add more game objects. Perhaps, an occasional UFO like in the original arcade classic.

In the next chapter we will use what we learned in previous projects to set up collision detection and finish off the game. However, a game with precise, clean, smooth moving lines deserves much more accurate collision detection than we used so far.

So, we will concentrate solely on implementing precise, efficient collision detection that will make our Asteroids simulator complete.

11
Things That Go Bump – Part II

The collision detection in this game is much more complex than the previous two. For this reason, the code will be quite heavily commented. Sometimes the comments will explain things in a bit more detail or in a slightly different way.

However, that doesn't mean it needs to be hard work. What we need to do is take a moment to consider a strategy that will work for us.

Hopefully, this approach will mean that by the end of the chapter, our collision detection solutions will appear straightforward.

Planning for collision detection

What we are trying to achieve can be put into the following two categories:

- What we want for the border:
  - Asteroids, bullets, and the ship need to know when they have collided with the border
  - Asteroids should reverse and head back into the game area when they touch the border
  - A bullet should reset itself at the border
  - The ship should subtract a life and then respawn in the centre

- What we want for the asteroids. We need to know and respond when:
  - ○ The ship touches an asteroid
  - ○ When a bullet touches an asteroid
  - ○ As in the original Asteroids game, we will not respond to asteroids bumping into each other

Although we will not be detecting an asteroid on asteroid collisions, you will see that when our collision detection nears completion, achieving asteroid on asteroid collision detection will not present much of an extra challenge. However, it will put extra strain on the device's CPU.

We know that we have object on border collisions to detect and object on asteroid collisions to detect.

Colliding with the border

It may sound obvious, but the border is simply four static straight lines. This makes a border collision a different problem to an asteroid collision.

All of the objects that we are interested in have vertices (or one vertex in the case of a bullet). This may at first suggest that we can simply compute the world location of each vertex from the model space and the centre of the object stored in `worldLocation`. We can, but this overlooks the fact that the asteroids and the ship rotate, which constantly causes a variation in the actual world locations of all the vertices.

We will need to translate and rotate the model space vertices, and then test if any of them have touched the border. We can do this in the object's `update` method for each frame, but we only need the rotated coordinates occasionally, when the object is very close to the border.

The first phase of border collision detection

This suggests that a preliminary check, a first phase of collision detection, is more efficient. It implies that the translation and rotation of the vertices will need to take place outside of the object itself.

What we will do is use a simple rectangle intersect check based on the centre of the object and its width and height. If this cheap method returns a hit, we will then rotate and translate each vertex and check their real-world coordinates individually against the location of the border.

Once the rotated game world locations of the vertices are calculated, the collision detection is simple.

```
if (any point falls outside the border){collision has occurred}
```

As we will see, a two-stage solution is appropriate for the asteroid detection as well. Also, rotation and translation is involved but it is far less important.

Colliding with an asteroid

Testing for collision with an asteroid is similar in some respects. We need to find out if any single vertex from the ship or a bullet crosses into the space contained by the vertices of the asteroid.

The first problem is that the asteroid is not only a moving target, but also a rotating one. We will not only have to rotate and translate all the vertices of the objects, but the asteroids as well.

We also need to calculate the line made between each pair of vertices on the asteroid. Fortunately, at this point, we can fall back on a clever algorithm devised and refined by mathematicians far greater than myself. We will use the crossing number algorithm. This is how it works.

The crossing number

We compute the line made by a pair of vertices and use the crossing number algorithm to see if a particular vertex from the object being tested crossed that line. If it did, we increment a variable from 0 to 1.

We test the same point against each and every line made by each vertex pair from an asteroid, incrementing our variable each time it does. If our variable is odd after testing the vertex against every line with the crossing number algorithm, we have a hit. If it is even, no collision has occurred.

Of course if no collision has occurred, we must proceed to test each and every vertex from the object being tested against each and every line formed out of the vertex pairs on the asteroid.

Here is a visual representation of the crossing number algorithm in action.

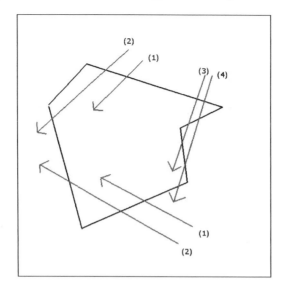

Of course with all these complex calculations going on, we will definitely want to do a simple first phase test to see if it is likely there has been a collision before doing the complex tests.

The first phase and overview of asteroid collision detection

The radius overlap test is quite appropriate when testing a single vertex, such as a bullet, a spinning triangle like a ship, or a rotating asteroid.

This is an overview of the whole process we will use for testing the collisions against asteroids:

1. Is the radius of the object being tested overlapped with the radius of an asteroid?
2. If yes, has the first vertex of the object crossed the first line of the asteroid?
3. If yes, `crossingNumber ++`.
4. Repeat step 2 with each line on the object.
5. If `crossingNumber` is odd, return true to calling code because a collision has occurred.

6. If `crossingNumber` is even, no collision has occurred (yet) repeat steps 2, 3, and 4 with the next vertex of the object being tested.

7. If all vertices tested and we reached here then no collision has occurred.

We will set up a collision detection class called `CD` with two static methods. The `detect` method will test for collisions with asteroids and be called for each bullet and ship against each and every asteroid in each frame.

The `contain` method will check for collisions with every asteroid, bullet, and ship against the border.

Doing the calculations outside the objects themselves means that we will need a whole bunch of data for the objects we will be testing, and the ones made accessible to the new `CD` class's methods.

The CollisionPackage class

We know that we need a certain set of data to carry out detections properly. This next class will hold all the data that our collision detection class's methods will need in order to do its job, and every object that we need to detect collisions for will have one.

When the time comes to rotate all the points to their real-world location, our collision package will need to know which way the object is facing. We have a float called `facingAngle`.

We will obviously need a copy of the model space vertices. As with the rotated location, we will not go through the trouble of updating every frame and will do so only after the first phase of collision detection shows that a collision is likely.

We will also hold the precomputed value for the length of the array that holds these vertices. It can potentially save time in the collision detection process.

Therefore, we will also need the world coordinates of the object. This, we will update every frame.

Each object will have a precomputed `radius` variable, which is the size of the object from its centre to its furthest vertex. This will be used in our `detect` method for radius overlapping, phase one detection.

We will also have a couple of `PointF` objects, `currentPoint`, and `currentPoint2`, which are just handy objects that will avoid us potentially summoning the garbage collector during an intensive part of the two collision detection methods.

Create a new class, call it `CollisionPackage`, and implement the members we have just discussed:

```
// All objects which can collide have a collision package.
// Asteroids, ship, bullets. The structure seems like slight
// overkill for bullets but it keeps the code generic,
// and the use of vertexListLength means there isn't any
// actual speed overhead. Also if we wanted line, triangle or
// even spinning bullets the code wouldn't need to change.

public class CollisionPackage {

    // All the members are public to avoid multiple calls
    // to getters and setters.

    // The facing angle allows us to calculate the
    // current world coordinates of each vertex using
    // the model-space coordinates in vertexList.
    public float facingAngle;

    // The model-space coordinates
    public PointF[] vertexList;

    /*
    The number of vertices in vertexList
    is kept in this next int because it is pre-calculated
    and we can use it in our loops instead of
    continually calling vertexList.length.
    */
    public int vertexListLength;

    // Where is the centre of the object?
    public PointF worldLocation;

    /*
    This next float will be used to detect if the circle shaped
    hitboxes collide. It represents the furthest point
    from the centre of any given object.
    Each object will set this slightly differently.
    The ship will use height/2 an asteroid will use 25
    To allow for a max length rotated coordinate.
    */
    public float radius;
```

```
    // A couple of points to store results and avoid creating new
    // objects during intensive collision detection
    public PointF currentPoint = new PointF();
    public PointF currentPoint2 = new PointF();
```

Next, we have a simple constructor that will receive all the necessary data from each object at the end of each object's constructor. Implement the `CollisionPackage` constructor as shown here:

```
public CollisionPackage(PointF[] vertexList, PointF worldLocation,
    float radius, float facingAngle){

        vertexListLength = vertexList.length;
        this.vertexList = new PointF[vertexListLength];
        // Make a copy of the array

        for (int i = 0; i < vertexListLength; i++) {
            this.vertexList[i] = new PointF();
            this.vertexList[i].x = vertexList[i].x;
            this.vertexList[i].y = vertexList[i].y;
        }



        this.worldLocation = new PointF();
        this.worldLocation = worldLocation;

        this.radius = radius;

        this.facingAngle = facingAngle;


    }


}
```

That's all the data we need for advanced collision detection.

Adding collision packages to the objects and making them accessible

Now, we have our `CollisionPackage` class. We will see how to add one to each object we need to monitor.

Adding a collision package to the Bullet class

Open up the `Bullet` class, and we will see how to make use of our `CollisionPackage` constructor on the simplest case (just a point). Add a new member for the collision package.

Add a new member of type `CollisionPackage` to the `Bullet` class:

```
CollisionPackage cp;
```

Now, we create a structure to pass in to our `CollisionPackage` constructor and initialize the collision package. Note that we send in a single element array with the model space coordinates that will be 0,0,0. Then, we send in the world location, 1, for the radius and the angle the bullet is facing. Enter the following code at the end of the `Bullet` class's constructor:

```
// Initialize the collision package
// (the object space vertex list, x any world location
// the largest possible radius, facingAngle)

// First, build a one element array
PointF point = new PointF(0,0);
PointF[] points = new PointF[1];
points[0] = point;

// 1.0f is an approximate representation
//of the size of a bullet
cp = new CollisionPackage(points, getWorldLocation(),
1.0f, getFacingAngle());
```

Finally for the `Bullet` class, we update the collision package in each frame by adding this code to the very end of the `Bullet` class's `update` method:

```
move(fps);

// Update the collision package
cp.facingAngle = getFacingAngle();
cp.worldLocation = getWorldLocation();
```

Now, our bullets are all set for detection.

Adding a collision package to the SpaceShip class

Open up the `SpaceShip` class and add these members. We will then see how to use them in the `SpaceShip` constructor:

```
CollisionPackage cp;

// Next, a 2d representation using PointF of
// the vertices. Used to build shipVertices
// and to pass to the CollisionPackage constructor
PointF[] points;
```

Here, we do something extra compared to the `Bullet` class. We add three more model space coordinates. OpenGL will not know about these and doesn't need them. They are positioned in the middle of each of the three lines, which make the ship. We do this to make it harder for a vertex of an asteroid to drift inside the ship without a vertex of the ship being inside the asteroid. This is a visual representation of the problem that we are solving. The ships vertices are heavily emphasized to highlight the problem. Refer to the following diagram:

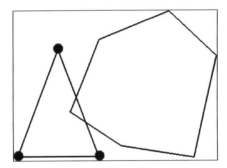

We can completely solve this problem by testing all the asteroids vertices against all of the ship's lines as well as what we are planning to do; test all the ship's vertices against all the asteroids lines. However, just adding a few extra points to the ship does produce near-perfect detection as shown next:

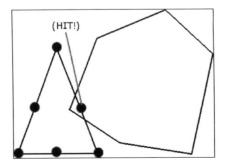

Now, right after the call to `setVertices()` in the `SpaceShip` constructor implement the code we just discussed:

```
setVertices(shipVertices);

// Initialize the collision package
// (the object space vertex list, x any world location
// the largest possible radius, facingAngle)

points = new PointF[6];
points[0] = new PointF(- halfW, - halfL);

points[2] = new PointF(halfW, - halfL);
points[4] = new PointF(0, 0 + halfL);

// To make collision detection more accurate we will define some
// more points on the midpoints of all our sides.
// It is possible that the point of an asteroid will pass through
// the side of the ship and we do not test for this!
// We only test for the point of a ship
// passing through the side of an asteroid!!
// This is computationally cheaper than running both tests.
// Although not as accurate we will see it is very close.
// We can think of this visually as
// adding extra sensors on the sides of our ship
// Here we use an equation to find the midpoint
// of a line which you can find an explanation of
// on most good high school math web sites.

points[1] = new PointF(points[0].x +
  points[2].x/2, (points[0].y + points[2].y)/2);

points[3] = new PointF((points[2].x + points[4].x)/2,
  (points[2].y + points[4].y)/2);

points[5] = new PointF((points[4].x + points[0].x)/2,
  (points[4].y + points[0].y)/2);

cp = new CollisionPackage(points, getWorldLocation(),
  length/2, getFacingAngle());

}// End SpaceShip constructor
```

Next as we did for the `Bullet` class, we synchronize the collision package each frame in the `SpaceShip` class's `update` method. We do this at the very end of the method after the call to `move()` has updated the ship's coordinates.

```
move(fps);

    // Update the collision package
    cp.facingAngle = getFacingAngle();
    cp.worldLocation = getWorldLocation();


}// End SpaceShip update()
```

Finally, we will add a collision package to the asteroids.

Adding a collision package to the Asteroid class

Open up the `Asteroid` class and add a `CollisionPackage` member:

```
CollisionPackage cp;
```

At the end of the `Asteroid` constructor, just after the call to `generatePoints()`, we initialize the `CollisionPackage` object:

```
// Define a random asteroid shape
// Then call the parent setVertices()
generatePoints();

// Initialize the collision package
// (the object space vertex list, x any world location
// the largest possible radius, facingAngle)
cp = new CollisionPackage
    (points, getWorldLocation(), 25, getFacingAngle());
```

Next, we add a helper method that reverses the direction of travel and *bounces* the asteroid back by a few pixels when a collision has been detected. We will call this method when we detect a collision with the border. Add the `bounce` method to the `Asteroid` class:

```
public void bounce(){

    // Reverse the travelling angle
      if(getTravellingAngle() >= 180){
        setTravellingAngle(getTravellingAngle()-180);
      }else{
        setTravellingAngle(getTravellingAngle() + 180);
      }
```

```
// Reverse velocity because occasionally they get stuck
setWorldLocation((getWorldLocation().x + -getxVelocity()/3),
(getWorldLocation().y + -getyVelocity()/3));

// Speed up by 10%
setSpeed(getSpeed() * 1.1f);

// Not too fast though
if(getSpeed() > getMaxSpeed()){
  setSpeed(getMaxSpeed());
}


}
```

As with the SpaceShip and Bullet classes, we will update the collision package in the update method just after the call to move at the very end of the update method:

```
move(fps);

// Update the collision package
cp.facingAngle = getFacingAngle();
cp.worldLocation = getWorldLocation();


}
```

Now, we need to do something that we didn't need to do for the other classes. Our crossing number algorithm uses lines not vertices, so we need to make a line out of the last vertex by joining it with the first. We didn't need to do this with the SpaceShip class because of the way our collision data code worked. The collision data code will test the points of the bullets and ship against the lines of the asteroids. Not the other way around.

Here is the extra code to add to the seventh point in the generatePoints method. In the following code, I have included the existing code on either side of the new highlighted code:

```
// left below 0
points[5] = new PointF();
i = -(r.nextInt(14)+11);
points[5].x =  i;
i = -(r.nextInt(12)+1);

points[5].y = i;

// We add on an extra point that we won't use in asteroidVertices[].
// The point is the same as the first.
```

```
// This is because the last vertex
// links back to the first to create a line.
// This line will need to be
// used in calculations when we do our collision detection.

// Here is the extra vertex- same as the first.
points[6] = new PointF();
points[6].x = points[0].x;
points[6].x = points[0].x;

// Now use these points to draw our asteroid
float[] asteroidVertices = new float[]{
// First point to second point
points[0].x, points[0].y, 0,
points[1].x, points[1].y, 0,
```

Now, we can talk about building the collision detection class itself.

The CD class outline

We will now implement the first phase of collision detection. As discussed, the algorithms we will use are computationally expensive, and we only want to use them when there is a realistic chance of a collision.

Therefore, we will check each bullet and the ship against every asteroid using the radius overlapping method discussed in *Chapter 3, Tappy Defender – Taking Flight*. We will check the asteroids, ship, and bullets against the border using a simplified rectangle intersection method.

After the next two sections, you will actually be able to play the game, but you will see that the basic collision detection that we have used so far is not satisfying enough for this type of game.

These first checks will decide whether we then move on to do the more accurate and computationally expensive checks.

We will implement these second phase checks in the sections *Precise collision detection with the border* and *Precise collision detection with an asteroid*, which will use the more advanced algorithms and put the data in our collision packages to full use.

To get started, create a new class and call it CD. Add a member PointF object and initialize it. We will use it to avoid creating new objects during the critical parts of the code.

```
private static PointF rotatedPoint = new PointF();
```

Now, let's discuss the methods.

Implementing radius overlapping for asteroids and ships

Let's add our first method to the CD class, to detect collisions between bullets and asteroids as well as the ship and asteroids. As we discussed, we are only implementing the first part of this method for now. Here is the implementation of the radius overlapping code.

The code works by making a hypothetical triangle with a missing side, and then using Pythagoras' theorem to calculate the missing side that is the distance between the centre points of the two objects. If the combined radii of the two objects is greater than the distance between the two object centers, we have an overlap.

Add the detect method with the radius overlapping code. Note that we return true if the radii overlap. This one line of code will be replaced with the more accurate detection later in this chapter.

```
public static boolean detect(CollisionPackage cp1,
    CollisionPackage cp2) {

    boolean collided = false;

    // Check circle collision between the two objects

    // Get the distance of the two objects from
    // the centre of the circles on the x axis
    float distanceX = (cp1.worldLocation.x)
        - (cp2.worldLocation.x);

    // Get the distance of the two objects from
    // the centre of the circles on the y axis
    float distanceY = (cp1.worldLocation.y)
        - (cp2.worldLocation.y);

        // Calculate the distance between the center of each circle
        double distance = Math.sqrt
            (distanceX * distanceX + distanceY * distanceY);

        // Finally see if the two circles overlap
        // If they do it is worth doing the more intensive
        // and accurate check.
        if (distance < cp1.radius + cp2.radius) {

        // Log.e("Circle collision:","true");
```

```
                   // todo  Eventually we will add the
                   // more accurate code here
                   // todo and delete the line below.

                       collided = true;
                   }

               return collided;
           }
```

Now, let's discuss the border.

Implementing rectangle intersection for the border

We will see if any asteroids, bullets, or the ship need containing within the border. As discussed, we will carry out a simple rectangle intersect test and return true if detected. Later, we will delete the return true and add the more sophisticated code.

Implement the contain method as shown next:

```
// Check if anything hits the border
public static boolean contain(float mapWidth, float mapHeight,
  CollisionPackage cp) {

  boolean possibleCollision = false;

     // Check if any corner of a virtual rectangle
     // around the centre of the object is out of bounds.
     // Rectangle is best because we are testing
     // against straight sides (the border)
     // If it is we have a possible collision.

     if (cp.worldLocation.x - cp.radius < 0) {
         possibleCollision = true;
       } else if (cp.worldLocation.x + cp.radius > mapWidth) {
         possibleCollision = true;
       } else if (cp.worldLocation.y - cp.radius < 0) {
         possibleCollision = true;
       } else if (cp.worldLocation.y + cp.radius > mapHeight) {
         possibleCollision = true;
       }

       if (possibleCollision) {
           // todo For now we return true
           return true;
```

```
        }

        return false; // No collision
    }
```

Now, we have two methods that we just need to call them on all the appropriate object combinations.

Performing the checks

We are really close to being able to play our game, albeit with simplified collision detection. First add some methods that handle what happens when certain collisions are detected and then see how we actually use our CD class.

Helper methods

First of all, we need a couple of helper methods to respond, when we detect various types of collisions.

We need a method for when the ship is destroyed and a method for when an asteroid is destroyed. The next two subsections cover this.

Destroying a ship

The death of a ship can be detected in two places, so it makes sense to add a method to handle the events that follow. In this next method, we reset the ship's location to the center of the map, play a sound, and decrement `numLives`.

If `numLives` is equal to zero, set `levelNumber` back to one, `numLives` to three, call `createObjects()` to redraw a level, pause the game, and then play a sound suitable to let the player know that he is starting again.

Now, add the `lifeLost` method to the `AsteroidsRenderer` class:

```
public void lifeLost(){
        // Reset the ship to the center
        gm.ship.setWorldLocation(gm.mapWidth/2, gm.mapHeight/2);
        // Play a sound
        sm.playSound("shipexplode");

        // Deduct a life
        gm.numLives = gm.numLives -1;
```

```
        if(gm.numLives == 0){
            gm.levelNumber = 1;
            gm.numLives = 3;
            createObjects();
            gm.switchPlayingStatus();
            sm.playSound("gameover");
        }
    }
```

We will handle what happens when an asteroid dies.

Destroying an asteroid

This method will be called when the ship or a bullet hits an asteroid. First, we set the asteroid that triggered the collision to setActive(false). It will not be drawn or updated any more.

Next, we play a sound and decrement numAsteroidsRemaining. Finally if numAsteroidsRemaining is equal to zero, the player has cleared an entire level. In that case, we increment levelNumber and numLives, play a victorious sound, and start a harder level by calling createObjects().

Now, add the destroyAsteroid() method to the AsteroidsRenderer class:

```
public void destroyAsteroid(int asteroidIndex){

gm.asteroids[asteroidIndex].setActive(false);
    // Play a sound
    sm.playSound("explode");
    // Reduce the number of active asteroids
    gm.numAsteroidsRemaining --;

    // Has the player cleared them all?
    if(gm.numAsteroidsRemaining == 0){
    // Play a victory sound

    // Increment the level number
    gm.levelNumber ++;

    // Extra life
    gm.numLives ++;

    sm.playSound("nextlevel");
    // Respawn everything
    // With more asteroids
```

```
        createObjects();


    }
    }
    }// End class
```

We can now call our new CD class's static methods and respond when we get a collision.

Testing for collisions in update()

First, we will check to see if the ship needs containing. We simply call CD.contain() with the mapWidth, mapHeight, and the ship's collision package. If there is a collision, the code calls lifeLost().

Add the collision detection code after all the code that updates the objects in the update method:

```
// End of all updates!!

// All objects are in their new locations
// Start collision detection

// Check if the ship needs containing
if (CD.contain(gm.mapWidth, gm.mapHeight, gm.ship.cp)) {

  lifeLost();

}
```

This is the code that detects if any of the asteroids are attempting to leave the asteroid simulator. It works exactly the same way as the previous block of code except that we loop through each asteroid, check if it is active, and call bounce on the asteroid if we detect a collision.

```
// Check if an asteroid needs containing
for (int i = 0; i < gm.numAsteroids; i++) {
  if (gm.asteroids[i].isActive()) {
      if (CD.contain(gm.mapWidth, gm.mapHeight,
      gm.asteroids[i].cp)) {

          // Bounce the asteroid back into the game
          gm.asteroids[i].bounce();
```

```
        // Play a sound
        sm.playSound("blip");


    }
  }


}
```

The code for the bullets looks a little more complicated, but it isn't really. The call to `CD.contain()` is identical, and we do so for each bullet. However, some last minute balancing of the game play is necessary for the bullet to be reset as it left the viewport (if that was before the border), because otherwise the ship can just spin round and destroy the asteroids from a great distance.

Enter the code to detect bullet collisions with the border and the edge of the viewport:

```
// Check if bullet needs containing
// But first see if the bullet is out of sight
// If it is reset it to make game harder
for (int i = 0; i < gm.numBullets; i++) {

    // Is the bullet in flight?
    if (gm.bullets[i].isInFlight()) {

    // Comment the next block to make the game easier!!!
    // It will allow the bullets to go all the way from
    // ship to border without being reset.
    // These lines reset the bullet when
    // shortly after they leave the players view.
    // This forces the player to go 'hunting' for the
    // asteroids instead of spinning round spamming the
    // fire button...
    // This code would be better with a viewport.clip() method
    // like in project 2 but seems a bit excessive just for these
    // few 15ish lines of code.

    // Start comment out to make easier
    handyPointF = gm.bullets[i].getWorldLocation();
    handyPointF2 = gm.ship.getWorldLocation();

    if(handyPointF.x > handyPointF2.x + gm.metresToShowX / 2){
        // Reset the bullet
        gm.bullets[i].resetBullet(gm.ship.getWorldLocation());
```

```
        }else
    if(handyPointF.x < handyPointF2.x - gm.metresToShowX / 2){
        // Reset the bullet
        gm.bullets[i].resetBullet(gm.ship.getWorldLocation());

    }else
    if(handyPointF.y > handyPointF2.y + gm.metresToShowY/ 2){
        // Reset the bullet
        gm.bullets[i].resetBullet(gm.ship.getWorldLocation());
    }else
    if(handyPointF.y < handyPointF2.y - gm.metresToShowY / 2){
        // Reset the bullet
        gm.bullets[i].resetBullet(gm.ship.getWorldLocation());
            }
        // End comment out to make easier

        // Does bullet need containing?
        if (CD.contain(gm.mapWidth, gm.mapHeight,
            gm.bullets[i].cp)) {

            // Reset the bullet
            gm.bullets[i].resetBullet
                (gm.ship.getWorldLocation());
            // Play a sound
            sm.playSound("ricochet");
    }

    }

}
```

You can run the game now and see how the CD.contain() method does a fairly good job of keeping everything within the asteroid simulator.

We will call our detect method to see if anything is bumping into an asteroid.

First, check the bullets. Note that we do a preliminary check to make sure the bullet is in flight, and the asteroid is active before we trouble our CD.detect method. Then, we just pass in the two collision packages and CD.detect does the rest. If a bullet collides with the border, we call resetBullet() on the appropriate bullet.

```
// Now we see if anything has hit an asteroid

// Check collisions between asteroids and bullets
// Loop through each bullet and asteroid in turn

for (int bulletNum = 0; bulletNum < gm.numBullets; bulletNum++) {
    for (int asteroidNum = 0; asteroidNum < gm.numAsteroids;
        asteroidNum++) {

        // Check that the current bullet is in flight
        // and the current asteroid is
        // active before proceeding
        if (gm.bullets[bulletNum].isInFlight() &&
            gm.asteroids[asteroidNum].isActive())

            // Perform the collision checks by
            // passing in the collision packages

            // A Bullet only has one vertex.
            // Our collision detection works on vertex pairs

        if (CD.detect(gm.bullets[bulletNum].cp,
            gm.asteroids[asteroidNum].cp)) {

            // If we get a hit...
            destroyAsteroid(asteroidNum);

            // Reset the bullet
            gm.bullets[bulletNum].resetBullet
                (gm.ship.getWorldLocation());
        }

    }
}
```

Now, we test for the ship. If a collision is detected, we call `destroyAsteroid()` followed by `lifeLost()`.

```
// Check collisions between asteroids and ship
// Loop through each asteroid in turn

for (int asteroidNum = 0; asteroidNum < gm.numAsteroids;
    asteroidNum++) {

    // Is the current asteroid active before proceeding
    if (gm.asteroids[asteroidNum].isActive()) {

        // Perform the collision checks by
        // passing in the collision packages
        if (CD.detect(gm.ship.cp, gm.asteroids[asteroidNum].cp)) {

        // hit!
        destroyAsteroid(asteroidNum);
        lifeLost();
        }
    }
}
```

At this point, you can play the game and our rudimentary collision detection will work. However, fly too close to an asteroid, and you will lose a life without touching it or merely shoot a bullet close and the asteroid is gone. We need to be able to skim the surface of the border or asteroid and only get a hit when a point actually crosses into the exact space of another object.

Precise collision detection with the border

To upgrade our `detect` method, we need to replace the return statement in the `if(possibleCollision)` block with the more precise detection code.

First, initialize `radianAngle` to be the radian equivalent of whichever direction (in degrees) our object is facing. The `Math` class uses radians as they are more mathematically useful in calculations than the easier to visualize degree measurement.

The variables `cosAngle` and `sinAngle` are just what the name suggests, and are used in the block of code which follows this one.

> It is worth mentioning that the `Math.cos()` and `Math.sin()` methods are relatively time consuming. We can speed up our collision detection class by precomputing 360 values for both `sin` and `cos` and then using a simple lookup method instead of this calculation.
>
> However, we maintain our goal of over 60 frames per second, so don't do so here.

Delete the return statement and add this code in the `if (possibleCollision)` block:

```
if (possibleCollision) {

    double radianAngle = ((cp.facingAngle/180)*Math.PI);
    double cosAngle = Math.cos(radianAngle);
    double sinAngle = Math.sin(radianAngle);
```

In the next block of code, enter a `for` loop that loops through each of the object's vertices, translates them from model-space to world-space coordinates, then uses our previously computed values for cosine and sine of the `facingAngle` object to rotate them to their precise locations in the game world.

```
//Rotate each and every vertex then check for a collision
// If just one is then we have a collision.
// Once we have a collision no need to check further
for (int i = 0 ; i < cp.vertexListLength; i++){
    // First update the regular un-rotated model space coordinates
    // relative to the current world location (centre of object)
    float worldUnrotatedX =
            cp.worldLocation.x + cp.vertexList[i].x;

    float worldUnrotatedY =
            cp.worldLocation.y + cp.vertexList[i].y;


    // Now rotate the newly updated point, stored in currentPoint
    // around the centre point of the object (worldLocation)
    cp.currentPoint.x = cp.worldLocation.x + (int)
        ((worldUnrotatedX - cp.worldLocation.x)
        * cosAngle - (worldUnrotatedY - cp.worldLocation.y)
        * sinAngle);
```

```
cp.currentPoint.y = cp.worldLocation.y + (int)
    ((worldUnrotatedX - cp.worldLocation.x)
    * sinAngle+(worldUnrotatedY - cp.worldLocation.y)
    * cosAngle);
```

Now all we do is see if the rotated and translated vertex falls outside of either the left, right, top, or bottom of the border/map. If it does, we return true; if not, the loop continues to check each and every vertex the same way (translate, rotate, check, and so on).

```
// Check the rotated vertex for a collision
if (cp.currentPoint.x < 0) {

  return true;
} else if (cp.currentPoint.x > mapWidth) {

  return true;
} else if (cp.currentPoint.y < 0) {

  return true;
} else if (cp.currentPoint.y > mapHeight) {

  return true;
}

}
```

You can run the game now and watch the bullets disappear with a satisfying thud into the border or fly your ship deadly close to the border.

Let's improve our asteroid collisions.

Precise collision detection with an asteroid

We did this last because there is a more complicated final step. As in the border detection, we will need to translate and rotate our object's vertices. However this time, we will need to do it for two objects.

Furthermore, once we rotated and translated the asteroid's vertices, we will need to handle them in pairs of vertices that form a line. These are lines that we will test against each and every vertex from the other object. This test is of course our crossing number method that we discussed.

We need to do all of this within the body of the `if (distance < cp1.radius + cp2.radius) { ...}`, where we previously just set the `collided` Boolean to `true`.

There is quite a lot of code, so we will split it into chunks and see what is going on at each stage. Also, the code indentation will not always be consistent from block to block in order to format it in the most readable way possible.

The next few blocks of code are the entire contents of the aforementioned, `if` block that needs replacing.

 As mentioned previously, we can use a sine and cosine lookup table here too.

We could make a method to rotate angles as we do this so often. But this is not as straightforward as it may seem. If we put the rotation code in a method, we will either have to put the following sine and cosine calculations in it, which will make it slow or precompute it before the method call and the `for` loops which is kind of untidy itself.

Also, if you consider that we need more than one value for both the sine and cosine of an angle, the method needs to *know* which value to use, and this isn't rocket science, but it starts to get even less compact than we might have initially imagined. So, I opted to avoid the method call altogether, even if the code is a little sprawling. Actually, if you place the whole lot in a method call, you still get nearly 60 FPS on an old Galaxy S2 phone. So if you want to tidy things up, go ahead; I just thought it was worth discussing why I did things this way.

Before we jump into the `for` loops, as we did with the border detection, we will compute a few things that won't change for the duration of this method. The sine and cosine of the facing angle from each of the two collision packages.

```
if (distance < cp1.radius + cp2.radius) {

        double radianAngle1 = ((cp1.facingAngle / 180) * Math.PI);
        double cosAngle1 = Math.cos(radianAngle1);
        double sinAngle1 = Math.sin(radianAngle1);

        double radianAngle2 = ((cp2.facingAngle / 180) * Math.PI);
        double cosAngle2 = Math.cos(radianAngle2);
```

```
        double sinAngle2 = Math.sin(radianAngle2);

        int numCrosses = 0;     // The number of times we cross a
        side

        float worldUnrotatedX;
        float worldUnrotatedY;
```

Now, we loop through all the vertices from `cp2`, then test each in turn with all the sides (vertex pairs) from `cp1`. Remember an asteroid has an extra vertex of padding that is the same as the first. Therefore, we can test the last side of the asteroid. We must always pass in the asteroid collision package as the *second* argument when calling `CD.detect()`.

In the next block of code, translate and then rotate the object being tested against an asteroid.

```
    for (int i = 0; i < cp1.vertexListLength; i++) {

        worldUnrotatedX = cp1.worldLocation.x + cp1.vertexList[i].x;
        worldUnrotatedY = cp1.worldLocation.y + cp1.vertexList[i].y;

        // Now rotate the newly updated point, stored in currentPoint
        // around the centre point of the object (worldLocation)
        cp1.currentPoint.x = cp1.worldLocation.x +
            (int) ((worldUnrotatedX - cp1.worldLocation.x)
            * cosAngle1 - (worldUnrotatedY - cp1.worldLocation.y) *
            sinAngle1);

        cp1.currentPoint.y = cp1.worldLocation.y +
            (int) ((worldUnrotatedX - cp1.worldLocation.x)
            * sinAngle1 + (worldUnrotatedY - cp1.worldLocation.y) *
            cosAngle1);

        // cp1.currentPoint now hold the x/y
        // world coordinates of the first point to test
```

Now using a pair of vertices at a time, from the asteroid, translate and rotate both to their final world-space coordinates ready for the next block of code, where we will use the vertex locations calculated in the previous block and this block.

```
    // Use two vertices at a time to represent the line we are testing
    // We don't test the last vertex because we are testing pairs
    // and the last vertex of cp2 is the padded extra vertex.
    // It will form part of the last side when we test vertexList[5]
```

```
for (int j = 0; j < cp2.vertexListLength - 1; j++) {

    // Now we get the rotated coordinates of
    // BOTH the current 2 points being
    // used to form a side from cp2 (the asteroid)
    // First we need to rotate the model-space
    // coordinate we are testing
    // to its current world position
    // First update the regular un-rotated model space coordinates
    // relative to the current world location (centre of object)

    worldUnrotatedX = cp2.worldLocation.x + cp2.vertexList[j].x;
    worldUnrotatedY = cp2.worldLocation.y + cp2.vertexList[j].y;

    // Now rotate the newly updated point, stored in worldUnrotatedX/y
    // around the centre point of the object (worldLocation)

    cp2.currentPoint.x = cp2.worldLocation.x +
            (int) ((worldUnrotatedX - cp2.worldLocation.x)
            * cosAngle2 - (worldUnrotatedY - cp2.worldLocation.y) *
            sinAngle2);

    cp2.currentPoint.y = cp2.worldLocation.y +
            (int) ((worldUnrotatedX - cp2.worldLocation.x)
            * sinAngle2 + (worldUnrotatedY - cp2.worldLocation.y) *
            cosAngle2);

    // cp2.currentPoint now hold the x/y world coordinates
    // of the first point that
    // will represent a line from the asteroid

    // Now we can do exactly the same for the
    // second vertex and store it in
    // currentPoint2. We will then have a point and a line (two
    // vertices)we can use the
    // crossing number algorithm on.

    worldUnrotatedX = cp2.worldLocation.x + cp2.vertexList[i + 1].x;
    worldUnrotatedY = cp2.worldLocation.y + cp2.vertexList[i + 1].y;

    // Now rotate the newly updated point, stored in worldUnrotatedX/Y
    // around the centre point of the object (worldLocation)
    cp2.currentPoint2.x = cp2.worldLocation.x +
            (int) ((worldUnrotatedX - cp2.worldLocation.x)
```

```
        * cosAngle2 - (worldUnrotatedY - cp2.worldLocation.y) *
        sinAngle2);

    cp2.currentPoint2.y = cp2.worldLocation.y +
        (int) ((worldUnrotatedX - cp2.worldLocation.x)
        * sinAngle2 + (worldUnrotatedY - cp2.worldLocation.y) *
        cosAngle2);
```

Here, we detect if the current vertex from either the ship or a bullet crosses the line formed by the current vertex pair of the asteroid. If it does, we increment `numCrosses`.

```
    // And now we can test the rotated point from cp1 against the
    // rotated points which form a side from cp2

    if ((((cp2.currentPoint.y > cp1.currentPoint.y) !=
            (cp2.currentPoint2.y > cp1.currentPoint.y)) &&
            (cp1.currentPoint.x < (cp2.currentPoint2.x -
        cp2.currentPoint2.x)    *(cp1.currentPoint.y -
            cp2.currentPoint.y) / (cp2.currentPoint2.y  -
    cp2.currentPoint.y) + cp2.currentPoint.x)){

        numCrosses++;

    }
```

Finally, we use the modulus operator to determine if `numCrosses` is odd or even. As discussed, we return `true` (collision) for odd and `false` (no collision) for even.

```
                }
                }
                // So do we have a collision?
                if (numCrosses % 2 == 0) {
                    // even number of crosses(outside asteroid)
                    collided = false;
                } else {
                    // odd number of crosses(inside asteroid)
                    collided = true;
                }

            }// end if
```

You can now fly your ship right up to the asteroids and only get hit when it really looks like you should. Refer to the following screenshot:

Now, all of our collision detection and our Asteroids simulator game is done!

Finishing touches

We can continue to improve our game. For example, it wouldn't be too hard to spawn two or three smaller asteroids when the current asteroid is destroyed. We just need an array to hold the smaller asteroids. When we deactivate the regular asteroid, the array activates some previously instantiated smaller ones at the same location as the regular one. We can then make some minor modifications to the way we count asteroids, and we will have a neat new feature.

The arcade classic, Asteroids, had a mean UFO that would turn up occasionally. It would be simple to design a UFO shape from lines, and have it randomly proceed from left to right, or right to left, moving up and down a bit as well.

Finally, we can add a hyperspace button. This is a kind of last resort for the player when they are sure that death is imminent. Tap the hyperspace button and the ship will respawn in a random location. We will just need to add a button to the array in the `InputController` class and a call to a new, simple `randomHyperspaceJUmp` method in the `Ship` class.

We can also add Google Play achievements and leaderboards and then publish the game. If you publish a game that uses OpenGL, you need to add this declaration to the `AndroidManifest.xml` file:

```
<uses-feature android:glEsVersion="0x00020000"
android:required="true" />
```

Try and add some of the improvements we talked about and perhaps some more of your own. If you publish your game or even if you don't, I would love to hear your ideas or see a link to your projects on `gamecodeschool.com`.

I think we are done!

Summary

I hope you have enjoyed our whirl-wind tour, making games for Android, and I hope you keep making lots of new games!

Index

A

Android Activity lifecycle
about 16
reference link 17
Android device
Tappy Defender, debugging on 41-43
Android Studio
file structure 18
installing 10, 11
URL 10
asteroid collision detection
about 331
crossing number 331, 332
phase 332
asteroids
drawing 309-314
moving 309-314
reference link, for games 251
Asteroids simulator game
about 1, 5, 252
asteroid, destroying 345, 346
checks, performing 344
collision package, adding to
    Asteroid class 339, 340
collisions, testing in update() 346-350
features 5
game controls 252
helper methods 344
improving 357, 358
rules 252
ship, destroying 344

B

backstory, Tappy Defender game
about 13, 14
enhanced draw method 100
BFXR
URL 82
Bob
animating 165-171
functionality, adding to 141-149
border collision
about 330
detection phase 330
Bullet class
collision package, adding to 336
creating 298-300
bullet collision detection 205-207

C

CD class
about 341
radius overlapping, implementing for
    asteroid 342, 343
radius overlapping, implementing for
    ships 342, 343
rectangle, implementing for border 343, 344
code structure, Tappy Defender game
about 16
Android Activity lifecycle 16, 17
collision detection
about 62
options 62
planning for 329, 330

collision package
  access, providing to 336
  adding, to Asteroid class 339, 340
  adding, to Bullet class 336
  adding, to objects 336
  adding, to SpaceShip class 337-339
CollisionPackage class 333-335
control buttons, HUD object 315-318
CopyOnWriteArrayList
  reference link 175
crossing number algorithm 65

D

design pattern, Tappy Defender game
  about 15
  control 15
  model 16
  reality check 16
  view 16
drone 190-195

E

endianness
  reference link 276
enemies
  building 52
  designing 53
  spawning 53, 54
  update method, handling 55-58
existing classes
  InputController class, adding 304-308
  reusing 301
  SoundManager class, adding 302-304

F

fire tiles
  adding 207-211
Flappy Bird apps, Google Play
  URL 15
flight, Tappy Defender game
  background, scrolling 58-60
fragment shader 253

G

game engine, Tappy Defender game
  layout, locking to landscape 104
  platform activity 101, 102
  PlatformView class 105
  upgrading 101
game loop, Tappy Defender
  class code, structuring 30-32
  coding 28
  game activity 32-34
  new class, creating for view 29, 30
  view, building 28, 29
GameObject class
  about 109-115
  functionality, adding to 293-297
GameObject super class
  building 271-281
GL Shader Language (GLSL) 254, 261
guard
  about 195
  route, generating for 195-203

H

home screen, Tappy Defender game
  AndroidManifest.xml file,
      configuring 27, 28
  building 19
  functionality, coding 24-26
  GameActivity, creating 27
  project, creating 19, 20
  UI, building 21-24
HUD
  displaying 71-73
HUD objects
  about 314
  control buttons, adding 315-318
  declaring 326-328
  drawing 326-328
  initializing 326-328
  life icons 323-325
  tally icons 319-322

I

identity matrix
    reference link 278
InputController class
    adding 304-308
installing
    Android Studio 10, 11
    JDK 7-10
iteration, Tappy Defender game
    about 89
    back button, handling 97
    enemy graphics, adding 89, 90
    exercise, in balance 91-95
    format time 96, 97

J

Java Development Kit (JDK)
    installing 7-10
Java SE Downloads
    URL 7

L

level designs, tough retro platformer project
    about 242
    cave 243
    city 244
    forest 245
    HUD 247, 248
    mountains 246, 247
life icons, HUD objects 323-326

M

machine gun
    building, with variable rate of fire 173-178
MachineGun class
    implementing 174-178
matrices
    about 254
    reference link 278
mechanics, Tappy Defender game 14, 101
MotionEvent class
    reference link 47
multiphase collision detection 150-157

O

objects
    collision package, adding to 336
OpenGL (Open Graphics Library)
    reasons, for using 252
    working 252
OpenGL ES 1 253
Open Graphics Library for Embedded
        Systems (OpenGL ES 2)
    about 1, 252
    Activity class 255
    benefits 253
    class, used for managing game 258, 259
    layout, locking to landscape 255
    preparing 255
    renderer 264-270
    simple shaders, managing 259-263
    using 254
    view 257
optimizations, collision detection
    multiple hitboxes 65
    neighbor checking 65, 66
options, collision detection
    crossing number algorithm 65
    radius overlapping 63, 64
    rectangle intersection 62, 63

P

persistence, Tappy Defender game
    adding 87-89
pickups
    about 180
    collecting 180-190
    drone 190-195
    guard 195-203
PlatformView class
    about 105
    basic structure 106-109
    enhanced draw method 132-134
    enhanced update method 131
    levels, creating 122-130
    view, through viewport 116-121
player input 157-165
PlayerShip object
    about 34-37
    drawing 38

Q

quadrants
  reference link 296

R

radius overlapping 63, 64
rectangle intersection 62, 63
route
  generating, for guard 195-203
rules, Tappy Defender game
  about 15, 101
  implementing 74-77

S

scene, Tappy Defender game
  Canvas object 39, 40
  drawing 37
  frame rate, controlling 41
  Paint object 39, 40
  PlayerShip, drawing 38
  plotting 37, 38
scores 314
shader program 253
sound FX, Tappy Defender game
  adding 82
  coding 85-87
  generating 82-84
  SoundPool class, used for playing
    sounds 85
SoundManager class
  about 137-141
  adding 302, 304
spaceship
  about 281, 282
  bringing, to life 293-297
SpaceShip class
  collision package, adding to 337-339
spaceship, controlling
  about 45
  boosters, adding to spaceship 47-50
  screen resolution, detecting 50-52
  touches, detecting 46
Star class
  update method, adding 290-292

static game border
  drawing 287-289

T

tally icons, HUD object 319-322
Tappy Defender game
  about 2, 100
  backstory 13, 14, 100
  best options 66-70
  code structure 16
  debugging, on Android device 41-43
  deploying 41
  design pattern 15
  ending 78-81
  finishing 98
  game engine, upgrading 101
  game loop, coding 28
  home screen, building 19
  iteration 89
  mechanics 14, 101
  persistence, adding 87-89
  planning 13
  PlayerShip object 34-37
  restarting 81
  rules 15, 101
  rules, implementing 74-77
  scene, drawing 37
  sound FX, adding 82
  sound FX, generating 82-84
tough retro platformer project
  about 3
  aesthetic props, adding 211, 212
  features 3, 4
  game rules 236
  level designs 242
  levels 236
  new platform tiles, adding 212-218
  new scenery objects, adding 218-226
  pause menu, with moveable
    viewport 234-236
  scrolling parallax backgrounds 226-234
  travelling, between levels 236-242

V

vertex shader 253

Thank you for buying
Android Game Programming by Example

About Packt Publishing

Packt, pronounced 'packed', published its first book, *Mastering phpMyAdmin for Effective MySQL Management*, in April 2004, and subsequently continued to specialize in publishing highly focused books on specific technologies and solutions.

Our books and publications share the experiences of your fellow IT professionals in adapting and customizing today's systems, applications, and frameworks. Our solution-based books give you the knowledge and power to customize the software and technologies you're using to get the job done. Packt books are more specific and less general than the IT books you have seen in the past. Our unique business model allows us to bring you more focused information, giving you more of what you need to know, and less of what you don't.

Packt is a modern yet unique publishing company that focuses on producing quality, cutting-edge books for communities of developers, administrators, and newbies alike. For more information, please visit our website at www.packtpub.com.

About Packt Open Source

In 2010, Packt launched two new brands, Packt Open Source and Packt Enterprise, in order to continue its focus on specialization. This book is part of the Packt Open Source brand, home to books published on software built around open source licenses, and offering information to anybody from advanced developers to budding web designers. The Open Source brand also runs Packt's Open Source Royalty Scheme, by which Packt gives a royalty to each open source project about whose software a book is sold.

Writing for Packt

We welcome all inquiries from people who are interested in authoring. Book proposals should be sent to author@packtpub.com. If your book idea is still at an early stage and you would like to discuss it first before writing a formal book proposal, then please contact us; one of our commissioning editors will get in touch with you.

We're not just looking for published authors; if you have strong technical skills but no writing experience, our experienced editors can help you develop a writing career, or simply get some additional reward for your expertise.

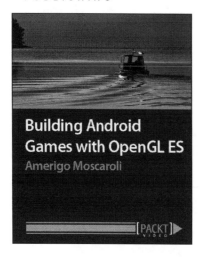

Building Android Games with OpenGL ES [Video]

ISBN: 978-1-78328-613-3   Duration: 01:42 hours

A comprehensive course exploring the creation of beautiful games with OpenGL ES

1. Create captivating games through creating simple and effective codes in Java.

2. Develop a version of the classic game Breakout and see how to monetize it.

3. Step-by-step instructions and theoretical concepts describe each activity before you implement them.

Unity Android Game Development by Example Beginner's Guide

ISBN: 978-1-84969-201-4   Paperback: 320 pages

Learn how to create exciting games using Unity 3D for Android with the help of hands-on examples

1. Enter the increasingly popular mobile market and create games using Unity 3D and Android.

2. Learn optimization techniques for efficient mobile games.

3. Clear, step-by-step instructions for creating a complete mobile game experience.

Please check **www.PacktPub.com** for information on our titles

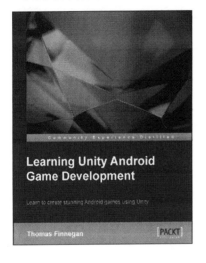

Learning Unity Android
Game Development

Learn to create stunning Android games using Unity

Thomas Finnegan   PACKT

Learning Unity Android Game Development

ISBN: 978-1-78439-469-1   Paperback: 338 pages

Learn to create stunning Android games using Unity

1. Leverage the new features of Unity 5 for the Android mobile market with hands-on projects and real-world examples.

2. Create comprehensive and robust games using various customizations and additions available in Unity such as camera, lighting, and sound effects.

3. Precise instructions to use Unity to create an Android-based mobile game.

Android NDK Game
Development Cookbook

Over 70 exciting recipes to help you develop mobile games for Android in C++

Sergey Kosarevsky
Viktor Latypov   [   ] open source ✤

Android NDK Game Development Cookbook

ISBN: 978-1-78216-778-5   Paperback: 320 pages

Over 70 exciting recipes to help you develop mobile games for Android in C++

1. Tips and tricks for developing and debugging mobile games on your desktop.

2. Enhance your applications by writing multithreaded code for audio playback, network access, and asynchronous resource loading.

3. Enhance your game development skills by using modern OpenGL ES and develop applications without using an IDE.

Please check **www.PacktPub.com** for information on our titles

Made in the USA
San Bernardino, CA
01 December 2018